WAR AT SEA AND IN THE AIR

WAR AT SEA AND IN THE AIR

EDITED BY ROBERT CURLEY, MANAGER, SCIENCE AND TECHNOLOGY

Britannica
Educational Publishing

IN ASSOCIATION WITH

ROSEN
EDUCATIONAL SERVICES

Published in 2012 by Britannica Educational Publishing
(a trademark of Encyclopædia Britannica, Inc.)
in association with Rosen Educational Services, LLC
29 East 21st Street, New York, NY 10010.

First Edition

Britannica Educational Publishing
Michael I. Levy: Executive Editor
J.E. Luebering: Senior Manager
Adam Augustyn: Assistant Manager
Marilyn L. Barton: Senior Coordinator, Production Control
Steven Bosco: Director, Editorial Technologies
Lisa S. Braucher: Senior Producer and Data Editor
Yvette Charboneau: Senior Copy Editor
Robert Curley: Manager, Science and Technology

Rosen Educational Services
Nicholas Croce: Editor
Nelson Sá: Art Director
Cindy Reiman: Photography Manager
Brian Garvey: Designer
Introduction by Greg Roza

Library of Congress Cataloging-in-Publication Data

War at sea and in the air / edited by Robert Curley.
    p. cm.—(Britannica guide to war)
"In association with Britannica Educational Publishing, Rosen Educational Services."
Includes bibliographical references and index.
ISBN 978-1-61530-677-0 (library binding)
1. Military art and science—History. 2. Naval art and science—History. 3. Air
warfare—History. 4. Military history. I. Curley, Robert, 1955-
U102.W278 2012
359.009—dc23

                                                        2011024848

Manufactured in the United States of America

On the cover: A nuclear-powered aircraft carrier of the U.S. Navy. *U.S. Navy photo by PH 3c Dusty Howell*

Pages 1, 25, 55, 78, 96, 125, 155, 169 Shutterstock.com

CONTENTS

The use of military aircraft and naval ships has become common in modern times, but warfare wasn't always fought at sea and in the air. The earliest battles between organized groups took place on land with crude weapons. The first warships were developed thousands of years ago. Warplanes, however, have been around for only about 100 years.

The earliest vessels used for war at sea were probably those used for everyday travel: dugouts, rafts, and hide boats. The oars used to power ships were probably one of the first naval implements. The ancient Egyptians built boats made of reeds that ended in a sharp point. They used these ships for ramming enemies on the Nile River. By 3000 BCE, they had made larger versions capable of distant sailing, trade, and warfare. Later, they developed wooden ships that had both oars and sails.

The Minoans were the first to build ships specifically for war, rather than modifying merchant ships for that purpose. Their warships were long, narrow, and agile. They had a long bow for ramming. The

Phoenicians and Greeks built vessels called biremes and triremes, which helped them rule the seas and spread their cultures. These ships had two and three sets of oars on each side instead of just one, allowing them to travel much faster.

At the end of the 4th century BCE, Demetrius I Poliorcetes of Macedonia introduced heavy missile weapons to warships. He had large crossbows and catapults mounted to the fronts of ships, which allowed them to attack other ships before ramming and boarding occurred.

Looking to increase their power in the Mediterranean, the Romans copied Greek triremes. They soon added spiked gangplanks to warships. After ramming an enemy, they dropped the gangplank to link the two ships together. This allowed Roman troops to board enemy ships and commence hand-to-hand combat.

In time, warships made more frequent use of heavy missile weapons. Some could hurl projectiles as large as 450 kg (1,000 pounds). Around the

An F/A-18F Super Hornet takes off from the U.S. aircraft carrier John C. Stennis. U.S. Navy photo by MC 3c Kenneth Abbate

7th century, the Byzantine Greeks began using Greek fire, a combustible material used to set enemy ships on fire.

Around 800 CE, the Vikings began building sturdy, double-ended, clinker-built ships. They had overlapping planks held together with iron nails and tarred rope. Their "great ships" had more than 30 rowers. The Vikings used "long ships" to travel long distances and conquer foreign lands. This type of ship remained popular in Europe through the 13th century.

By the middle of the 14th century, several European navies began using mounted guns. King Henry VIII of England built ships called carracks with gun ports so cannons could be set up below the deck. This proved to be more stable and effective than previous warships.

Carracks were replaced by galleons, which were longer, leaner, and even more stable. They could carry more heavy guns, and some had up to three tiers of canons. Evolving into the formidable 70- to 100-gun ship of the line, this type of heavily armed ship ruled the seas for three centuries. In the mid-1700s, navies began adding frigates and other smaller ships to their fleets. These ships were more maneuverable and were used as escort, patrol, and scouting ships.

As the Industrial Revolution took hold in Europe and America, militaries began building steam-powered "ironclad" ships. Navies around the world instantly recognized the value of these armoured vessels. Ironclads featured more effective forms of propulsion, armament, and armour. Important developments of this time included the paddle wheel, screw propeller, and more powerful guns. In the late 19th century, British engineer Robert Whitehead produced the first self-propelled torpedo. These innovations paved the way for the construction of modern battleships.

Commissioned in 1869, HMS *Monarch* was the first true turret warship. It had four 12-inch (300-mm) guns in two turrets. It had both sails and a steam engine. HMS *Devastation* was commission four years later. It was larger than the *Monarch*, and was powered by steam alone. The U.S. Navy followed the Royal Navy in the 1880s, creating heavily armoured ships with guns of various sizes for numerous tasks. Swift cruisers were also developed during this time.

By 1904, navies around the world had realized that firing large guns of uniform calibre from longer ranges was more effective than using guns of multiple sizes at closer ranges. Using this knowledge, the British developed a new type of warship: the dreadnought. The first one, HMS *Dreadnought*, had 10 12-inch (300-mm) guns for attacking other battleships and 3-inch (75-mm) guns for fighting off destroyers. Other countries—including Germany, the United States, Japan, France, and Russia—soon produced versions of the dreadnought. These ships and their guns grew increasingly larger and more powerful.

Other important warships were developed in the years leading up to World

War II, including the battle cruiser and destroyer. These ships would play a large role in the outcome of that conflict. On some smaller ships internal combustion engines replaced steam engines. They were easier to start and stop quickly and were more suitable for the operations of lighter vessels.

As the airplane grew more dependable in the early 1900s, navies developed aircraft carriers to transport them around the world. The first carriers during World War I were modified U.S. ships. They allowed the U.S. Navy to scout large areas of ocean. By World War II, aircraft carrier technology had improved so much that it became a bigger threat than the battleship itself. Landing craft and other amphibious vehicles played a large role in World War II, and they have remained an important asset to navies around the world.

Since the end of World War II, naval technology has entered a new era. In 1954, the United States commissioned USS *Nautilus*, the first nuclear submarine. Soon after, nuclear-powered surface ships took to the seas as well. Around the same time, navies around the world began to replace their guns with extremely accurate guided missiles. Carried by a multitude of small, fast surface vessels as well as stealthy submarines, guided missiles may prove particularly dangerous for aircraft carriers.

Unlike warships, warplanes have been in use for only 100 years. Prior to the advent of the airplane, some militaries used hot air balloons, primarily for reconnaissance. In 1794, the French military became the first to use hot air balloons. They were also used during the American Civil War.

Wilbur and Orville Wright received the first contract for a military airplane from the U.S. Army in 1908. Early military airplanes were used strictly for reconnaissance. The first airships to carry explosives were zeppelin airships made in Germany. Arming airplanes proved to be difficult at first. In 1915, the French devised a method that allowed a mounted machine gun to shoot bullets between the blades of a spinning propeller. The French had instant success with this invention against the Germans; however, the technology soon fell into German hands.

By the end of World War I, airplanes had improved so much that they proved their worth in warfare. They were used as fighter planes and bombers. They were used to stage ground attacks and stop submarines. In some instances they were used to transport supplies.

In the time between the two world wars, great improvements were made in military aircraft as countries raced to modernize their air forces. By 1939, fighter planes had transformed from cloth-covered biplanes into all-metal monoplanes. They could fly faster, farther, and higher than previous planes. Other advancements included improved flight instruments, retractable landing gear, and sleeker aerodynamics.

Bombers also improved dramatically. In 1931, the Boeing Aircraft Company produced the B-9 bomber. This metal monoplane could travel twice as fast as previous bombers. Soon after, Boeing added other features to the bombers, including a closed cockpit, more engines, greater armour, and defensive machine gun turrets. Militaries also began using dive bombers. This was a smaller plane that dove toward the ground and released a bomb just before climbing back into the sky.

During World War I, several militaries had recognized the potential of aircraft carriers. Between the wars, many important technical advances in aircraft made carriers a more practical option. Planes with foldable wings allowed them to be stored more efficiently aboard a ship. Hooks under the planes' tails snagged on cables strung across the decks of carriers in order to bring them to a halt quickly.

Air superiority became a deciding factor during the most decisive battles of World War II. Single-seat fighters proved to be very effective. These fighters included the German Messerschmitt, the British Spitfire and Hurricane, and the U.S. Mustang and Wildcat. The technology continued to improve during the war. By 1942, fighters had more powerful guns, stronger engines, and more effective aerodynamics. Also by this time, massive bombers—such as the U.S. B-29, nicknamed the Superfortress—were carrying large loads of explosives to targets thousands of miles away.

Aircraft carriers replaced large-gun battleships as the dominant naval weapons during the Second World War.

Fighters were able to reach distant locations previously out of their combat range. Carriers also transported dive bombers and torpedo planes, which proved to be highly successful in battle. Aircraft were also used for reconnaissance, transport, and training during World War II. The helicopter proved its value in combat, too, but was used mainly for reconnaissance.

Jet fighters had made an appearance by the end of World War II, although their use was limited. They were much faster than propeller-driven planes, but they had serious deficiencies in range and handling. After the war, improved jet airplanes quickly replaced piston-engine planes as the military aircraft of the future.

Several militaries—including Soviet, British, and American forces—began experimenting with improved aerodynamic designs. Sleeker shapes, such as delta-shaped wings, led to better performance by reducing drag. In 1947, U.S. pilot Chuck Yeager became the first person to travel at supersonic speeds in the rocket-powered Bell X-1.

Other developments followed soon after, including the introduction of slats and slotted flaps to help increase lift. Turbojets became more powerful, and the afterburner helped fighters reach even greater speeds. Radar became smaller and more dependable. This facilitated the change from optically ranging gun sights to radar-ranging sights. Jets were soon armed with air-to-air missiles that utilized radar guidance and infrared homing. The US F-86 and the Soviet MiG-15 were the two most effective fighter jets during the Korean War.

Continual improvements in fighter jets resulted in steadily increasing engine power and improved aerodynamics. In the 1960s, fighter jets were capable of reaching speeds between Mach 1.5 and Mach 2.3. It became clear that improved air-to-air missiles made dog fighting obsolete, so fewer jet fighters included guns in their armament. The introduction of surface-to-air missiles—designed to stop high-altitude bombers—resulted in the development of jet fighters configured and armed for quick surface attacks.

The newest fighter jets have reached even greater speeds. However, many modern jet designers have sacrificed speed for improved maneuverability, range, takeoff and landing qualities, and "stealth," or the ability to reduce an aircraft's visibility to radar and other warning devices. Almost all air-to-air combat occurs at subsonic speeds, the opposing jets often well out of each other's visual range.

Since the end of World War II, the use of military helicopters has become commonplace. They were first used with significant impact during the Korean War. The use of military helicopters grew during the Vietnam War. They have been used to insert airmobile infantry, evacuate casualties, transport artillery and ammunition, and mount rescue missions.

Highly armed helicopters are also used as ground-attack craft.

Previously, warship and military aircraft designers believed that "bigger is better." Modern trends, however, focus more on small, speedy, well-armed craft. Starting in the early 1980s, the U.S. military began developing stealth technology for jets. The aim was to make fighters that were immune to radar detection at normal combat ranges. These aircraft have unconventional shapes designed to thwart radar. The first stealth aircraft was the F-117A Nighthawk ground-attack fighter jet. The second was the Northrop B-2 Spirit strategic bomber. Recently, stealth technology has also been applied to naval ships as well.

As modern militaries look to the future, reducing the loss of life and property while making warfare more precise are taking centre stage. The use of unmanned aerial vehicles, for instance, is becoming more common. Unmanned aircraft were used as early as World War II for training purposes, but over time, as electronic technologies have grown more sophisticated and commonplace, militaries have realized their value for reconnaissance and scouting. In the future unmanned aerial vehicles are likely to be used in direct air-to-air combat, and even unmanned naval vessels may become a reality.

CHAPTER 1

EARLY WARSHIPS

When men first set out to sea in large boats and ships to do battle with their enemies, they relied on their own muscle to move and fight. Rows and banks of oarsmen laboured to bring their vessels into contact with each other, and armed men prepared to board and fight hand-to-hand. Later the force of the wind was harnessed through sails to do the work of oarsmen, and in the 14th century gunpowder weapons appeared. Guns and sails were a deadly addition, making it possible to build fleets that could roam the seas and harm an enemy before the ships even closed with each other. In the 19th century the steam engine, the great innovation of the Industrial Revolution, replaced the sail at a time when naval guns were becoming more and more accurate and powerful. With the invention of the steam turbine at the turn of the 20th century, warships were able to hunt their enemies around the world and strike them when they were barely visible on the horizon.

THE AGE OF OAR AND RAM

The first craft fitted purposely to make war were conversions of the dugouts, inflatable bladders, papyrus rafts, or hide boats used in everyday transport. It is probable that the conversion at first consisted simply of a concentration of weapons in the hands of a raiding party. In time conversions added offensive and defensive powers to the craft itself. As vessels became more seaworthy and

USS Carl Vinson, *a nuclear-powered aircraft carrier of the U.S. Navy, in the Indian Ocean,* 2005. *Department of Defense photo by Petty Officer 3rd Class Dusty Howell, U.S. Navy*

more numerous, warships designed as such developed both as marauders and as defenses against marauders. The first craft designed and built especially for combat may have sailed in the fleets of Crete and Egypt 5,000 years ago.

EGYPT

The first recorded appearance of warships is on the Nile River, where Egypt's history has centred since antiquity. These boats were built of bundles of reeds lashed together to form a narrow, sharp-ended hull and coated with pitch, and they were hardly suited for tempestuous seas. By 3000 BCE larger wooden seagoing versions of the reed craft sailed for distant cruising, trade, and conquest.

Egyptian wooden ships had both oars and sails, being fitted with a bipod (inverted V) mast and a single, large, square sail. The whole mast could be lowered when under oars. Large Egyptian ships had more than 20 oars to a side, with two or more steering oars. The war galley was built to the same pattern but was of stouter construction. Modifications that could be easily incorporated in a merchant ship's hull under construction included elevated decks fore and aft for archers and spearmen, planks fitted to the gunwales to protect the rowers, and a small fighting top high on the mast to accommodate several archers. Some galleys had a projecting ram, well above the waterline, which may have been designed to crash through the gunwale of a foe, ride up on deck, and swamp or capsize him.

CRETE

By about 2000 BCE Crete had evolved into a naval power exercising effective control of the sea in the eastern Mediterranean. Little record exists of Minoan seapower, yet these maritime people may have been the first to build a warship designed as such from the keel up, rather than as a modification of a merchant ship. Thus it was probably the Minoans who began to differentiate between war craft and merchantmen and between the rowing galley and sailing vessel.

Sometime in the 2nd millennium BCE the commodious merchantman evolved as a beamy "round ship" powered by sails and emphasizing cargo capacity at the expense of speed. By contrast, the fast fighting "long ship" was narrower, faster, and more agile than the tubby cargo ship. Developing as both predator on and protector of maritime trade and

coastal cities, it hoisted its sails for cruising but depended on oars when in action.

The Cretan warship had a single mast and a single bank of oars. The sharply pointed or "beaked" bows suggest an emphasis on the tactical use of the ram.

PHOENICIA

Beginning about 1100 BCE, the Phoenicians dominated the eastern Mediterranean for about three centuries. Information about Phoenician ships is fragmentary, but they appear to have been built primarily for trading, with a capacity to fight effectively if necessary.

Phoenician trading ships were apparently galleys, mounting a single pole mast with a square sail and with steering oars to port and starboard. Their war galleys show a Cretan influence: low in the bow, high in the stern, and with a heavy pointed ram at or below the waterline. Oars could be carried in a staggered, two-bank arrangement, allowing more oars to be mounted in a ship of a given length and increasing power and momentum. Because the ram was the principal weapon, the vessel's slender build and greater rowing power were important in providing more speed for the decisive shock of battle.

GREECE

Unlike the Egyptians, for whom wood was scarce and costly, the Aegean peoples had an abundance of timber for shipbuilding. The earlier Greek warships were used more to carry attack personnel than as fighting vessels. No mention is made in the *Iliad*, for instance, of sea warfare. Even the pirates of the time were sea raiders seeking their booty ashore rather than in sea actions. The so-called long penteconter, mentioned by Herodotus, was employed in exploring, raiding, and communicating with outlying colonies. Light and fast, with 25 oars to a side, it played an important role in the early spread of Grecian influence throughout the Mediterranean. As the Greek maritime city-states sped the growth of commerce and thus the need for protection at sea, there evolved a galley built primarily for fighting. The first galleys, called uniremes (Latin: *remus*, "oar"), mounted their oars in a single bank and were undecked or only partially decked. They were fast and graceful with high, curving stem and stern. In Homeric times some carried an *embolon*, a beak or ram, which became standard in succeeding centuries.

BIREMES AND TRIREMES

The bireme (a ship with two banks of oars), probably adopted from the Phoenicians, followed and became the leading warship of the 8th century BCE. Greek biremes were probably about 80 feet (24 metres) long with a maximum beam around 10 feet (3 metres). Within two or three generations the first triremes (ships with three vertically superimposed banks of oars) appeared. This type gradually took over as the primary warship, particularly after the Greeks' great sea victory at the Battle of Salamis (480 BCE).

Like its predecessors, the trireme mounted a single mast with a broad, rectangular sail that could be furled. The mast was lowered and stowed when rowing into the wind or in battle. Built on an entirely different system from the Egyptians—with keel, frames, and planking—these were truly seagoing warships.

After Salamis, the trireme continued as the backbone of the Greek fleet, with the ram continuing as its primary weapon. Its keel, like those of its predecessors, formed the principal-strength member, running the length of the ship and curving upward at each end. The ram, usually shod in bronze, formed a forward prolongation that gained effectiveness from the heavy keel back of it. Additional longitudinal strength came from a storming bridge, a gangway along the centreline from bow to stern along which the crew raced to board when a foe was rammed. Gradually, with ships becoming steadily heavier, boarding assumed greater importance and the ram lost some of its importance.

A trireme of the 5th century BCE may have had a length of about 38 metres (125 feet), a beam of 6 metres (20 feet), and a draft of 1 metre (3 feet). Manned by about 200 officers, seamen, and oarsmen (perhaps 85 on a side), with a small band of heavily armed *epibatai* (marines), under oars it could reach seven knots (seven nautical miles per hour; one knot equals 1.15 statute miles per hour or 1.85 km per

THE BATTLE OF SALAMIS

The Battle of Salamis (480 BCE) was the first great naval battle recorded in history. It took place during the Greco-Persian Wars, which was a series of wars fought over a period of almost half a century by Greek city-states and the invading Persian empire. By 480 the Persian king Xerxes and his army had overrun much of Greece, and his navy of about 800 galleys had bottled up the smaller Greek fleet of about 370 triremes in the Saronic Gulf. The Greek commander, Themistocles, devised a clever stratagem: feigning retreat, he lured the Persian fleet into the narrow strait at Salamis, between the island of Salamis and the Athenian port-city of Piraeus, where he calculated the massed Persian ships would have difficulty maneuvering and the Greeks might have a chance if their armoured marines could board the Persian ships. As the Persians emerged from the narrowest part of the strait, the Greek triremes enveloped the head of their column and attacked furiously, ramming or sinking many Persian vessels and boarding others. The Greeks sank about 300 Persian vessels while losing only about 40 of their own. The rest of the Persian fleet was scattered, and as a result Xerxes had to postpone his planned land offensives for a year, a delay that gave the Greek city-states time to unite against him.

hour). Extremely light and highly maneuverable, the classical trireme represented the most concentrated application of human muscle power to military purposes ever devised. The oarsmen sat on three levels, which were slightly staggered laterally and fore and aft to achieve the maximum number of oarsmen for the size of the hull. In rowing, the oarsmen slid back and forth on leather cushions strapped to their buttocks; this enabled full use of the powerful muscles of the thighs and abdomen.

With only scant room for provisions, such warships could not remain long at sea, and a voyage usually consisted of short hops from island to island or headland to headland. Even the largest triremes put into shore and beached for the night, resuming the passage in the morning, weather permitting. Light construction and little endurance made short distances between bases essential and frequent refits imperative.

LATER DEVELOPMENTS

The trireme reached its peak development in Athens. By the middle of the 4th century BCE, Athenians employed quadriremes (four-bank seating), with quinqueremes appearing soon thereafter. In the late 4th and early 3rd century BCE an arms race developed in the eastern Mediterranean, producing even larger multibanked ships. Macedonia's rulers built 18-banked craft requiring crews of 1,800 men. Ptolemaic Egypt capped them with 20s and 30s. Ptolemy III even laid down a 40 (tesseraconter) with a design length of over 120 metres (400 feet) and calling for a crew of 4,000 rowers. The vessel was never actually used. (The multiplicity of "banks," once a puzzle to historians, signifies the number of rowers on each oar or row of oars rather than an almost unimaginable vertical piling-up of banks.)

This same arms race brought other changes of significance. Until the late 4th century BCE, maneuver, marines, and the ram constituted a warship's offensive strength, and archers provided close-in fire. Demetrius I Poliorcetes of Macedonia is credited with introducing heavy missile weapons on ships at the end of the century, starting a trend that has continued to the present day. Demetrius' ships mounted crossbow-like catapults, for hurling heavy darts, and stone-throwing machines of the type the Romans later called ballistae. From this time on, large warships carried these weapons, enabling them to engage a foe at standoff ranges, though ramming and boarding also continued. Temporary wooden turrets—forecastles and sterncastles—were similarly fitted to provide elevated platforms for archers and slingers.

Following the fragmentation of the brief empire of Alexander the Great, sea power developed elsewhere. The city-state of Rhodes built a small but competent fleet to protect its vital shipping. Meanwhile to the west, Carthage, a state with ancient maritime origins, rose to prominence on the north coast of Africa and by about 300 BCE had become the foremost Mediterranean naval power. Carthage's navy consisted probably of the same ram-galley types developed by its ancestral Phoenicians and by the Greeks.

ROME

Coincidentally, across the sea to the north the city-state of Rome expanded to include most of the southern Italian peninsula, with its extensive seacoast and maritime heritage. Rome's growth southward collided with Carthage's ambitions in Sicily, leading to the First Punic War, which began in 264 BCE. Unlike their seafaring opponents, the Romans were not a naval power. When in the fourth year of the war Carthage sent a fleet against Sicily, Rome realized its fatal disadvantage and moved to remedy it. The Greek city-states it had conquered had long seagoing experience. Employing their shipbuilders and learning also from the foe, Rome built a fleet of triremes and quinqueremes, the latter patterned after a Carthaginian warship that ran aground in Roman territory early in the war.

Not content with copying the enemy's tactics, the Romans took land warfare to sea and forced the Carthaginians to fight on Roman terms. Each Roman galley had fitted in the bow a hinged gangplank with a grappling spike or hook (the *corvus*) in the forward end, thus providing a boarding ramp. They added to the crews many more marines than warships usually carried.

The Phoenicians and Greeks had emphasized ramming, with boarding as a secondary tactic. A Roman captain rammed and then dropped the gangplank. Ram and *corvus* locked the galleys together, and the Roman marines boarded, overwhelming the opponent. The Roman fleet had extraordinary success in the great naval Battle of Mylae off northeast Sicily, destroying or capturing 44 ships and 10,000 men. After other victories, and some defeats, by the end of the First Punic War, 241 BCE, Rome had become the leading sea power.

As the Roman navy evolved, so did its warships. Though pictorial evidence is ambiguous, it seems clear that the gangplank and *corvus* disappeared as the Romans gained experience in sea warfare. Later Roman warships appear to have been conventional fully decked ram-galleys mounting one or two wooden turrets (probably dismountable) for archers. To the single mast with rectangular sail was added a bowsprit carrying a small sail, the artemon. Falces, or long spars tipped with blades, were used by Julius Caesar's fleet against the sailing vessels of the Veneti of northwestern Gaul to cut their rigging and immobilize them. Catapults and ballistae served as mechanical artillery, and it was under their fire that Caesar's legions landed in England.

Early Roman warships were all large; to escort merchantmen and combat pirates Rome found need for a lighter type, the liburnian. Probably developed by the pirates themselves, this was originally a light, fast unireme to which the Romans added a second bank of oars. In the Battle of Actium, 31 BCE, Octavian's skilled fleet commander, Agrippa, used his liburnians to good effect. Although polyremes continued to be built after Actium, the liburnian became the predominant Roman man-of-war.

THE BYZANTINE EMPIRE

With the breakup of the western Roman Empire, naval organization and activity in the west decayed. In the eastern Roman Empire, however, the need for sea power was well appreciated. During the 11 centuries that the Roman Empire centred on Constantinople, the Byzantine rulers maintained a highly organized fleet. Their original type of warship was the liburnian, called in Greek the *dromōn*; it was built in several different sizes, the heavier designed to bear the weight of battle and the lighter single-bank dromons serving as cruisers and scouts.

Throughout the eastern Roman Empire's existence warships changed little except in rig and armament. An average large dromon measured up to 46 metres (150 feet) in length, with 100 oars and one or two fighting towers for marines. At some point early in the Christian era, the lateen sail, three-cornered and suspended from an angled yard, probably adopted from the Arabs, came into general use. Eastern warships had two or three masts. In a departure from classical customs, these were left in place in battle. Contemporary pictures show rams above the waterline.

Missile-launching weapons grew in size, some hurling projectiles as large as 450 kg (1,000 pounds) up to 685 metres (750 yards). Greek fire, a combustible material for setting fire to enemy ships, was invented in the 7th century or earlier. The various compounds passing under the name used a blend of some of the following: pitch, oil, charcoal, sulfur, phosphorus, and salt. As the composition of Greek fire was improved, tubes shaped into the mouths of savage monsters were placed in the bows of war galleys and the flaming substance, which water merely spread, was hurled on the enemy. Greek fire was an important factor in terrifying and repelling the Muslim fleet in sieges of Constantinople from the early 8th century on.

Viking Vessels

By the beginning of the Viking period, about 800 CE, the early and primitive Scandinavian craft had evolved into the well-known Viking ship, a sturdy, double-ended, clinker-built (i.e., with overlapping planks) galley put together with iron nails and caulked with tarred rope. It had a mast and square sail, which was lowered in battle; high bow and stern, with removable dragon heads; and a single side rudder on the starboard (steerboard) quarter.

Viking vessels were essentially large open boats. Like the Homeric Greeks, the Vikings at first made no distinction between war and cargo ships, the same vessel serving either purpose as the occasion demanded. Later, however, they built larger ships specifically designed for war. By 1000 CE they sailed three categories of these: those with fewer than 20 thwarts (40 rowers); those with up to 30; and the "great ships" with more than 30, which might be considered the battleship of the time. Expensive and unwieldy, though formidable in battle, the great ships were never numerous. The middle group, maneuverable and fast, proved most valuable.

Viking "long ships" played an important role in exploration (reaching Greenland and America before Columbus), in the consolidation of kingdoms in Scandinavia, and in far-ranging raids and conquests. In them the Norsemen invaded the British Isles and established themselves in Normandy, whence their descendants under William I the Conqueror crossed the Channel in 1066.

THE AGE OF GUN AND SAIL

To about the end of the 13th century, the typical ship in northern European waters remained a clinker-built, single-masted, square-rigged descendant of the long ship. In that century, and even more in the 14th, changes began that would bring an end to the long dominance of the oar in battle. About 1200 CE came one of the great steps in the history of sail: the introduction, probably in the Netherlands, of the stern rudder. This rudder, along with the deep-draft hull, the bowsprit and, in time, additional masts, transformed the long ship into the true sailing ship, which could beat into the wind as well as sail with it.

Until the 15th century, northern ships probably continued to have single masts, though in the Mediterranean a two-mast rig carrying lateen (fore-and-aft) sails had existed for some time. Then change came rapidly in the north, spurred on by Henry V of England's construction of large and strongly built warships for his cross-Channel French campaigns. The remains of one of these, the *Grâce Dieu*, reflected the clinker-built construction of the Viking long ship, but they had a keel to beam ratio of about 2.5:1 and now carried a second mast.

Some historians believe that the *Grâce Dieu* carried a third mast. At any rate, in a few decades ships had three and, by the end of the century, large vessels mounted four masts carrying eight or more sails. A three-master carried a large sail on each mast and in addition a main topsail and the spritsail under the bowsprit—the rig, in fact, of Christopher Columbus' *Santa Maria* in 1492. Ships, no longer dependent on fair winds, could and did range the world.

The beamier round sailing ship used for commerce also became the warship when the need arose. In times of war, temporary wooden castles were added at the bow and stern to provide bulwarked platforms for archers and slingers. A complement of men-at-arms embarked, in addition to the ship's seamen. Tactics were usually simple and straightforward, opposing fleets closing and attempting to beat down each other's archers before grappling and boarding. At war's end, off came the castles, and the ship went back to trading.

The trading vessel that could be promptly adapted to war did not, however, fulfill the need of the European nations for navies. The coming of gunpowder and the period of world exploration brought changes that were to cause the sailing man-of-war to become more and more distinct from the merchantman.

GUN-ARMED WARSHIPS

The employment of guns afloat, bringing a slow but progressive revolution in warship construction and naval tactics, had its first small beginnings by the 14th century. The first guns used at sea, undoubtedly hand weapons, were probably in Mediterranean galleys in the 13th or early 14th century. Such weapons played a minor role. In fact, in the numerous sea battles of the Greeks, Genoese, Moors, Turks, and Venetians during this period there is no mention of guns. But by the middle of the 14th century, the English, French, Spanish, and other navies mounted guns. Most were relatively small swivel pieces or breech-loading deck guns located in the castles fore and aft, but heavier guns were added later. The Mediterranean galleys of Venice, Turkey, and Spain at first simply mounted a heavy gun rigidly in a timber bed that was fixed to fire the gun forward over the bow. By the late 15th century these rigid mounts gave way to sliding mounts for the main centreline bow gun, as the pieces were called. Though some of these pieces were quite large, the light structure of a galley meant that there was only one large gun per vessel.

European guns were originally built up of wrought-iron bars welded together to form a tube, then banded with a thick iron hoop. Initially, they were breechloaders with an open trough at the rear of the barrel through which the ball was loaded and a cylindrical chamber, filled with powder, inserted and wedged tight. They were replaced after 1500 by brass muzzle-loaders, cast in one piece. Some of these muzzle-loaders attained great size for their day; by the mid-16th century even some 60-pounders (firing 60-pound [27-kg] solid shot) were mounted in the largest ships. In this century also, increasing knowledge of iron metallurgy led to the production of cast-iron cannon that slowly replaced the brass guns in ships, though brass remained predominant for the lighter calibre well into the 19th century.

The Portuguese and Spanish, and then the French, seem to have been the first to cover transoceanic distances with cannon-armed warships. Vasco da Gama reached Calicut in India in 1498 with a squadron of cannon-armed carracks, and the Portuguese gained a number of signal victories over their Muslim opponents in the East in the early years of the 16th century using standoff artillery tactics that their foes could not match. The Spanish were patrolling the waters of the Caribbean in ships well-provided with wrought-iron breech-loading cannon by the 1520s or '30s, if not before, and heavily armed French raiders were not far behind.

Henry VII of England created the first true oceangoing battle fleet. The "king's ships" carried many guns, but most of these weapons were small breechloaders. Following him, Henry VIII initiated gunports in English warships, a development that was to have a far-reaching effect on man-of-war design. Neither stability nor structural strength favoured heavy guns in the high castles built upon the deck, so that Henry's introduction of gunports, at first low in the waist of the ship and afterward along the full broadside, made possible the true heavy-gun warship. The cutting of gunports in the hull must also have been a factor in causing the northern nations to shift from clinker-built ships to caravels with flush-fitting planks, a change that took place in the early 1500s.

The armament of an English man-of-war of the early 16th century consisted of four or five short-barreled cannon, or curtals, a similar number of demicannon, and culverins. The average cannon, a short-range gun, hurled an iron ball of about 50 pounds (23 kg), and the demicannon one of 32 pounds (14 kg). The culverin, a longer and stronger gun, fired a smaller shot over a longer range and was likely to be more accurate at other than point-blank range. Supplementing these standoff "ship killers," in descending size of ball fired (down to only several ounces), were the smaller demiculverin, saker (quarter culverin), falcon (half saker), falconet, and robinet.

A great warship of the 16th century mounted a total of large and small pieces approximating the numbers mounted in battleships of World War II. For its original complement in 1514, Henry VIII's best-known warship, the *Henry Grâce à Dieu*, had 186 guns. Most of these were small, but they also included a number of iron "great guns."

As the 17th century advanced, guns and gunpowder improved. Gun carriages were given heavy wooden sides called brackets, which had sockets for the gun trunnions and were joined by similar flat timbers called transoms. The carriage was supported on wooden trucks and hauled out after recoil by heavy tackle.

FROM OAR TO SAIL

The coming of mighty men-of-war did not mean the immediate end of oared warships. In fact, some types of galleys

The Battle of Lepanto, Oct. 7, 1571, in which the fleets of Spain, Venice, and the Papal States defeated the Turks in the last great sea battle involving galleys; in the National Maritime Museum, London. © Photos.com/Jupiterimages

and oared gunboats continued to serve well into the 19th century.

THE GALLEASS

The Battle of Lepanto (1571), in which a combined European fleet defeated the Turkish fleet, differed little from traditional galley warfare with two exceptions. First, the scale of the action was very large, with more than 200 cannon-armed galleys on each side. Each of those galleys was propelled by 50 to 200 oarsmen and carried at least 50 additional men to fight and to man the guns and sails. Second, the European line of battle included six Venetian galleasses, a compromise type developed in the transition from oar to sail. These huge vessels, which depended on sail as well as oar, bristled with guns, including heavy ones in broadside. Although cumbersome to maneuver, their concentrated fire contributed importantly to victory.

Galleasses outside the Mediterranean differed somewhat from Venice's in that they were basically full-rigged sailing ships carrying broadsides of heavy guns and a bank of auxiliary oars for mobility. The hybrid existed only in small numbers and soon passed out of fashion to the north.

THE GALLEON

The "great ships" of Henry VII and Henry VIII were carracks: starting basically with the lines of beamy, seaworthy merchant ships, designers had added stronger timbers, masts, sailpower, broadside guns, and high-built forecastles and aftercastles. In the galleon, the successor to the carrack, the general principles of design of sailing men-of-war were established, and they ruled, without fundamental change, for three centuries. The galleon retained certain characteristics of the galley, such as its slender shape, and in fact it had a greater length-to-beam ratio than the carrack. But the carrack's high-built forecastle, which tended to catch the wind and thus make the ship unmaneuverable, was eliminated from the galleon's design. The resulting ship was much more seaworthy. Like carracks, the larger galleons might carry a single mizzenmast or two relatively small masts, the second being called the bonaventure.

In the longer, leaner galleon, the number of heavy guns was increased until they ran the full length of the ship's broadside in one or two tiers (and later three).

The galleon came into favour in northern Europe during the middle of the 16th century. The far-ranging experience of mariners and improved construction techniques led to great fighting ships that were both lower in the water and more seaworthy than their predecessors. The sides now sloped inward from the lowest gun deck up to the weather deck. This "tumble home" helped concentrate the weight of the large broadside guns toward the centreline, improving the ship's stability.

By this time it had become normal for warships to mount powerful broadsides of 28 or more ship-smashing guns, a much heavier armament in proportion to their size than their predecessors. For their handy, maneuverable ships, the British had relatively large cannon carried in broadsides. Thus they were designed for off-fighting, permitting the English fleet to get the most out of its ships' superior maneuvering qualities. When the Spanish Armada arrived in 1588, the British sought and fought a sea battle with ship-killing guns, rather than the conventional fleet engagement of the past that concentrated on ramming, boarding, and killing men in hand-to-hand combat. With superior ability and long-range culverins, the English ships punished the invading fleet outside the effective range of the heavy but shorter-range cannon the Spanish favoured. This historic running battle of July 1588 closed one era and opened a greater one of big-gun sailing navies.

SHIP OF THE LINE

The late Elizabethan galleon that began the true fighting ship of the line reached its culmination in England's *Prince Royal* of 1610 and the larger *Sovereign of the Seas* of 1637, along with similar great ships in other European navies. These two English ships mounted broadside guns on three decks; the *Sovereign of the Seas*, the most formidable ship afloat of its time, carried 100 guns. In this mobile fortress displacing approximately 1,500 tons, there was some reduction of height; the bonaventure mizzen disappeared, leaving the standard three masts that capital ships thereafter carried.

Soon ships began to be standardized into different categories. James I organized his ships into four ranks, and, by the mid-17th century, six "rates" existed as a general concept, though not yet a system. The number of guns a ship carried determined its rate, with a first-rater mounting 100 guns and a sixth-rater 18. An important improvement came in the standardization of batteries in the higher rates so that guns on the same deck were of the same weight and calibre rather than mixed, as originally in the *Sovereign of the Seas*. Near the end of the century, guns began to be described by their weight and calibre, with the 32-pounder long gun favoured as the standard lower-deck weapon for British warships.

The frequent hard-fought sea battles of the 17th century, particularly in the Anglo-Dutch wars, led to the column formation of heavy warships called line ahead. In the line formation, each warship followed in the wake of the ship ahead so that every ship in the line had a clear field of fire for a broadside discharge of its guns. The adoption of line-ahead tactics made it necessary to standardize the battle line, which had consisted of ships of widely varying strength. Now only the more powerful warships were considered suitable "to lie in the line of battle." Hence the origin by the 1700s of the term line-of-battle ship, or the ship of the line, and, in the second half of the 19th century, the derived term battleship—ships

THE BATTLE OF TRAFALGAR

The Battle of Trafalgar (Oct. 21, 1805) was a naval engagement of the Napoleonic Wars that was fought west of Cape Trafalgar, Spain, between Cádiz and the Strait of Gibraltar. It was there that a fleet of 33 ships (18 French and 15 Spanish) under Admiral Pierre de Villeneuve of France fought a British fleet of 27 ships under Admiral Horatio Nelson.

At the end of September 1805, Villeneuve had received orders to leave Cádiz and land troops at Naples to support the French campaign in southern Italy. On October 19–20 his fleet slipped out of Cádiz, hoping to get into the Mediterranean Sea without giving battle. Nelson caught him off Cape Trafalgar on October 21.

Villeneuve ordered his fleet to form a single line heading north, and Nelson ordered his fleet to form two squadrons and attack Villeneuve's line from the west, at right angles. By noon the larger squadron, led by Admiral Cuthbert Collingwood in the Royal Sovereign, *had engaged the rear (south) 16 ships of the French-Spanish line. At 11:50 AM Nelson, in the* Victory, *signaled his famous message: "England expects that every man will do his duty." Then his squadron, with 12 ships, attacked the van and centre of Villeneuve's line, which included Villeneuve in the* Bucentaure. *The majority of Nelson's squadron broke through and shattered Villeneuve's lines in the pell-mell battle. Six of the leading French and Spanish ships, under Admiral Pierre Dumanoir, were ignored in the first attack and about 3:30 PM were able to turn about to aid those behind. But Dumanoir's weak counterattack failed and was driven off. Collingwood completed the destruction of the rear, and the battle ended about 5:00 PM. Villeneuve himself was captured, and his fleet lost 19 or 20 ships—which were surrendered to the British—and 14,000 men, of whom half were prisoners of war.*

Nelson was mortally wounded by a sniper, but when he died at 4:30 PM he was certain of his complete victory. About 1,500 British seamen were killed or wounded, but no British ships were lost. Trafalgar shattered forever Napoleon's plans to invade England and established British naval supremacy for more than 100 years.

that could hit the hardest and endure the most punishment.

Some first-raters were built to carry as many as 136 guns, but, because the biggest ships were often cumbersome, relatively few were built. The handier 74-gun third-rater proved particularly successful, combining sufficient hitting power with better speed and maneuverability. Most of the ships of the line of the late 18th and early 19th centuries were 74s. One of these might be approximately 50 metres (163 feet) long with two full gun decks, the lower mounting the heaviest guns, by the Napoleonic Wars usually 32-pounders. The upper gun deck customarily carried 24-pounders, while the forecastle and quarterdeck mounted lighter guns. The bigger ships were similar but had three covered gun decks instead of two. Viscount Nelson's *Victory*, launched in 1765 and preserved in dry dock as it was at Trafalgar in 1805, is a classic example of this powerful type.

Warships gradually improved in design through the 17th and 18th centuries. New types of sails, providing more canvas and more versatile combinations for varying weather conditions, such as staysails and the jib sail, came into use in the 17th century. Soon thereafter the steering wheel replaced the old whip staff, or tiller.

FRIGATES AND SMALLER VESSELS

Ships of the line, first to fourth rates, had strong, fast frigates as consorts. This ancestor of the modern cruiser evolved during the mid-18th century for scouting, patrol, and escort, as well as for attacking enemy merchantmen. The frigate carried its main battery on a single gun deck, with other guns on forecastle and quarterdeck. Like ships of the line, they varied in size and armament, ranging from about 24 guns in early small frigates to as many as 56 in some of the last. Two classic

USS United States, *a naval frigate launched in 1797, was commanded by U.S. Navy Capt. Stephen Decatur during the War of 1812.* Library of Congress, Washington, D.C.

examples, still preserved, are the U.S. Navy's *Constitution*, with 44 guns, and *Constellation*, with 38.

Smaller vessels aided frigates in their blockade, escort, commerce raiding, and other duties. The single-masted cutter served as scout and coastal patrol craft. Brig and schooner-rigged types, generally called sloops of war, by the time of the American Revolution grew into the three-masted, square-rigged "ship sloop." Called a corvette on the Continent, the fast ship sloop complemented frigates on the fringes of the fleet. Smaller sloops, schooners, brigs, and luggers were widely used for special service. Fleets also needed ordnance and supply ships and other auxiliaries; these were usually merchantmen taken into service in war emergency. Converted merchantmen, such as John Paul Jones's *Bonhomme Richard*, often played combat roles. Fleets also had various special types, such as fire ships and bomb ketches. The latter, with two large mortars hurling bombs of about 90 kg (200 pounds), were developed by France in the late 1600s and were used with devastating effect against Barbary pirate ports.

THE AGE OF STEAM AND IRON

As the Industrial Revolution unfolded in the 19th century, the age of wooden-hulled sailing ships gave way to that of steam-powered iron ships. Phenomenal changes took place in nearly every aspect of warship design, operation, and tactics. These changes ended the reign of the majestic ship of the line by the mid-1800s, but another half century elapsed before it was clear what form its replacement as the backbone of fleets would take.

TOWARD THE IRONCLAD

The change from wood to iron came slowly, in considerable part because the introduction of steam power required new techniques and experience in shipbuilding. The general use of iron for warships awaited the full realization of the value of the shell gun and the resulting need for armour, which were first demonstrated in the employment of armoured batteries in the Crimean War and in the battle between the *Monitor* and *Merrimack* in the American Civil War. The changes may be summarized under three headings: propulsion, armament, and armour.

PROPULSION

Steam for propulsion of vessels was tried with varying success in several countries during the late 18th century. Engines and supporting machinery were at first not adequate for this fundamental advance in ship capability, but useful steam craft appeared in the early 1800s, suitable for operation on inland and coastal waterways. The earliest steam warship was the *Demologos* of the U.S. Navy (renamed *Fulton* after its designer, Robert Fulton). Built in the War of 1812, this well-gunned, double-hulled, low-powered ship cruised briefly in the New York Harbor area before the war ended and later was destroyed by an accidental fire.

The earliest steam warships in action were small paddle wheelers used by British and American navies against pirates and other weak foes. As engines gradually improved, navies experimented with them in standard warships, first as auxiliaries to sail, which was then essential for endurance. The paddle wheels were particularly vulnerable to enemy fire. In 1843, through the drive of Captain Robert Field Stockton of the U.S. Navy and the inventive skill of John Ericsson, a Swede whom Stockton brought to America, the United States launched the world's first screw-driven steam man-of-war, USS *Princeton*, a large 10-gun sloop.

The screw propeller was an old idea going back to Archimedes, but, with Stockton's assistance, Ericsson had made it effective for large warships, as Sir Francis Pettit Smith was doing at about the same time in England for large merchantmen. By the mid-1840s, boilers, engines, and machinery had improved to the point that thereafter practically all of the new warships had steam propulsion, though they also still carried sails.

Among the advances of this period were two other milestones. In 1834 Samuel Hall of England patented a type of steam condenser that made it possible to use fresh instead of corrosive salt water for boilers. In 1824 James Peter Allaire of the United States invented the compound-expansion steam engine, in which the steam was used in a second cylinder at a lower pressure after it had done its work in the first. Eventually it was made practical by progress in metallurgy and engineering; in 1854 John Elder, shipbuilder on the River Clyde, installed a successful two-stage engine in the merchant steamer *Brandon*. The higher efficiency was of great importance for ocean-keeping navies.

ARMAMENT

The basic changes in armament that were to take place in the 19th and 20th centuries had begun in the 18th century. In the British navy steps to make possible heavier long-range guns began with the introduction of strong springs to take up the first shock of the gun's recoil after firing, aided by inclined-plane wedges behind the trucks to coax the gun forward into firing position after recoil. Flintlocks pulled by a lanyard, instead of match, fired the guns. Sights also improved. In the early 1800s navies began to employ mercury fulminate in percussion caps to initiate firing. Efficient percussion locks came into use within a few years.

Smoothbore guns were still inaccurate, and successful efforts were made to bring back the rifled barrels, as well as the breech loading, of early guns, thus increasing their speed and accuracy of fire. The bore of a rifled gun barrel had spiral grooves cut into it that caused a projectile fired from it to spin in flight; if this projectile was shaped in the form of a cylinder with a cone-shaped forward tip, spin enabled it to fly through the air with its pointed end forward at all times. This improved aerodynamics gave the shell a more accurate course of flight and a longer range. Because a projectile could not be rammed down the muzzle of a rifled barrel, the use of rifling had to await the design of an efficient breech-loading mechanism. In the 1840s, Italian and Austrian inventors brought out sliding-wedge breechblocks. Later the French developed an interrupted screw system, originally an American invention. A British firm produced a rifled breech-loading gun that the Royal Navy used until 1864, when a number of accidents brought a temporary reversion to muzzle-loaders. But defects were eventually remedied, and breech loading brought phenomenal increases in rates of fire.

French 165-mm (6.5-inch) cast-iron rifled guns in the Crimean War demonstrated superiority in range, destructive power, and accuracy. They helped impress all of the navies with the need for rifling. Slower-burning powder was also badly needed. Black powder had gradually been improved during 600 years of use in firearms, but it still retained its primary defect, too-rapid burning (and

hence the creation of gas pressures so high that they could burst a gun barrel upon firing). The use of rapid-burning powder required keeping the size of the charge down (and therefore the range) to prevent the bursting of even the best guns. Just before the American Civil War the U.S. Army developed large, perforated, dense grains of black powder that burned more slowly and thus were a start toward the controlled burning ultimately achieved with smokeless powder.

A development equal in importance to the rifling of naval guns was the replacement of solid iron cannonballs with large shells that exploded upon impact. Shell guns in warships' main batteries were preceded by bombs fired from mortars, small shell guns, and solid hot shot heated to cherry red. A principal architect in bringing big shell guns to sea was Henri-Joseph Paixhans, a general of French artillery. The first large shell guns from Paixhans' design, chambered howitzers firing a 28.5-kg (62.5-pound) shell (thicker-walled than bombs to penetrate before exploding) was tested in 1824 against a moored frigate with remarkable accuracy and incendiary effect.

The new guns began to come into use afloat in the 1830s, a French squadron firing them in the bombardment of Vera Cruz, Mexico. The U.S. Navy began installation of the new guns, including 16 eight-inch (20-cm) shell guns in the three-decker *Pennsylvania*, along with 104 32-pounder solid-shot guns. The

British made similar installations. There was good reason for navies to proceed cautiously, as the production of shell guns at first encountered many manufacturing problems. (Indeed, in a gala demonstration of the 12-inch shell guns on the USS *Princeton* for President John Tyler, one of the guns blew up, killing the secretary of the navy and several others.) In the event, improvements in metallurgy, gun construction, and fire control—along with the maneuverability of steam warships—at last led to the important extension of range that the big gun had promised from the beginning.

In 1853 the dramatic destruction of a weaker Turkish squadron by a Russian fleet in the harbour of Sinop of Turkey's Black Sea coast attracted world attention and increased interest in shell guns. England, the United States, and others built big steam frigates (as they were misleadingly called) with big shell guns. Their great striking power and maneuverability under steam made them the capital ships of the day, superseding the ship of the line for a brief time before the ironclads took over.

Larger guns, increased powder charges, and greater tube pressures were made possible by the replacement of cast iron by built-up wrought-iron guns (later, cast steel and, eventually, forged steel were used). Hoops were shrunk on over the powder chamber and breech end of the tube to give the strength required for the greater internal pressures sustained by these guns upon firing.

ARMOUR

The use of larger guns with more penetrating power and explosive shells made armour plating imperative. Among early experiments were floating armoured batteries built for the Crimean War. Heavy wrought-iron plates over a thick wooden backing gave these flat-bottomed vessels outstanding protection as they carried large-shell guns close inshore.

Other developments followed swiftly. The British soon built the first iron-hulled floating batteries. The French followed with the *Gloire*, the first seagoing armoured warship, protected throughout her entire length by a wrought-iron belt of 10.9- to 11.9-cm (4.3- to 4.7-inch) armour backed by 66 cm (26 inches) of wood. Displacing 5,617 tons, it mounted 36 large shell guns and could steam at 13.5 knots; a three-masted sailing rig supplemented the engines. *Gloire* was the first of a series of ironclads laid down by Napoleon III; 13 similar ships soon followed, then two-decker armoured rams. Great Britain countered with the *Warrior*, the first iron-hulled, seagoing, armoured man-of-war. Much larger than the *Gloire*, it displaced 9,210 tons, mounted 28 7-inch (180-mm) shell guns, had slightly lighter armour, carried sails, and was one knot faster.

These first ironclads were commissioned on the eve of the American Civil War, in which ironclads were destined to take a decisive part. The war itself produced several spectacular developments, including pioneer submarines, the first aircraft carriers (to handle balloons for observation), and the torpedo boat, one of several means the Confederates explored in trying to break the blockade. These little craft had weak steam engines and mounted a torpedo lashed to a spar projecting from the bow. Called Davids, they were weak but definite forerunners of the torpedo boat and the versatile destroyer.

Ironclad warships were crucial, perhaps decisive, in the North's victory over the South. Partial ironclads appeared early on the western rivers and spearheaded Union general Ulysses Grant's victories in 1862. River and coastal ironclads (ultimately, mostly monitors) dominated the war against the South in attacks from the sea and in decisive support of land operations from the Mississippi system to the Chesapeake Bay and James River. Most memorable of the combats was the duel between the *Monitor* and *Virginia* (better known as the *Merrimack*). The battle ended in a draw with neither ship seriously injured, but the repercussions of this first duel between completely ironclad warships swept the world. On April 4, scarcely more time than required for a ship to cross the Atlantic, Great Britain ordered the 131-gun ship of the line, the *Royal Sovereign*, to be cut down, armoured, and fitted with turrets. Only three and a half weeks later Great Britain laid down the *Prince Albert*, the Royal Navy's first iron-hulled turret ship, mounting four turrets.

The Union Navy ordered 66 coastal and river monitors; these were low freeboard ships that were unsuitable for high-seas action and rarely suitable for long voyages. Many were not completed in time for war service. Besides the *Virginia*, the Confederates began a number of other ironclads. Several of these rendered valuable service and probably lengthened the war, but most had to be destroyed before completion. Out of a combination of characteristics of the *Monitor* and *Virginia* types evolved the battleship, which was next to rule the sea.

THE BATTLE OF THE *MONITOR* AND *MERRIMACK*

On March 9, 1862, during the American Civil War, the Confederate warship Merrimack *and the Union warship* Monitor *engaged in a gun duel at Hampton Roads, Va., a harbour at the mouth of the James River, in what came to be known as history's first engagement between ironclad warships. It was the beginning of a new era of naval warfare.*

When the Federal forces lost Norfolk Naval Shipyard in Portsmouth, Va., in April 1861, they burned several warships, including the heavy steam frigate Merrimack. *The Confederates raised* the Merrimack, *installed a ram and slanting casemates made from railroad track over thick wooden backing, and renamed it* Virginia. *The 263-foot (80.2-metre) masterpiece of improvisation, mounting 10 guns, including four rifled ones, resembled, according to one contemporary source, "a floating barn roof." Commanded by Commo. Franklin Buchanan and supported by several other Confederate vessels, the* Virginia, *with yard workmen still on board finishing up, sailed on March 8, 1862, for its trial run. Defying concentrated fire of ship and shore batteries, it virtually decimated a Union fleet of wooden warships off Newport News, Va.—destroying the sloop* Cumberland *and the 50-gun frigate* Congress, *while the frigate* Minnesota *ran aground. The* Virginia *then retired with the ebbing tide.*

The Union ironclad Monitor, *under the command of Lieut. John Worden, arrived from New York the same night. This "Yankee Cheese Box on a raft" represented an entirely new concept of naval design. Displacing fewer than 1,000 tons, less than one-third of the* Virginia, *the* Monitor *had a boxlike iron hull supporting an iron-plated wooden raft on which revolved the turret. The 172-foot- (52-metre-) long vessel had little freeboard except for the thickly armoured rotating turret within which were mounted two 11-inch (280-mm) smoothbores. The* Monitor *had many deficiencies. Not really a seagoing warship, it had nearly sunk on its voyage down and did sink on its next sea voyage.*

Thus the stage was set for the dramatic battle, with crowds of Union and Confederate supporters watching from the decks of nearby vessels and the shores on either side. Soon after 8:00 AM the Virginia *opened fire on the* Minnesota, *and the* Monitor *appeared. They passed back and forth on opposite courses. Both crews lacked training; firing was ineffective. The* Monitor *could fire only once in seven or eight minutes but was faster and more maneuverable than her larger opponent. After additional action and reloading, the* Monitor's *pilothouse was hit, driving iron splinters into Worden's eyes. The ship sheered into shallow water, and the* Virginia, *concluding that the enemy was disabled, turned again to attack the* Minnesota. *But her officers reported low ammunition, a leak in the bow, and difficulty in keeping up steam. At about 12:30 PM the* Virginia *headed for its navy yard; the battle was over.*

The Virginia's *spectacular success on March 8 had not only marked an end to the day of wooden navies but had also thrilled the South and raised the false hope that the Union blockade might be broken. The subsequent battle between the two ironclads, though actually indecisive, was generally interpreted as a victory for the* Monitor *and produced feelings of combined relief and exultation in the North.*

On May 9, 1862, following the Confederate evacuation of Norfolk, the Virginia *was destroyed by its crew. The* Monitor—*with 16 crewmen—was lost during a gale off Cape Hatteras, N.C., on Dec. 31, 1862. The wreck of the* Monitor *was located in 1973, and in 2002 marine salvagers raised the ship's gun turret and other artifacts from the wreckage. Conservation work on these artifacts can be viewed by the public at the Mariner's Museum in Newport News.*

Toward the Battleship

The later 19th century continued to be a time of great flux in warship design. European states tried numerous arrangements of guns and armour, such as centreline turrets, a central armoured citadel with large guns on turntables at each corner, lightly armoured big guns topside in barbettes (open-top breastworks), torpedoes in even the largest vessels, and substitution of high speed for armour.

For a time even the ancient ram was revived. When the Austrians won the Battle of Lissa from the Italians in 1866 by ramming, its value for the future seemed confirmed. Hence for years most large ships carried rams, which proved to be more dangerous to friend than foe when ships were sunk in peacetime collisions.

This period also saw a fundamental advance in underwater weaponry with the invention of the locomotive torpedo. After being presented with the idea by an Austrian naval captain in 1864, a British engineer named Robert Whitehead produced a projectile that was driven by compressed air and was designed to strike a ship's unprotected hull below the waterline. The Whitehead torpedo, as it was quickly adapted by the European navies, was about 16 inches (410 mm) in diameter and had a range of about 1,000 yards (914 metres) at approximately seven knots.

Engines for all the types of warships steadily improved as stronger metals made possible higher steam pressures and weight reduction. In the 1870s a third cylinder was added onto the two-stage compound steam engine to make the triple expansion engine, and in the 1890s a fourth cylinder was added. These improvements on the traditional reciprocating steam engine provided a marked increase in speed that was surpassed only by the radical innovation of the steam turbine at the end of the century.

Ships

A trend toward the centreline-turret, big-gun battleship finally became clear. In it were combined the seagoing hull, armour, and habitability of the *Virginia*, *Gloire*, and *Warrior* with the revolving turret and big guns of the *Monitor*.

HMS *Monarch*, 8,300 tons, mounting four 12-inch (300-mm) guns in two turrets, and commissioned in 1869, was perhaps the first true seagoing turret warship. HMS *Devastation*, 9,330 tons, four 12-inch (300-mm) guns in two turrets, and massively armoured, was completed four years later without sail and was a next step toward the ultimate 20th-century battleship, a ship with an armoured citadel around the propulsion plant, powder magazines, and handling rooms. Rising out of it, protecting big guns and crews, were barbettes and turrets. The main battery shrank to a few powerful guns, but these took the place of many in broadside because of their great size and ability to fire through a wide arc of bearings.

The change was vividly illustrated by the "new navy" the United States began building in the 1880s, consisting not of improved monitors but of powerful sea-going capital ships with mixed-calibre main batteries. Displacing 11,700 tons, these vessels had 18-inch (460-mm) belt armour and a speed of 15 knots and mounted four 13-inch (330-mm) guns in two turrets. They also mounted eight 8-inch (200-mm) guns in four turrets, smaller guns for defense against torpedo boats, and six torpedo tubes. The plan was, as in other navies, to employ the heavy guns against an enemy ship's armour-protected machinery and magazines while the faster-firing eight-inch guns attacked its relatively unprotected superstructure.

The armoured cruiser was developed in this period as a large, fast vessel armed with intermediate-calibre guns and protected by armoured deck and medium-weight belt armour. Designed for commerce protection and raiding, as well as to cooperate with the battle line in fleet action, it was considered powerful enough and sufficiently protected to fight any ship capable of catching it and able to outrun battleships. Some even held it should become the principal warship.

Less heavily armoured was the protected cruiser, the engines and magazines of which were shielded by an armoured deck, but which lacked an armour belt. Unprotected cruisers had little or no armour, carried fairly light guns, and were designed primarily for scouting, patrolling, and raiding.

Carrying the new self-propelled torpedo, the torpedo boat had great potential, particularly under conditions of low visibility. Small, unseaworthy, and useful only in restricted waters with the then-short-range, slow torpedoes, the new boats did not immediately live up to expectations; nevertheless, as craft and torpedo improved, they were soon regarded as a major menace.

ARMOUR

Early hull armour had been of wrought iron backed by wood. To increase resistance against ever more powerful rifled guns, compound armour of steel backed with iron was devised to combine steel's surface hardness with iron's resiliency. The firm Schneider & Cie in France invented an oil-tempering process to produce a homogeneous steel plate that had good resiliency and greater resistance than compound armour. The later addition of nickel further improved its resistance.

Steel-armour-piercing shells came into use in the late 1880s, again threatening the armoured ship. Accordingly, an American engineer, Hayward Augustus Harvey, perfected a face-hardening process, applying carbon to the face of the steel plate at very high temperatures for an extended period and tempering. Harvey nickel-steel armour superseded earlier types. Then, in 1894, the Krupp firm of Germany devised hot-gas tempering, based on Harvey's process, which in turn became standard with world navies. Later, the addition of chromium to nickel steel was found to be a further improvement.

ARMAMENT

The impact of developments in guns and powder exceeded even that of warship design in their effect upon navies. In the two decades after the American Civil War the main difficulties with breech mechanisms were resolved. Better guns, along with breech-loading, made possible both longer ranges and higher rates of fire.

New powders were equally important. About 1880 brown or cocoa powder appeared, employing incompletely charred wood. It burned slower than black powder and hence furnished a sustained burning that was effective ballistically but did not create excessive pressures within the gun barrel. To take advantage of this for longer-range firing, gun-barrel lengths jumped to 30–35 times bore diameter.

Several nations began to achieve success with smokeless powder of nitrated cellulose and usually some nitroglycerin. With greater striking power available, armour-piercing projectiles became more formidable. These were originally solid shot designed simply to punch through armour plate. In the 1890s, better steel and fuses made it possible to add an explosive charge. The resulting semi-armour-piercing shells became highly destructive, and in time all of the armour-piercing projectiles carried explosive charges.

In 1881 the British Admiralty advertised for an anti-torpedo-boat gun to fire cased ammunition at a rate of 12 shots per minute. Benjamin Berkeley Hotchkiss, an American ordnance engineer with a factory in Paris, produced a series of one-, three-, and six-pounder rapid-fire guns that vastly increased the rate of fire for small guns.

CHAPTER 2

MODERN WARSHIPS

The age of the modern warship has seen advances in speed, power, and precision that would have been inconceivable to seamen even in the industrial 19th century. Reciprocating steam engines fired by coal-burning boilers gave way first to oil-fueled steam turbines and diesel engines, then to gas turbines and nuclear-powered steam. Naval guns reached farther with greater accuracy, and then the combat range of naval fleets was lengthened beyond the horizon first with carrier-launched airplanes, then with missiles launched by all sorts of craft. Early warning systems, first based on maintaining a screen of smaller vessels patrolling well in advance of the main fleet, were surpassed by patrol airplanes, which in turn were succeeded by radar and satellite communication.

THE AGE OF BIG GUN AND TORPEDO

From the late 19th century through World War I, the greatest driving force in warship development was the rivalry between the big gun and the torpedo. Improvements in these weapons had immense influence on the design and use of surface warships, from the huge dreadnought battleships to the small torpedo boat.

GUNS

By 1900 a major change had occurred in the handling of the very heavy main guns, those of 280 to 340 mm (11 to 13.5 inches) calibre that fired shells weighing up to 600 kg (1,300 pounds). In the 1890s such weapons often fired no faster than once every five minutes, compared to the five to 10 rounds per minute fired by a 150-mm (6-inch) gun. As power control became easier and more precise, the big guns became more effective. By 1900 it was possible for a 300-mm (12-inch) gun to fire one or two aimed shots per minute.

Meanwhile, the standard of heavy-gun marksmanship began to improve. Although rifled guns had grown bigger and muzzle velocity had increased throughout the late 19th century, there had been no corresponding improvement in fire control. For this reason, effective battle ranges had not extended much beyond 3,000 to 4,000 metres (10,000 to 13,000 feet). Then it was discovered that a ship's roll and pitch could be systematically compensated for, so that each shot could be fired at the same angle to the sea and reach almost exactly the same range. Greater accuracy could be achieved by firing groups of shells, or salvos, bunched around the estimated range. The pattern of splashes raised by a salvo would then make corrections possible. By the end of World War I, fire control had improved enough that guns firing 15,000 to 20,000 metres (30,000 ro 66,000 feet) could attain a hit rate of 5 percent. This meant that a ship firing 10 heavy guns at the rate of once or twice per minute could expect a hit after two or three minutes.

Increased range was valuable for two reasons. First, a ship that could hit at ranges beyond the capabilities of its enemies could stand off and destroy them at leisure. Second, improved gun range increased protection against the new, longer-range torpedoes.

TORPEDOES

Modifications and adaptations of the original Whitehead design quickly made the torpedo a formidable weapon. Directional control was greatly improved in the 1890s by the use of a gyroscope to control the steering rudders. Another significant improvement was the use of heat engines for propulsion. British firms, introducing both heat engines and contrarotating propellers, advanced to the high-performance, steam-driven Mark IV torpedo of 1917. Concurrently with this development, an American firm, E.W. Bliss Company, successfully used a turbine to drive a modified Whitehead design. (This Bliss-Leavitt torpedo remained in extensive use until World War II.) By 1914, torpedoes were usually 460 or 530 mm (18 or 21 inches) in diameter and could reach almost 4,000 metres (13,000 feet) at 45 knots or 10,000 metres (33,000 feet) at close to 30 knots.

ARMOUR

The torpedo threat forced ship designers to provide battleships with underwater protection. Schemes to place coal bunkers near the outside of the ship proved impractical, but research during World War I showed that the basic idea of keeping the underwater explosion at a distance from the interior of the ship was correct. In the Royal Navy, existing ships were fitted with external bulges or "blisters" to keep the explosion farther outboard, and new ships were built with specially designed layers of compartments designed to absorb the shock of explosion.

During the war it also became apparent that the longer firing ranges meant that more shells would fall onto a ship's deck than on its side armour. Because these ranges were experienced at the Battle of Jutland, ships designed afterward with stronger deck armour were called post-Jutland.

PROPULSION

While weapons were the main driving force in warship development, changes in propulsion were also important. In 1890, propulsion was exclusively by reciprocating (i.e., piston) steam engines, which were limited in power and tended to vibrate. To escape these limits, warship designers adopted steam turbines, which ran more smoothly and had no inherent limits. Turbines were applied to destroyers from about 1900 and to battleships from 1906.

The main drawback of turbine propulsion was that really efficient turbines ran too fast to drive efficient propellers. The solution was to reduce turbine speeds to acceptable propeller speeds through gearing. By 1918, single-reduction gearing was commonplace. Late in the interwar period, the U.S. Navy adopted double-reduction gearing, which permitted even higher turbine speeds without requiring propellers to run any faster.

Fuel also became a major issue. Coal was relatively inexpensive and easily available; however, it did not burn cleanly and was difficult to transfer from ship to ship at sea. Oil, on the other hand, burned cleanly, and it could be transferred easily at sea. Also, it had a higher thermal content than coal, so that the same weight or volume of oil could drive a ship much farther. The United States shifted to oil fuel in new ships in about 1910 and converted its remaining coal-burning warships after World War I. Beginning with the Queen Elizabeth class of battleships in 1915–16, Britain switched to oil. The other navies followed suit after the war.

In contrast to the steam engine, a gasoline or diesel engine often needed no tending at all, could be very compact, and could start and stop quite easily. Such engines made it possible to build small, fast coastal minesweepers, subchasers, and motor torpedo boats. Internal combustion was thought to be especially suitable to subchasers, which would have to stop their engines while listening for a submarine and then start them up suddenly when something was heard.

BATTLESHIPS

A battleship entering service in 1900 typically mounted a mixed battery of four heavy (280- to 340-mm, or 11- to 13.5-inch) guns in two twin turrets, about a dozen secondary guns of 150 to 225 mm (6 to 9 inches), and small, fast-firing guns of

75 mm (3 inches) or less for beating off torpedo-boat attacks. These ships usually displaced 12,000 to 18,000 tons.

By 1904 studies reinforced by battle experience in the Spanish-American and Russo-Japanese wars indicated that fire from large guns at longer ranges was more effective than mixed-battery fire closer in. Only bigger shells could do serious damage to well-armoured ships. Moreover, the shells fired from guns of many different calibres produced a confusing pattern of splashes in the water that made the correcting of aim and range quite difficult. Effectively increasing range, then, depended upon abandoning the multiple-calibre pattern of previous battleship armament in favour of a single-calibre armament. Several navies reached this conclusion simultaneously, but the British were the first to produce such a ship, HMS *Dreadnought*, completed in 1906. Displacing about 18,000 tons, it carried 10 12-inch (300-mm) guns; its only other armament consisted of 3-inch (75-mm) weapons intended to fight off destroyers.

The *Dreadnought* gave its name to an entirely new class of battleships of the most advanced design. By 1914 the Royal Navy had 22 dreadnoughts (another 13 were completed during World War I), Germany built a total of 19 (five completed after 1914), and the United States completed 22 (14 of them after 1914). Japan and Italy built six, while Russia and France each built seven. Not all of these ships were strictly equivalent. Unlike its immediate German and American contemporaries, the *Dreadnought* had steam

turbines in place of reciprocating engines. These enabled it to attain a speed of 21 knots, which was hitherto achieved only by cruisers. (Contemporary battleships were generally limited to about 18 knots.) Thus, in mobility as well as in size, the *Dreadnought* began a new era.

HMS *Dreadnought* also marked a beginning of rapid development in big-gun firepower. In 1909 the Royal Navy laid down HMS *Orion*, the first "super dreadnought," which displaced 22,500 tons and was armed with 13.5-inch (340-mm) guns. The U.S. Navy followed with ships armed with 14-inch (350-mm) guns. Then, on the eve of World War I, the Royal Navy went a step further with HMS *Queen Elizabeth*, armed with 15-inch (380-mm) guns and capable, in theory, of 25 knots. World War I stopped the growth of British and German battleships, but the United States and Japan continued to build ships exceeding 30,000 tons displacement. In 1916 both countries adopted the 400-mm (16-inch) gun, which fired a shell of approximately 950 kg (2,100 pounds). Such guns could be aimed to hit at ranges as great as 20,000 metres (66,000 feet).

The battleship saw little combat in World War I, yet, despite submarines, aircraft, and destroyers, the outcome of the war still hinged upon control of the sea by the battleship. Had superiority in battleships passed to Germany, Britain would have been lost, and the Allies would have lost the war. The one moment when this might have happened was the only large-scale clash of battleships, the Battle of Jutland.

THE BATTLE OF JUTLAND

The Battle of Jutland was the only major encounter between the British and German fleets in World War I and in fact was the biggest naval battle in history. Fought on May 31–June 1, 1916, in the Skagerrak, an arm of the North Sea, about 100 km (60 miles) off the coast of Jutland (Denmark), the battle came to an indecisive end. Both sides claimed victory, however— Germany because it had destroyed or damaged many more ships, Britain because it retained control of the North Sea.

Adm. Reinhard Scheer, who became commander in chief of Germany's High Seas Fleet in January 1916, planned to contrive an encounter on the open sea between his fleet and some part of the British fleet in separation from the whole, so that the Germans could exploit their momentary superiority in numbers to achieve victory. Scheer's plan was to ensnare Adm. David Beatty's squadron of battle cruisers at Rosyth, midway up Britain's eastern coast, by strata-gem and destroy it before any reinforcements could arrive from the Grand Fleet's main base at Scapa Flow, in Scotland's Orkney Islands.

To set the trap, five battle cruisers of the German High Seas Fleet, together with four light cruisers, were to sail northward, under Adm. Franz von Hipper's command, from Wilhelmshaven, Ger., to a point off the southwestern coast of Norway. Scheer himself, with the battle squadrons of the High Seas Fleet, was to follow, 80 km (50 miles) behind, to catch Beatty's forces in the gap once they had been lured eastward across the North Sea in pursuit of Hipper. But the sig-nal for the German operation to begin, made in the afternoon of May 30, was intercepted and partially decoded by the British; and before midnight the whole British Grand Fleet was on its way to a rendezvous off Norway's southwestern coast and roughly across the planned route of the German fleet.

At 2:20 PM on May 31, when Adm. John Jellicoe's Grand Fleet squadrons from Scapa Flow were still 105 km (65 miles) away to the north, Beatty's advance guard of light cruisers—8 km (5 miles) ahead of his heavier ships—and Hipper's scouting group learned quite accidentally of one another's proximity. An hour later the two lines were drawn up for battle, and in the next 50 minutes the British suffered severely, and the battle cruiser Indefatigable was sunk. When Beatty's other battle cruisers came up, however, the German cruisers, in their turn, sustained such damage that Hipper sent a protective screen of destroyers in to launch a torpedo attack. The British lost another battle cruiser, the Queen Mary, before the German High Seas Fleet was sighted by a British patrol to the south, at 4:35 PM. On this report Beatty ordered his ships north-ward, to lure the Germans toward the Grand Fleet under Jellicoe's command.

Not until 6:14 PM, after Jellicoe's squadrons and Beatty's had been within sight of one another for nearly a quarter of an hour, was the German fleet precisely located—only just in time for Jellicoe to deploy his ships to the best advantage. Jellicoe arrayed the Grand Fleet end-to-end in a line so that their combined broadsides could be brought to bear on the approaching German ships, who could in turn reply only with the forward guns of their lead-ing ships. The British ships in effect formed the horizontal stroke and the German ships the vertical stroke of the letter "T," with the British having deployed into line at a right angle to the German ships' forward progress. This was the ideal situation dreamed of by tacticians of both navies, since by "crossing the T" one's forces temporarily gained an overwhelming superiority of firepower.

For the Germans this was a moment of unparalleled risk. Three factors helped prevent the destruction of the German ships in this trap: their own excellent construction, the steadiness and discipline of their crews, and the poor quality of the British shells. The battle cruisers Lützow and Derfflinger and the battleship König led the line and were under broadside fire from some 10 British battleships, yet their main guns remained undamaged and they fought back to such effect that one of their salvoes fell full on the battle cruiser Invincible and blew it up. This success, however, did little to relieve the intense bombardment from the other British ships, and the German fleet was still pressing forward into the steel trap of the Grand Fleet.

Relying on the magnificent seamanship of the German crews, Scheer extricated his fleet from the appalling danger into which it had run by a simple but, in practice, extremely difficult maneuver. At 6:30 PM he ordered a turn of 180° for all his ships at once; it was executed without collision; and the German battleships reversed course in unison and steamed out of the jaws of the trap, while German destroyers spread a smoke screen across their rear. The smoke and worsening visibility left Jellicoe in doubt about what had happened, and the British had lost contact with the Germans by 6:45 PM.

Yet the British Grand Fleet had maneuvered in such a way that it ended up between the German High Seas Fleet and the German ports, and this was the situation Scheer most dreaded, so at 6:55 PM Scheer ordered another reverse turn, perhaps hoping to pass around the rear of the British fleet. But the result for him was a worse position than that from which he had just escaped: his battle line had become compressed, and his leading ships found themselves again under intense bombardment from the broadside array of the British ships. Jellicoe had succeeded in crossing the Germans' "T" again. The Lützow now received irreparable damage, and many other German ships were damaged at this point. At 7:15 PM, therefore, to cause a diversion and win time, Scheer ordered his battle cruisers and destroyers ahead to virtually immolate themselves in a massed charge against the British ships.

This was the crisis of the Battle of Jutland. As the German battle cruisers and destroyers steamed forward, the German battleships astern became confused and disorganized in trying to execute their reverse turn. Had Jellicoe ordered the Grand Fleet forward through the screen of charging German battle cruisers at that moment, the fate of the German High Seas Fleet would likely have been sealed. As it was, fearing and overestimating the danger of torpedo attacks from the approaching destroyers, he ordered his fleet to turn away, and the two lines of battleships steamed apart at a speed of more than 20 knots. They did not meet again, and when darkness fell, Jellicoe could not be sure of the route of the German retreat. By 3:00 AM on June 1 the Germans had safely eluded their pursuers.

In all, the British lost three battle cruisers, three cruisers, eight destroyers, and 6,274 offi- cers and men in the Battle of Jutland. The Germans lost one battleship, one battle cruiser, four light cruisers, five destroyers, and 2,545 officers and men. The losses inflicted on the British, though greater, were not enough to affect the numerical superiority of their fleet over the German in the North Sea, where their domination remained practically unchallengeable dur- ing the course of the war. Henceforth, the German High Seas Fleet chose not to venture out from the safety of its home ports.

Fought in May 1916 in mist, fog, and darkness, Jutland revealed the strengths and weaknesses of battleships and battle cruisers. Three British battle cruisers were lost. Several German battleships, thanks to watertight subdivision and efficient damage-control systems, sur- vived despite more hits. But the British advantage in numbers was decisive, and Germany turned to the submarine to counter the Allied blockade.

CRUISERS

HMS *Dreadnought* made earlier large cruisers obsolete, since it was nearly as fast as any of these ships. Consequently, the Royal Navy built a series of ships it called battle cruisers. These were as large as the newest battleships and were armed with battleship guns, but they were much faster (initially a top speed of 25 knots, compared with the 21 knots of battleships). The first was HMS *Invincible*, completed in 1907. Many of these ships were built: 10 for the Royal Navy before 1914, seven for Germany, and four for Japan.

Battle cruisers gained their superior speed by sacrificing heavy armour; as a consequence, they could not stand up to battleships. This was proved at the Battle of Jutland, where the *Invincible* was blown in two by a single salvo and sunk along with two other battle cruis- ers. These losses led many to argue that the battle cruiser was a mistake, but dur- ing the war Britain laid down six more, three of which were eventually com- pleted. The last of them, HMS *Hood*, launched in 1918, could be described as a new stage in warship development. It was so large, at 41,200 tons, that it could combine contemporary battleship armour and armament (equivalent to that of HMS *Queen Elizabeth*) with the very high speed of 31 knots. Although classed as a battle cruiser, it was actually the first of a new generation of very fast battleships.

At the other end of the cruiser spec- trum were small, fast "scout" cruisers used for reconnaissance and escort duties. These ships displaced from 3,000 to 7,000 tons and, by 1915, attained speeds as high as 30 knots. They were armed with guns of smaller calibre, usually 150 or 190 mm (6 or 7.5 inches). The British built many of this type of cruiser, as well as larger types that were nevertheless smaller than their battle cruisers.

DESTROYERS

The self-propelled torpedo had its greatest impact on the design of small surface ships. Beginning in the 1880s, many nations built hundreds of small steam torpedo boats on the theory that they could bar coastal waters to any enemy. Because their hulls could be crammed with machinery, torpedo boats were quite fast. By the early 1890s, speeds as high as 25 knots were being reported. As a defense against this new fast threat, Britain deployed oversized torpedo boats, calling them torpedo boat destroyers. These craft were successful in hunting down torpedo boats, and eventually they were renamed destroyers.

The first destroyers were essentially coastal craft, displacing only about 200 tons, but their larger successors could accompany battle fleets to sea. There it soon became apparent that a destroyer was in effect a superior sort of torpedo boat, capable of delivering its weapon against capital ships during or immediately after a fleet engagement. By 1914, 800- or even 1,000-ton ships were quite common.

During World War I British destroyer design changed radically, creating what became the postwar formula of the V and W destroyer classes: four 4-inch (100-mm) guns superimposed fore and aft, a high forecastle forward for greater seakeeping ability, and two sets of twin (later triple) torpedo tubes amidships. These vessels, displacing about 1,200 tons and capable of 34 knots, made all earlier British destroyers obsolete.

When Germany adopted unrestricted submarine warfare in February 1917, shipping losses soon forced the diversion of destroyers from fleet duty to convoy protection and antisubmarine warfare. Destroyers were not ideally suited to the escort role, as they had limited steaming range and their high-speed design made them less seaworthy than the merchant ships they were required to escort. The Royal Navy therefore built several types of specialized convoy escort, but the U.S. Navy found it easier to mass-produce its current destroyer design. These vessels, equipped with hydrophones and depth charges, as well as guns and torpedoes, overcame the submarine threat and had a large share in the safe convoy of two million American troops to Europe without loss of a single soldier.

THE AGE OF THE AIRCRAFT CARRIER

Although naval strategists continued to extol the battleship and battle cruiser after World War I, these capital ships soon were swept away by the new art of naval aviation. Conventional naval guns were limited to a range of perhaps 35 km (20 miles), but by World War II the aircraft carrier—a ship capable of launching, recovering, and storing aircraft that could themselves destroy ships—had extended the battle range of surface fleets by as much as 500 km (300 miles). In doing so, it had a profound effect on naval warfare.

THE LAST CAPITAL SHIPS

In 1922 the Five-Power Naval Limitation Treaty, signed in Washington, D.C., by emissaries of the victorious Allies of World War I plus Japan, changed the character of navies by limiting battleship inventories. With a few exceptions, new battleship construction was prohibited until 1931, and most remaining pre-dreadnought battleships were ordered scrapped. The new battleships allowed by the treaty could not mount guns of greater calibre than 16 inches (410 mm), and they could not displace more than 35,000 tons.

Battleships were defined as warships armed primarily with guns over 8 inches (200 mm) in calibre or displacing more than 10,000 tons. This definition of a battleship in effect defined a new kind of cruiser, which would displace about 10,000 tons and would be armed with 8-inch (200-mm) guns. In 1930 a new treaty, signed in London, extended the battleship-building "holiday" through 1936 and divided cruisers into two classes: ships armed with guns of up to 155 mm (6.1 inches) and ships armed with guns of 155 to 200 mm (6.1 to 8 inches). In U.S. parlance the former were light, and the latter heavy, cruisers.

One peculiarity of the Washington Treaty was that it defined warship size by devising new "standard" tonnages, which excluded the weight of fuel and reserve feed water. (Standard tonnage remains a means of measuring ship displacement in many cases, and it is used here when ship tonnages are listed.) The effect of the London Treaty's limit on cruiser tonnage was the saving of weight in warship design. Several navies used aluminum in structures not contributing directly to the strength of their ships, and there was considerable interest in welding (which was lighter than riveting) and in more efficient hull structures. Lighter machinery was also developed. The U.S. Navy, for example, built higher-pressure, higher-temperature boilers and more efficient turbines.

Most of the battleships that survived the scrappings were rebuilt during the 1920s and '30s with added deck armour and with new blisters to improve their resistance to underwater explosions. In many cases, lighter engines and boilers were fitted, so that weight and internal volume were freed for other purposes such as improved fire-control computers.

New battleships were also built. The Treaty of Versailles limited Germany to 10,000-ton capital ships, but in the 1930s that country built three large cruisers of about 12,000 tons, each armed with six 275-mm (11-inch) guns. These so-called pocket battleships, by combining heavy armour with great speed (provided by diesel engines), could defeat any contemporary cruiser. They also reignited the race in battleship construction. In 1935 France produced the *Dunkerque*; at

26,500 tons, armed with eight 325-mm (13-inch) guns, and reaching 30 knots, this was the first of the new generation of "fast battleships" presaged by HMS *Hood*. In 1937, after the Washington and London treaties had expired, Japan laid down the *Yamato* and *Musashi*. These two 72,800-ton ships, armed with 460-mm (18.1-inch) guns, were the largest battleships in history.

As World War II began, Britain was constructing five battleships of the King George V class. These displaced about 36,000 tons and carried 350-mm (14-inch) guns. The United States completed five 35,000-ton battleships before entering the war and one in 1942, and four 45,000-ton Iowa-class ships were built during wartime. The Iowa ships, carrying 400-mm (16-inch) guns, were the last battleships completed in the United States. Germany completed five ships (including the 42,000-ton *Bismarck* and *Tirpitz* and the 32,000-ton *Scharnhorst*), France completed four, Italy completed three, and Japan completed two. Most of these fast battleships could exceed 30 knots.

Before the war began, the new arts of dive-bombing and torpedo-bombing from carrier-based aircraft did not promise enough velocity and destructive power to penetrate battleship armour. But by the end of the war, even modern capital ships maneuvering at sea could be sunk by carrier aircraft. In October 1944 and April 1945, U.S. carrier-based airplanes sank the *Musashi* and *Yamato*; more than any other event, these marked the end of the long reign of the battleship.

AIRCRAFT CARRIERS

The airplane had just begun to go to sea on the eve of World War I. In November 1910 the American scout cruiser USS *Birmingham* launched the first airplane ever to take off from a ship, and two months later a plane was landed on an improvised flight deck built onto the armoured cruiser USS *Pennsylvania*. In 1913 a British cruiser, HMS *Hermes*, was converted to carry aircraft. In 1916, flying-off decks were built aboard several British ships, and by 1918 the Royal Navy had a converted passenger liner, HMS *Argus*, that could land and launch planes on a flight deck extending from bow to stern. The *Argus* was thus the prototype for a revolutionary type of ship—the aircraft carrier.

WORLD WAR I AND THE INTERWAR PERIOD

Aircraft carriers were valuable in World War I primarily because their planes vastly extended a ship's ability to scout, or reconnoitre, large areas of ocean. The wartime Royal Navy developed a series of torpedo-carrying seaplanes and carrier-based light bombers, but both the aircraft and their weapons were too weak to pose a serious threat. For this reason, the aircraft carrier was considered an essential element of the fleet but not a replacement of the battleship.

Throughout the interwar period, naval aircraft performance gradually improved, and dive bombers and torpedo bombers made aircraft carriers effective ship killers. In the opinion of many experts, this made other carriers so vulnerable that the only way to protect them was to find and destroy the enemy's carriers first. Another option was to protect the carrier with its own fighters. This option was not practical without some means of detecting an enemy air attack at a great distance, so that defending fighters could be sent up in time. The key to such a defense was radar. The phenomenon of radar was observed in the 1920s, and by the late 1930s prototype sets with huge antennas were operating. Radar was first installed aboard British and U.S. carriers in 1940–41.

As another defensive measure, in 1936 the Royal Navy decided to provide its new carriers with armoured hangars, the armour including part of the flight deck. The U.S. Navy, on the other hand, built its flight decks of wood, on the theory that damage from bombs to the decks could be repaired relatively easily. (Substantial armour lower in the ships was intended to preserve them from more serious bomb damage.)

Aircraft carrier operation required three elements: a means of launching from the ship, a means of recovering aircraft aboard ship, and a means of stowage. Landing aircraft were caught by arresting wires strung across the deck that engaged a hook fastened under the planes' tails. Originally, arresting wires were needed to keep the very light wood-and-cloth airplanes of the World War I era from being blown overboard by gusts of wind. After heavier steel-framed and steel-skinned airplanes were introduced, wires were no longer necessary. The Royal Navy abandoned arresting gear about 1926. The U.S. and Japanese navies continued to use it, but for a very different purpose: to keep landing airplanes from rolling into aircraft that were stowed at the forward end of the flight deck. In British practice this was unnecessary, because aircraft were stowed below immediately upon landing, so that each pilot faced a clear deck when he landed. Stowage was accomplished by elevator lifts, which were usually located in two or three places along the centreline of the flight deck.

WORLD WAR II

The Washington Treaty of 1922 permitted each of the major powers to convert two capital ships to carriers, within a 33,000-ton limit. New carriers could not displace more than 27,000 tons, and no carrier could have guns of more than 8 inches (200 mm). The United States and Japan converted heavy battle cruisers just under construction into the USS *Lexington* and *Saratoga* and the Japanese *Akagi* and *Kaga*. These ships actually exceeded the 33,000-ton limit, the U.S. vessels carrying about 80 aircraft and the Japanese about 40. Two new U.S. carriers built in the 1930s to treaty specifications were the *Yorktown* and *Enterprise*, which displaced more than 20,000 tons and carried about 80 aircraft. Their Japanese equivalents were the *Hiryu* and *Soryu*, which operated about 50 aircraft. Britain, which had suspended new capital-ship construction during the war, converted two light battle cruisers completed in 1916, HMS *Courageous* and *Glorious*. For economic reasons Britain did not build a new carrier to the treaty specifications until 1935, when HMS *Ark Royal* was laid down.

Under a new treaty of 1936, new carriers were limited to 23,000 tons, but the limit on the total number of carriers was removed. In response, the Royal Navy laid down the Illustrious class of 23,000-ton carriers. These vessels did not enter service until after the outbreak of World War II in 1939. With the commencement of war, the United States produced the 27,500-ton Essex class. Carrying more than 100 aircraft, these vessels became the principal fleet carriers of the Pacific Theatre. Between 1940 and 1943, the United States also designed a series of 45,000-ton ships partly inspired by Britain's Illustrious carriers. Completed after the war ended in 1945, this Midway class was the first of the U.S. carriers to be built with armoured flight decks.

During the war Britain built second-line carriers, called light fleet carriers, which were designed for quick construction. These became the Colossus and Majestic classes, vessels of approximately 15,000 tons that carried about 40 aircraft each. The U.S. war program, meanwhile, included the conversion of

a series of cruisers into light carriers of the 11,000-ton Independence class.

For protecting merchant convoys from submarine attack, escort carriers were built in large numbers, mainly in the United States. Many were converted merchant ships, and others were specially built on hulls originally designed for merchant service. The Royal Navy also added flight decks to some tankers and grain carriers, without eliminating their cargo role. These were called MAC ships, or merchant aircraft carriers.

Carriers played a dominant role in every aspect of operations at sea in World War II. The Pacific conflict began with the Japanese carrier strike against Pearl Harbor and ended with American and British carriers operating with impunity against the Japanese homeland. In between, the Battle of the Coral Sea, in May 1942, was the first naval battle in history in which opposing fleets fought without ever coming in sight of each other. A month later off Midway atoll, carriers again played the decisive role. The Battle of Midway reinforced a conviction already clear, especially from British operations in the Mediterranean with and without air support, that control of the sea also meant control of the air over the sea. In the autumn of 1942 the Solomon Islands campaign underlined the importance of both aircraft and submarines in fleet operations, emphasizing that modern sea power was a trident of air, surface, and undersea forces.

THE BATTLE OF MIDWAY

In May 1942, a U.S. fleet had turned back a Japanese invasion force that was attempting to seize control of the Coral Sea (between Australia and New Caledonia) by establishing air bases at Port Moresby in southeastern New Guinea and at Tulagi in the southern Solomons. Despite this setback in the southern Pacific Ocean, Japan was continuing with plans to seize the U.S. naval facilities and airfield at Midway Island, 2,100 km (1,300 miles) northwest of Honolulu in the central Pacific, as well as bases in the Aleutian Islands in the northern Pacific. Seeking a showdown with the numerically inferior U.S. Pacific Fleet, Adm. Yamamoto Isoroku had sent out the bulk of the Japanese fleet, including four heavy and three light air-craft carriers, with orders to engage and destroy the American fleet and invade Midway.

Battle of Midway, June 3–6, 1942. National Archives, Washington, D.C.

U.S. intelligence had divined Japanese intentions after breaking the Japanese naval code, however, and the Americans were ready: three heavy aircraft carriers of the U.S. Pacific Fleet were mustered. These ships were stationed 560 km (350 miles) northeast of Midway and awaited the westward advance of Yamamoto's armada. Whereas the Japanese had no land-based air support, the Americans from Midway and from Hawaii could commit about 115 land-based planes.

The battle began on June 3, 1942, when U.S. bombers from Midway Island struck ineffectually at the Japanese carrier strike force about 350 km (220 miles) southwest of the U.S. fleet. Early the next morning Japanese planes from the strike force attacked and bombed Midway heavily, while the Japanese carriers again escaped damage from U.S. land-based planes. But as the morning progressed the Japanese carriers were soon overwhelmed by the logistics of almost simultaneously sending a second wave of bombers to finish off the Midway runways, zigzagging to avoid the bombs of attacking U.S. aircraft, and trying to launch more planes to sink the now-sighted U.S. naval forces. A wave of U.S. torpedo bombers was almost completely destroyed during their attack on the Japanese carriers at 9:20 AM, but at about 10:30 AM 36 carrier-launched U.S. dive-bombers caught the Japanese carriers while their decks were cluttered with armed aircraft and fuel. The U.S. planes quickly sank three of the heavy Japanese carriers and one heavy cruiser. In the late afternoon U.S. planes disabled the fourth heavy carrier (scuttled the next morning), but not before its aircraft had badly damaged the U.S. carrier Yorktown. On June 6, a Japanese submarine fatally torpedoed the Yorktown and an escorting American destroyer; that day a Japanese heavy cruiser was sunk. The Japanese, however, appalled by the loss of their carriers, had already begun a general retirement on the night of June 4–5 without attempting to land on Midway.

The Battle of Midway brought the Pacific naval forces of Japan and the United States to approximate parity and marked a turning point of the military struggle between the two countries. Fought almost entirely with aircraft, the battle destroyed Japan's first-line carrier strength and most of its best trained naval pilots. Together with the Battle of Guadalcanal later that year, Midway ended the threat of further Japanese invasion in the Pacific.

DESTROYERS AND ESCORT SHIPS

Most destroyers built between the two world wars repeated Britain's V and W formula, sometimes with more powerful guns or with more torpedo tubes and generally displacing from 1,300 to 1,500 tons. The London Treaty of 1930 prohibited destroyers larger than 1,500 tons, but by the late 1930s several navies had exceeded the limits.

Besides delivering a bomb with enough velocity to damage a capital ship, the dive bomber forced the addition shipboard of large numbers of automatic guns, of 40 mm (1.50 inch) or less, to supplement the more powerful but slower-firing 75- to 125-mm (3- to 5-inch) antiaircraft guns. The Royal Navy converted some of its small World War I cruisers into antiaircraft ships, replacing their single 6 inch (150 mm) guns with twin 4 inch (100 mm) weapons controlled by special antiaircraft directors. The Japanese built large destroyers (the Akitsuki class) for much the same role; these were armed with a special 100-mm (3.94-inch) gun. The U.S. Navy provided virtually all of its destroyers with effective antiaircraft guns.

As in World War I, destroyers were used for convoy escort against submarines, if only because they were available in large numbers. However, they were not especially suited to that purpose; like their pre-1914 forebears, they were still primarily fast fleet escorts optimized to deal with surface torpedo attack. The likelihood of such attack declined as radar became widely available, but aircraft remained an important threat to major fleet units, so that the destroyer naturally evolved into an antiaircraft escort.

One important exception to the general abandonment of surface torpedo attack was the Imperial Japanese Navy. By 1941 Japanese doctrine envisaged concentrated night attacks by cruisers and destroyers carrying large numbers of unusually powerful, oxygen-fueled, wakeless torpedoes. These torpedoes were the Type 93 Long Lances, which proved extremely effective in the U.S.-Japanese naval battles around the Solomon Islands in 1942–43.

The submarine threat in World War II placed Britain, the United States, and Japan in desperate need of escorts for merchant convoys. Besides converting existing destroyers, each navy built huge numbers of specialized escorts adapted to mass-production techniques. Britain led in these measures, building relatively small escorts of limited endurance, which it called corvettes, and much larger escorts, which it called frigates. The U.S. Navy built a somewhat faster equivalent, which it called a destroyer escort. The Japanese built a series of escorts roughly equivalent to the British corvettes.

TORPEDO BOATS

In the 1930s the German, Italian, British, and U.S. navies regained interest in motor torpedo boats, which had been largely discarded after World War I. All four navies built them in substantial numbers to fight in narrow seas during World War II. Against convoys in the English Channel and the North Sea, the Germans used their S-boats (Schnellboote, "fast boats"; often called E-boats by the British). The U.S. Navy's PT (Patrol Torpedo) boats harassed Japanese traffic in the South Pacific. Some of these wooden-hulled craft, which were powered by diesel or

The PT 20, a patrol torpedo boat of the U.S. Navy, World War II. U.S. Navy Photograph

gasoline engines, could reach speeds of 40 knots. In addition to torpedoes, they could carry significant gun armament.

Amphibians

The internal combustion engine made possible the most spectacular naval innovation of World War II, the shallow-draft landing craft used to bring large forces quickly to enemy beaches during amphibious assaults. The most famous example of these was the LST (landing ship, tank), a large beaching craft that could embark and disembark troops and vehicles directly from shore to shore. Another famous example were various landing craft of intermediate size that the U.S. and Royal navies used to deploy troops, vehicles, and supplies onto foreign shores. Landing craft were carried over oceanic distances by ships and then launched at the time of assault.

The LST

The landing ship, tank was first designed during World War II to disembark military forces without the use of dock facilities or the various cranes and lifts necessary to unload merchant ships. LSTs gave the Allies the ability to conduct amphibious invasions at any location on a foreign shore that had a gradually sloped beach.

Specially designed landing ships were first employed by the British in Operation Torch, the invasion of North Africa in 1942. The British recognized the need for such ships after the debacle at Dunkirk in 1940, when they left behind tons of badly needed equipment because no vessels were available with the capability to bridge the gap between the sea and the land. Following the evacuation, Prime Minister Winston Churchill sent his minister of supply a memorandum posing the question,

What is being done about design-ing and planning vessels to transport tanks across the sea for a British attack on enemy coun-tries? These must be able to move six or seven hundred vehicles in one voyage and land them on the beach, or, alternatively, take them off the beaches.

As an interim measure, three shallow-draft tankers were converted to LSTs. The bows were redesigned so that a door, hinged at the bottom, and a 21-metre- (68-foot-) long double ramp could be fitted to the vessels. These modifications made it possible for vehicles to disembark directly from the ship to the beach. Both the new design and the vessel were con-sidered unsatisfactory, but the concept was sound.

At the request of the British, the Americans undertook the redesign and production of LSTs in November 1941, and John Niedermair of the Bureau of Ships designed a ship with a large ballast system. Deep-draft ships were necessary to cross the ocean, and shallow-draft ves-sels were required to bridge the water gap. A newly proposed ballast system gave one ship both capabilities: when at

sea the LST took on water for stability, and during landing operations the water was pumped out to produce a shallow-draft vessel. The American-built LST Mk2, or LST(2), was 328 feet (100 metres) in length and 50 feet (15 metres) wide. It could carry 2,100 tons. Built into the bow were two doors that opened outward to a width of 14 feet (4.25 metres). Most Allied vehicles could be transported on and off-loaded from LST(2)s. The lower deck was the tank deck, where 20 Sherman tanks could be loaded. Lighter vehicles were carried on the upper deck. An elevator was used to load and off-load vehicles, artillery, and other equipment from the upper deck; in later models a ramp replaced the elevator. The vessel was powered by two diesel engines, and it had a maximum speed of 11.5 knots and a cruising speed of 8.75 knots. LSTs were lightly armed with a variety of weap-ons. A typical American LST was armed with seven 40-mm (1.50-inch) and twelve 20-mm (.75-inch) antiaircraft guns.

LSTs were in great demand in both the Pacific and Europe. They were used in the invasions of Sicily, Italy, Normandy, and southern France. At Normandy the Americans' employment of LSTs enabled them to meet their off-loading require-ments following the destruction of their Mulberry artificial harbour in a storm. In the Southwest Pacific theatre, General Douglas MacArthur employed LSTs in his "island-hopping campaigns" and in the invasion of the Philippines. In the Central Pacific, Admiral Chester Nimitz used them at Iwo Jima and Okinawa.

U.S. troops landing with Higgins assault boats on a beach in French Morocco, November 1942. U.S. Army Photo

Landing Craft

The development and use of specialized craft for tactical deployment on hostile shores was first undertaken by the Japanese, who in the early 1930s employed the first landing craft with a ramp in the bow to permit the rapid deployment of troops. This design was copied by the British and Americans, who eventually incorporated it into 60 different types of landing craft and landing ships.

In the 1930s the U.S. Marine Corps and Navy, anticipating the need for amphibious assaults, experimented with small landing boats. Private firms were contracted to develop boats based on criteria outlined by the Navy. Early in World War II, Andrew Higgins, a New Orleans boatbuilder, produced the basic design for the Landing Craft, Vehicle, Personnel (LCVP), a landing craft with a ramp in the bow. Often simply called the Higgins boat, the LCVP could carry 36 combat-equipped infantrymen or 8,000 pounds (3,600 kg) of cargo from ship to shore. During the war the United States produced 23,398 of the craft.

In addition to the basic infantry assault craft, the U.S. Army needed a vessel to transport and land its medium battle tank, and in 1942 the Navy accepted a 50-foot (15.25-metre) Higgins design, the prototype for the Landing Craft, Mechanized (LCM). During the war 11,392 LCMs were produced by the United States.

In 1940 the British designed and manufactured the Landing Craft, Tank (LCT), initially to conduct amphibious raids. Eight different models of this vessel were produced, the Mk4 being the most commonly used. A total of 1,435 were mass-produced in the United States. The LCT Mk4 was capable of carrying and deploying six medium tanks.

In addition to transport landing craft, the United States developed and deployed a number of specialized craft. In these cases additional letters were typically added to the standard abbreviations to designate the special task. For example, LCT(R) designated a Landing Craft, Tank, mounted with rockets, and LCG(L) designated a Landing Craft, Gun (Large), a craft equipped with naval guns to engage fortified beach defenses with direct fire.

LCTs and LCVPs could not have been built without using diesel power plants. Only because their engines and fuel consumed so small a portion of their total displacement could these craft carry such massive loads on shallow drafts.

THE AGE OF THE GUIDED MISSILE

By the middle of World War II, carrier-borne aircraft had become so effective that the aircraft carrier was clearly replacing the battleship as the core of the modern navy. After the war, the development of jet aircraft and nuclear-powered ship propulsion magnified the range and speed of operations, but they did not alter the central role of the carrier.

At the same time, though, a new equalizer was being developed: the antiship guided missile. This weapon, which could be mounted onto the smallest surface vessels as well as aircraft and submarines, was especially dangerous to aircraft carriers because it could be launched outside antiaircraft range and, being unmanned, could not be distracted easily by defensive fire. The main defense was to provide the fleet with its own guided missiles capable of destroying either the missile or its launching platform.

Propulsion

The diesel engine, adapted to warships even before World War II, has remained in use in the navies of the world, as have steam turbines. But steam propulsion reached its ultimate development with the use of the energy released by nuclear fission to heat the boilers of steam turbines. In addition, the gas turbine, a turbine in which the combustion of fuel generates a stream of gases that turns the rotor, has become available for ship propulsion.

Nuclear Power

Nuclear power was proposed for ships, particularly submarines, in 1945, and by 1955 the United States had a nuclear submarine, USS *Nautilus*, in service. Other navies followed suit, so that within 20 years Britain, the Soviet Union, France, and China all operated nuclear submarines. In the 1950s the United States also developed nuclear power plants for surface ships, subsequently installing them aboard aircraft carriers and their escorts. The Soviet Union and France followed with more limited programs in the 1970s and '80s.

For a surface ship, the advantage of nuclear power is effectively infinite range at high speed. The disadvantage is the high cost, which has limited such power to a few valuable ships built by the wealthiest powers—in most cases, the United States.

Gas Turbines

Gas turbines share with internal combustion piston engines the great virtues of quick starting and stopping as well as relatively simple operation. They are also quite reliable. Their main defect is that they are efficient only over a relatively narrow speed range. For this reason, the first gas turbine warships employed combination power plants, such as combined steam and gas turbine (COSAG) or combined diesel and gas turbine (CODAG). Using such a plant, a relatively small ship, such as a frigate, could achieve much higher speed than with a conventional steam turbine. The next step was to combine two gas turbines, one sized for cruising and the other for high speed. Such an arrangement might be either combined gas and gas (COGAG), with both plants able to operate together, or combined gas or gas (COGOG), with only one plant being used at a time.

Systems employing the gas turbine prove useful in smaller escort ships such as destroyers and frigates, although they are also installed in cruiser-sized vessels. A related system, called combined diesel, electric, and gas turbine (CODLAG), is especially valuable in antisubmarine warfare. In order to minimize engine noise, which might interfere with sonar sensors, diesel generators power electric motors, which in turn drive the ship's propellers. For higher speeds, electricity is supplemented or replaced by gas turbines.

ARMOUR

The role of armour has greatly declined since 1945 because aircraft, the greatest threat to warships, now carry guided missiles and bombs capable of penetrating the thickest deck armour that any viable ship can accommodate. At the same time, warships' new missile weaponry has occupied much more space than did the earlier guns, shells, and powder. Modern weapon systems also require room for computers and radars and for their operators. To cover such spaces with anything but the lightest plating would add enormous weight and thus require very large and expensive hulls. The high cost of protection (in ship size as well as money) is a major reason for the abandonment of heavy, extensive armour in the guided-missile era.

Armour has not been abandoned altogether, however. Thin armour, for example, can protect aircraft and missiles from the steel splinters of exploding warheads and thus could keep a ship hit elsewhere from being destroyed by a huge explosion of jet fuel or its own missiles. For this reason most modern warships have adopted thin (about 25- or 50-mm, or one- or two-inch) splinter protection around their missile magazines.

Aircraft carriers, at least in the U.S. Navy, have retained armoured flight decks, though in their case the armour provides structural strength as well as limited protection.

AIRCRAFT CARRIERS

Since World War II the heavy attack aircraft carrier has developed three roles: to deliver air strikes (both conventional and nuclear) against sea and shore targets; to provide a long-range air-defense umbrella for other ships; and to support antisubmarine operations (leaving it to other ships actually to destroy the submarines). In order to carry out these roles, jet carriers have become so huge that only a first-rate power can afford to build and operate them. Today only the United States and France operate full-scale carriers (although the 38,000-ton French *Charles de Gaulle* is closer in size to the carriers of the immediate post-World War II period than to the 80,000-ton, 1,000-foot [300-metre] behemoths built by the United States since the 1970s). The Soviet Union considered building large carriers, but the idea was abandoned by Russia after the collapse of the Soviet system in 1991.

Navies that cannot afford the large carrier have divided its three roles among escort ships and light aircraft carriers. The light aircraft carriers have been given the role of antisubmarine warfare, along with limited ground-attack and air-protection capabilities.

USS Kitty Hawk, *a conventionally powered aircraft carrier of the U.S. Navy launched in 1960, in the Philippine Sea.* U.S. Navy photo by Photographer's Mate 2nd Class William H. Ramsey

LARGE CARRIERS

The main technical development in aircraft carrier design during World War II was the hydraulic catapult, but this was barely powerful enough to launch the heavier jet aircraft coming into service after 1945. The problem was solved in 1951, when the British first tested an effective catapult driven by steam from a ship's boilers.

Jet aircraft landed at much higher speeds than had propeller-driven planes, making the installation of better arresting gear necessary. Also, landing control had to be improved, because the approaching pilot had to make crucial decisions much more quickly. As in the case of the steam catapult, the British supplied the solution, in the form of the angled deck and the mirror (later the Fresnel-lens) landing sight. By building an extension of the flight deck to one side and angling the landing strip onto that extension, the British system allowed a pilot to land away from aircraft parked at the end of the flight deck. If he missed the arresting wires, the pilot could fly off to try again. In this way mistakes became much less serious. The mirror landing sight, in effect, allowed the pilot to see his own position relative to the required glide path and to make corrections instantly. Previously, an officer on deck, observing the landing, had generally ordered the corrections.

By 1955 the modern jet aircraft carrier had emerged, with steam catapults, an angled deck, and a mirror landing system. The first full jet carrier was USS *Forrestal*, commissioned in 1955. The 60,000-ton Forrestal carriers were built with rectangular extensions to the after part of the flight deck; these considerably widened the deck and allowed the angled landing strip to be merely painted on rather than extended over the side. The elevators were shifted to the edge of the flight deck, so that they could operate while aircraft were landing and taking off.

The first nuclear-powered carrier, USS *Enterprise*, was commissioned in 1961. It was equipped with eight nuclear reactors and steamed for more than three years before refueling was necessary. The *Enterprise* displaced 75,700 tons, carried 100 jet aircraft, and could reach more than 30 knots. Beginning in 1975, 10 Nimitz-class carriers superseded the *Enterprise*. These 81,600-ton carriers were powered by only two nuclear reactors, yet they reached speeds comparable to the *Enterprise*, and their uranium cores needed replacement only once every 13 years. The smaller propulsion system created more room for the storage of aviation fuel, which greatly extended the operation of the 90 aircraft carried on these ships. The last Nimitz carrier was commissioned in 2009, and in that year the keel was laid for the first Gerald R. Ford-class carrier. Scheduled to enter service every five years beginning in 2015, the 10 Gerald R. Ford carriers will be approximately the same size as

USS Forrestal, *the first full jet aircraft carrier of the U.S. Navy, at sea, 1959.* U.S. Navy Photograph

the Nimitz carriers, but various technological improvements are expected to reduce the number of crewmembers to as few as 2,500 (as opposed to some 3,250 crewmembers manning a Nimitz carrier). Onboard electric-power generation will be greatly increased over that of the Nimitz carriers, mainly to accommodate a revolutionary electromagnetic aircraft launch system, or EMALS. EMALS would replace the classic steam-powered catapult with a 100-metre- (330-foot-) long "linear synchronous motor," an electric motor containing a series of magnetic coils that would accelerate the launcher

The USS *Enterprise*

The USS Enterprise, *launched in 1960 and commissioned by the U.S. Navy in 1961, was the first nuclear-powered aircraft carrier in the world. Powered by eight nuclear reactors (two for each of its four propellers), the* Enterprise—*displacing about 75,000 tons and having a flight deck of 1,101 by 252 feet (336 by 77 metres)—cruises more than 200,000 miles (320,000 km) over three years before requiring refueling. In addition to endurance, its nuclear reactors give the ship greater space for aviation fuel, ordnance, and stores—important advantages over oil-powered carriers. With a top speed of more than 30 knots, it is said to be the fastest warship afloat. The* Enterprise *has served in conflicts from the Cuban missile crisis in 1962 to the Iraq War that began in 2003. It is scheduled for decommissioning about 2012–14.*

USS Enterprise, *commissioned in 1961, the first nuclear-powered aircraft carrier of the U.S. Navy.* J.E. Williams, PHC/U.S. Navy Photo

and connected aircraft along the carrier's deck. Electromagnetic launching would reduce stress on the aircraft and launching mechanisms; also, energy generated by the system could be adjusted to aircraft of differing weights. Arresting gear would also be based on electromagnets.

Large U.S. carriers are expected to have a service life of 50 years, and over such a period of time construction and operating costs can climb into the tens of billions of dollars. Such costs place large carriers out of reach of all except the wealthiest countries or those countries willing to spend vast sums for military security or international prestige. In the 1970s and '80s the Soviet Union considered building large nuclear-powered carriers similar to those of the United States. The keel for the first such ship was laid in 1988, but after the collapse of the Soviet Union in 1991 the unfinished vessel was scrapped. In 2001 the 38,000-ton *Charles de Gaulle*, a nuclear-powered ship designed to carry 40 aircraft, entered service with the French navy. After that, France canceled plans for further nuclear-powered carriers, though it left open the possibility of building a conventionally powered catapult-equipped carrier to complement its nuclear carrier.

LIGHT CARRIERS

The expense of large carriers is due partly to the huge amounts of fuel, ammunition, and maintenance required to keep as many as 80 aircraft operational, but it is also due to the complexity and size of the catapults and arresting gear needed for jets. In the late 1960s Britain developed a jet fighter, the Harrier, that was capable of taking off vertically or (with a heavy payload) after a short roll. A carrier equipped with these V/STOL (vertical/short takeoff and landing) jets could be much smaller than a full jet carrier, because it would need neither catapults nor arresting gear. In the 1970s and '80s, Britain built three such ships—HMS *Invincible*, *Illustrious*, and *Ark Royal*. These 20,000-ton ships carried eight Sea Harriers and about a dozen antisubmarine helicopters. They

HMS Invincible, *a light aircraft carrier of the Royal Navy.* Department of Defense (Image Number: DN-ST-90-04616.JPEG)

also incorporated a further British contribution to aircraft carrier design: an upward-sloping "ski jump" at the end of the short (170-metre, or 558-foot) flight deck to assist the Sea Harriers in short takeoff. The Invincible-class ships were designed primarily for antisubmarine warfare, but in 1982 the newly commissioned HMS *Invincible* took on the job of providing air cover for amphibious assault forces in the Falkland Islands War, and in 2003 HMS *Ark Royal* performed similar duties at the opening of the Iraq War. In 1998 Britain announced plans to replace the Invincible ships after 2010 with two much larger (65,000-ton) carriers, HMS *Queen Elizabeth* and HMS *Prince of Wales*, that would be able to handle conventional fixed-wing jets as well as the V/STOL Harriers.

The Italian and Spanish navies also constructed light carriers for helicopters and V/STOL jets. Like the Invincible-class ships, they were powered by gas turbines. The Soviet Kiev class, four ships displacing 40,000 tons, carried a larger complement of rotary and V/STOL craft plus a significant battery of antiship missiles, designed to give the ships a surface-fighting capability similar to that of a cruiser in addition to their antisubmarine and fleet-protection duties. The Kiev ships were followed in 1985 with the launching of the *Kuznetsov*, a 60,000-ton carrier with a ski-jump flight deck that could launch conventional fixed-wing aircraft without need for a V/STOL capability.

In the 1960s, '70s, and '80s the United States constructed the Iwo Jima, Tarawa, and Wasp classes of amphibious assault ships, descendants of the World War II escort carriers that could transport close to 2,000 marines as well as their weapons and vehicles. The Tarawa and Wasp classes, besides carrying helicopters and Harriers, were built with well decks for the launching of landing craft. The Wasp class was built specifically to launch air-cushion landing craft (LCACs). However, as the U.S. Marine Corps since 2009 has begun to deploy new tilt-rotor aircraft, which can launch and land vertically or with a short roll and also ferry assault troops quickly to shore much like a transport plane, the U.S. Navy has constructed new America-class assault ships, in which the space for the old well deck is used to create more hangar space.

Occupying a position between cruisers and the through-deck light carriers are helicopter carriers, whose flight decks occupy only the after section of the ship. The 17,000-ton Moskva class of the Soviet Union, introduced in 1967, is a prominent example.

Since the collapse of the Soviet Union, some of the Cold War naval powers have found it difficult to justify the expense of even light aircraft carriers. In the 1990s Russia decommissioned its Soviet-era Kiev ships without replacing them, finally scrapping three and selling one to India. This left Russia with one aircraft carrier, the *Kuznetsov*, as Ukraine in 1998 sold that carrier's unfinished sister ship to China. In the United Kingdom, HMS *Invincible* was decommissioned in 2005, and in 2010 the British government, in a major reduction of defense spending, announced the immediate decommissioning of the *Ark Royal*. The remaining Invincible-class ship, HMS *Illustrious*, had been scheduled for replacement in 2012 by the new *Queen Elizabeth*, but that ship is now budgeted to carry only helicopters and will be decommissioned in 2019, immediately upon the completion of its sister ship, the *Prince of Wales*. These moves have effectively removed any capability of the Royal Navy to launch fixed-wing aircraft from the sea until at least 2020.

Meanwhile, emerging nations wishing to assert their growing wealth and prestige have made a point of acquiring aircraft carriers. China, for instance, converted the unfinished Kuznetsov-class carrier to a training ship—part of its effort to build up its own future aircraft-carrier force. In 2009 India, which had a history of converting retired light carriers from other countries to its own use, laid down the keel of a 40,000-ton vessel that would be the first aircraft carrier to be built in an Indian shipyard.

FLEET ESCORT SHIPS

In the surface ships supporting aircraft carriers, the most important trend after 1945 has been an amalgamation of types. In 1945 cruisers were armoured big-gun ships that were capable of operating independently for protracted periods. Destroyers were part of the screen protecting a main fleet, and frigates were slower ships designed for merchant convoy protection against air and submarine threats—primarily the latter.

This series of distinctions began to collapse in the late 1950s. First, in order to hunt the new fast submarines, frigates had to match destroyer speeds. This made them more like small destroyers. At the same time, most cruisers were converted to carry long-range antiaircraft missiles. This conversion made it clear that cruisers were not solitary raiders or ship killers but fleet escorts—in effect, super destroyers. In the event, all three types have become capable of antiaircraft, antisubmarine, and antiship warfare, although individual classes often specialize in one role.

The most prominent trend in armament has been a shift from guns to guided missiles. Beginning in the mid-1950s, existing ships had at least some of their guns replaced by missiles, and thereafter new ships were built with missiles making up their main batteries. The ranges of these weapons vary from about 7.5 km (four nautical miles) for a short-range antimissile missile to more than 550 km (300 nautical miles) for a long-range antiship missile. Some of these travel at more than twice the speed of sound.

Main guns have become fewer and smaller. The most prominent guns now are dual-purpose weapons (for antiaircraft as well as surface fire) measuring from 75 to 125 mm, or three to five inches. Close-in protection against missiles is provided by fully automatic or Gatling-type guns of 20 to 40 mm (0.75 to 1.5 inch). All guns are now remotely controlled and directed by radar. Stealth technologies have increasingly been brought to bear on the design of fleet escort ships, which now incorporate smooth surfaces coated with materials intended to reduce reflections to an enemy's radar receiver.

CRUISERS

The era of big-gun cruisers ended with the completion of ships laid down during World War II. In 1961 the United States commissioned USS *Long Beach*, the first vessel designed from the keel

The guided-missile cruiser USS Long Beach, *the first surface vessel powered by nuclear reactors, 1966.* U.S. Navy Photograph

up as a guided-missile cruiser and the first surface warship to steam under atomic energy. This 14,000-ton ship was followed by a series of nuclear-powered U.S. cruisers that ended, in the 1970s, with the 10,400-ton Virginia class. This class has been supplemented since the 1980s and '90s by the 7,400-ton, gas-turbine-powered Ticonderoga cruisers. Both the Virginia and Ticonderoga ships are fitted with a broad array of weaponry, including surface-to-air and antiship missiles, tube-launched and rocket-launched antisubmarine torpedoes, and two 125-mm (5-inch) and two 20-mm (0.75-inch) guns. In addition, they are supplied with Tomahawk cruise missiles, which can be fitted with conventional or nuclear warheads. The Ticonderoga vessels carry two submarine-hunting helicopters, and they are equipped with the extremely sophisticated Aegis radar system for tracking hostile targets and directing missile defense.

As the guided-missile cruiser has evolved into an escort for aircraft carriers, it has ceased to be built by navies that had allowed their large carrier capacities to expire. Britain, for example, sold its County-class ships (which were officially classed as destroyers but were effectively cruisers) in the 1970s and '80s, relying thereafter on smaller escorts to protect its light carriers.

The Soviet Union, on the other hand, laid down the first of four 22,000-ton, nuclear-powered Kirov cruisers in 1973. With armament, speed, and steaming range comparable to the Virginias, these cruisers were logical escorts for the new nuclear-powered aircraft carriers that were expected to give the Soviet navy the ability to project its power around the world. They also had a heavy complement of long-range antiship missiles typical of Soviet guided-missile cruisers, giving them a ship-killing role similar to that of the old big-gun cruisers. Since the collapse of the Soviet Union, however, these ships, with no aircraft carriers to escort, have been of dwindling strategic use to Russia. This has left the United States as the only naval power with a fleet of guided-missile cruisers; its Ticonderoga ships are expected to serve in aircraft-carrier task forces well into the 21st century.

DESTROYERS AND FRIGATES

Because of the high cost of cruisers, smaller escort ships have become the backbone of lesser navies in the guided-missile age. The destroyer has completed its transition, begun during World War II, from surface-ship killer to antiaircraft escort. To this duty has been added antisubmarine warfare, the traditional role of the frigate. Often the frigate is distinguished from the destroyer only by its lesser displacement, armament, and speed.

As submarines have become faster, many classes of destroyer and frigate have adopted the helicopter (often housed in a hangar in the after section) as

The radar room of the destroyer USS John Young. U.S. Navy Photo

a help in hunting them down. Like cruisers, they bristle with an array of sonar and radar sensors and satellite receivers and are packed with electronic gear for the swift detection and identification of hostile targets and the computation of firing data. Such complex equipment, packed into ships that must also have high speed (30 knots and more), excellent seakeeping ability, and long endurance, means that destroyers and frigates have become larger than their World War II predecessors. Guided-missile destroyers range from 3,500 to 8,000 tons displacement, while frigates range between 1,500 and 4,000 tons.

CHAPTER 3

SUBMARINES

Submarines were conceived at least on paper as early as the 16th century, but they first became a major factor in naval warfare during World War I (1914–18), when Germany employed them to destroy surface merchant vessels. In such attacks submarines used their primary weapon, a self-propelled underwater missile known as a torpedo. Submarines played a similar role on a larger scale in World War II (1939–45), in both the Atlantic (by Germany) and the Pacific (by the United States). Since the 1960s the nuclear-powered submarine, capable of remaining underwater for months at a time and of firing long-range nuclear missiles without surfacing, has been an important strategic weapon platform fielded by the world's biggest military powers. At the same time, nuclear-powered attack submarines, armed with torpedoes as well as antiship and antisubmarine missiles, have become a key element of naval warfare, even as sophisticated modern versions of the traditional nonnuclear submarine have remained formidable weapon platforms in the service of navies around the world.

EARLY HAND-POWERED SUBMERSIBLES

The first serious discussion of a "submarine"—a craft designed to be navigated underwater—appeared in 1578 from the pen of William Bourne, a British mathematician and writer on naval subjects. Bourne proposed a completely enclosed boat that could be submerged and rowed underwater. It consisted of a wooden frame covered with waterproof leather; it was to be submerged by reducing its volume by contracting the sides through the use of hand vises. Bourne did not actually construct his boat, and Cornelis Drebbel (or Cornelius van Drebel), a Dutch inventor, is usually credited with building the first submarine. Between 1620 and 1624 he successfully maneuvered his craft at depths of from 4 to 5 metres (12 to 15 feet) beneath the surface during repeated trials in the Thames River, in England. King James I is said to have gone aboard the craft for a short ride. Drebbel's submarine resembled that proposed by Bourne in that its outer hull consisted of greased leather over a wooden frame; oars extended through the sides and, sealed with tight-fitting leather flaps, provided a means of propulsion both on the surface and underwater. Drebbel's first craft was followed by two larger ones built on the same principle.

A number of submarine boats were conceived in the early years of the 18th century. By 1727 no fewer than 14 types had been patented in England alone. In 1747 an unidentified inventor proposed an ingenious method of submerging and returning to the surface: his submarine design had goatskin bags attached to the hull with each skin connected to an aperture in the bottom of the craft. He planned to submerge the vessel by filling the skins with water and to surface by forcing the water out of the skins with a "twisting rod." This arrangement was a forerunner of the modern submarine ballast tank.

First Use in War

The submarine was first used as an offensive weapon in naval warfare during the American Revolution (1775–83). The *Turtle*, a one-man craft invented by David Bushnell, a student at Yale, was built of wood in the shape of a walnut standing on end. Submerged, the craft was powered by propellers cranked by the operator. The plan was to have the *Turtle* make an underwater approach to a British warship, attach a charge of gunpowder to the ship's hull by a screw device operated from within the craft, and leave before the charge was exploded by a time fuse. In the actual attack, however, the *Turtle* was unable to force the screw through the copper sheathing on the warship's hull.

Robert Fulton, famed U.S. inventor and artist, experimented with submarines several years before his steamboat *Clermont* steamed up the Hudson River. In 1800, while in France, Fulton built the submarine *Nautilus* under a grant from Napoleon Bonaparte. Completed in May 1801, this craft was made of copper sheets over iron ribs. A collapsing mast and sail were provided for surface propulsion, and a hand-turned propeller drove the boat when submerged. A precursor of a conning tower fitted with a glass-covered porthole permitted observation from within the craft. The *Nautilus* submerged by taking water into ballast tanks, and a horizontal "rudder"—a forerunner of the diving plane—helped keep the craft at the desired depth. The submarine contained enough air to keep four men alive and two candles burning for three hours underwater; later a tank of compressed air was added.

The *Nautilus* was intended to attach an explosive charge to the hull of an enemy ship in much the same manner as the *Turtle*. Fulton experimentally sank an old schooner moored at Brest but, setting out to destroy British warships, was unable to overtake those he sighted. France's interest in Fulton's submarine waned, and he left for England, offering his invention to his former enemy. In 1805 the *Nautilus* sank the brig *Dorothy* in a test, but the Royal Navy would not back his efforts. Fulton then came to the United States and succeeded in obtaining congressional backing for a more ambitious undersea craft. This new submarine was to carry 100 men and be powered by a steam engine. Fulton died before the craft was actually finished, however, and the submarine, named *Mute*, was left to rot, eventually sinking at its moorings.

During the War of 1812 between the United States and England, a copy of the *Turtle* was built, which attacked HMS *Ramillies* at anchor off New London, Conn. This time the craft's operator succeeded in boring a hole in the ship's copper sheathing, but the screw broke loose as the explosive was being attached to the ship's hull.

AMERICAN CIVIL WAR AND AFTER

The next U.S. attempt at submarine warfare came during the Civil War (1861–65) when the Confederate States resorted to "unconventional" methods to overcome the Union Navy's superior strength, exerted in a blockade of Southern ports.

In 1862 Horace L. Hunley of Mobile, Ala., financed the building of a Confederate submarine named *Pioneer*, a craft that was 10.4 metres (34 feet) long and was driven by a hand-cranked propeller operated by three men. It probably was scuttled to prevent its capture when Union forces occupied New Orleans (although some records say the *Pioneer* was lost with all those aboard during a dive while en route to attack Union ships).

The second submarine developed by the same builders was a remarkably advanced concept: a 7.6-metre (25-foot) iron boat intended to be propelled by a battery and electric motors. Not surprisingly, no suitable motors could be found, so a propeller cranked by four men was again adopted. The submarine sank without loss of life in heavy seas off Mobile Bay while seeking to attack the enemy.

The third submarine of the Confederacy was the *H.L. Hunley*, a modified iron boiler lengthened to between 11 and 12 metres (36 and 40 feet). Ballast tanks and a system of weights submerged the craft; it could travel at a speed of 6.4 km (4 miles) an hour, powered by eight men cranking its propeller. On the night of Feb. 17, 1864, the submarine, armed with an explosive "torpedo" mounted at the end of a long spar projecting from its forward end, attacked the Union warship *Housatonic* in Charleston harbour. The torpedo's detonation exploded the warship's magazines: the *Housatonic* sank in shallow water with the loss of five men, but the *Hunley* was also destroyed by the explosion, and its crew was killed.

THE *H.L. HUNLEY*

The first submarine to sink an enemy ship was a Confederate invention of the American Civil War. The H.L. Hunley *was designed and built at Mobile, Ala., and named for its chief financial backer, Horace L. Hunley. Less than 40 feet (12 metres) long, the submarine held nine crewmen, eight of whom propelled the vessel by hand-cranking a single screw. Its commander controlled steering and depth. Its armament consisted of a "torpedo," filled with 90 pounds (40 kg) of gunpowder, towed behind the submarine at the end of a 200-foot (30-metre) line. The* Hunley *was to dive under an enemy warship and drag the torpedo against its hull. After a successful test against a barge, the* Hunley *was moved by railroad to Charleston, S.C. There, in practice runs and in attempts to attack blockading Union warships, the vessel suffered several disasters, sinking three times and drowning a number of crewmen, including Hunley himself.*

Manned for a fourth time, the Hunley *was fitted with a torpedo on the end of a long spar, and the craft made several successful dives. On Feb. 17, 1864, it successfully attacked the Union sloop* Housatonic, *sinking the vessel. The* Hunley, *however, was lost shortly after the attack, along with all its crewmen. The vessel lay in only 30 feet (9 metres) of water some 4 miles (6 km) offshore until it was found by preservationists in 1995. It was raised intact in 2000 and brought ashore so that the crewmen's remains could be removed for burial and the vessel itself restored for display at the Charleston Museum.*

One of the more intrepid submarine inventors of the same period was Wilhelm Bauer, a noncommissioned officer of Bavarian artillery who built two boats, *Le Plongeur-Marin* (1851) and *Le Diable-Marin* (1855). The first boat sank in Kiel harbour on Feb. 1, 1851, but Bauer and his two assistants escaped from a depth of 18 metres (60 feet) after the craft had been on the bottom for five hours. His second craft, built for the Russian government, was successful and reportedly made 134 dives before being lost at sea. In September 1856, during the coronation of Tsar Alexander II, Bauer submerged his submarine in Kronshtadt harbour with several musicians on board. An underwater rendition of the Russian national anthem was clearly heard by persons inside ships in the harbour.

TOWARD DIESEL-ELECTRIC POWER

A major limitation of the early submarines was their lack of a suitable means of propulsion. In 1880 an English clergyman, George W. Garrett, successfully operated a submarine with steam from a coal-fired boiler that featured a retractable smokestack. The fire had to be extinguished before the craft would submerge (or it would exhaust the air in the submarine), but enough steam remained in the boilers for traveling several miles underwater.

Similarly, the Swedish gun designer Torsten Nordenfelt constructed a steam-powered submarine driven by twin propellers. His craft could be submerged by vertical propellers to a depth of 15 metres (50 feet) and was fitted with one of the first practical torpedo tubes. Several navies built submarines to Nordenfelt's design.

In an effort to overcome the problems of propulsion, two French naval officers built the 50-metre (146-foot) submarine Le Plongeur in 1864, powered by an 80-horsepower compressed-air engine, but the craft quickly exhausted its air tanks whenever it got under way. Development of the electric motor finally made electric propulsion practicable. The submarine Nautilus, built in 1886 by two Englishmen, was an all-electric craft. This Nautilus, propelled by two 50-horsepower electric motors operated from a 100-cell storage battery, achieved a surface speed of six knots (nautical miles per hour; one knot equals 1.15 statute miles per hour or 1.85 km per hour). But the battery had to be recharged and overhauled at short intervals, and the craft was never able to travel more than 130 km (80 miles) without a battery recharge. In France, Gustave Zédé launched the Gymnote in 1888; it, too, was propelled by an electric motor and was extremely maneuverable but tended to go out of control when it dived.

The end of the 19th century was a period of intensive submarine development, and Zédé collaborated in a number of designs sponsored by the French navy. A most successful French undersea craft of the period was the Narval, designed by Maxime Laubeuf, a marine engineer in the navy. Launched in 1899, the Narval was a double-hulled craft, 34 metres (111.5 feet) long, propelled on the surface by a steam engine and by electric motors when submerged. The ballast tanks were located between the double hulls, a concept still in use today. The Narval made a large number of successful dives. Further French progress in submarines was marked by the four Sirène-class steam-driven undersea craft completed in 1900–01 and the Aigrette, completed in 1905, the first diesel-driven submarine of any navy.

Similarly, there were submarine successes in the United States by rival inventors John P. Holland (an Irish immigrant) and Simon Lake. Holland launched his first undersea craft in 1875. This one and its successors were significant in combining water ballast with horizontal rudders for diving. In 1895, in competition with Nordenfelt, Holland received an order from the U.S. Navy for a submarine. This was to be the Plunger, propelled by steam on the surface and by electricity when submerged. The craft underwent many design changes and finally was abandoned before completion. Holland returned the funds advanced by the navy and built his next submarine (his sixth) at his own expense. This was the Holland, a 53.25-foot (16.25-metre) craft launched in 1897 and accepted by the navy in 1900. For underwater propulsion the *Holland* had an electric motor, and it was propelled on the surface by a gasoline engine. The submarine's armament consisted of a bow torpedo tube, for which three torpedoes were carried, and two dynamite guns. With its nine-man crew the *Holland* was a successful boat; it was modified many times to test different arrangements of propellers, diving planes, rudders, and other equipment.

Holland's chief competitor, Simon Lake, built his first submarine, the *Argonaut I*, in 1894; it was powered by a gasoline engine and electric motor. This and Lake's other early boats were intended as undersea research craft. In 1898 the *Argonaut I* sailed from Norfolk, Va., to New York City under its own power, predating the cruises of the French *Narval* and marking the first time an undersea craft operated extensively in the open sea. Lake's second submarine was the *Protector*, launched in 1901.

Of the major naval powers at the turn of the century, only Britain remained indifferent toward submarines. Finally, in 1901, the Royal Navy ordered five of the Holland-design undersea craft. Germany completed its first submarine, the *U-1* (for *Unterseeboot 1*), in 1905. This craft was 42 metres (139 feet) long, powered on the surface by a heavy oil engine and by an electric motor when submerged, and was armed with one torpedo tube. Thus, the stage was set for the 20th-century submarine, a craft propelled on the surface by diesel engines and underwater by battery-powered electric motors, submerging by diving planes and taking on water ballast, and armed with torpedoes for sinking enemy ships. The quarters inside these early craft were cramped, generally wet, and stank from diesel oil.

WORLD WAR I

By the eve of World War I all of the major navies included submarines in their fleets, but these craft were relatively small, were considered of questionable military value, and generally were intended for coastal operations. The most significant exception to the concept of coastal activity was the German Deutschland class of merchant U-boats, each 96 metres (315 feet) long with two large cargo compartments. These submarines could carry 700 tons of cargo at 12- to 13-knot speeds on the surface and at seven knots submerged. The *Deutschland* itself became the *U-155* when fitted with torpedo tubes and deck guns, and, with seven similar submarines, it served in a combat role during the latter stages of the war. In comparison, the "standard" submarine of World War I measured slightly over 60 metres (200 feet) in length and displaced less than 1,000 tons on the surface.

The prewar submarines generally had been armed with self-propelled torpedoes for attacking enemy ships. During the war submarines also were fitted with deck guns. This permitted them to approach enemy merchant ships on the surface and signal them to stop for searching (an early war policy) and later to sink small or unarmed ships that did not warrant expenditure of torpedoes. Most war-built submarines had one and sometimes two guns of about 75- or 100-mm (3- or 4-inch) calibre; however, several later German submarines carried 150-mm (6-inch) guns (including the Deutschland class in military configuration).

An important armament variation was the submarine modified to lay mines during covert missions off an enemy's harbours. The Germans constructed several specialized submarines with vertical mine tubes through their hulls; some U-boats carried 48 mines in addition to their torpedoes.

Also noteworthy was the development, during the war, of the concept of an antisubmarine submarine. British submarines sank 17 German U-boats during the conflict; the early submarine-versus-submarine successes led to British development of the R-class submarine intended specifically for this role. These were relatively small craft, 50 metres (163 feet) long and displacing 410 tons on the surface, with only one propeller (most contemporary submarines had two). Diesel engines could drive them at nine knots on the surface, but once submerged, large batteries permitted their electric motors to drive them underwater at the high speed of 15 knots for two hours. (Ten knots was a common speed for submerged submarines until after World War II.) Thus, they were both maneuverable and fast. Advanced underwater listening equipment (asdic, or sonar) was installed, and six forward torpedo tubes made them potent weapons.

Although these submarines appeared too late to have any actual effect on the war, they pioneered a new concept in the development of the submarine.

All World War I-era submarines were propelled by diesels on the surface and by electric motors submerged, except for the British Swordfish and K class. These submarines, intended to operate as scouts for surface warships, required the high speeds then available only from steam turbines. The K-boats steamed at 23.5 knots on the surface, while electric motors gave them a 10-knot submerged speed.

WORLD WAR II

Interest in submarines continued high within the world's navies during the period between World Wars I and II. Britain, France, and Japan built improved types, and during this period the U.S. Navy built its first large long-range submarine, the *Argonaut*. Completed in 1928, it was 381 feet (116 metres) long, displaced 2,710 tons on the surface, was armed with two six-inch (150-mm) guns and four forward torpedo tubes, and could carry 60 mines. The *Argonaut*, the largest non-nuclear submarine ever built by the U.S. Navy, led to the highly successful Gato and Balao classes of U.S. submarines used in World War II.

During the 1930s the rejuvenated Soviet shipyards began producing large numbers of submarines, primarily coastal craft, in an attempt to make the Soviet Union a sea power without major expenditures for surface warships. But though the Soviet program achieved quantity, their ships were unsuitable for operations against the German navy, their crews were poorly trained, and Soviet bases were blocked by ice much of the time.

World War II saw extensive submarine campaigns on all of the world's oceans. In the Atlantic the principal German U-boat was the VII type, a relatively small but effective craft when properly employed. The Type VIIC variant was 67 metres (220.25 feet) long, displaced 769 tons on the surface, and was powered by diesel-electric machinery at a speed of 17 knots on the surface and 7.5 knots submerged. Armament consisted of one 90-mm (3.5-inch) deck gun, various antiaircraft guns, and five torpedo tubes, four forward and one aft. Either 14 torpedoes or 14 tube-launched mines were carried. Manned by a crew of 44, these submarines had a surface endurance of 10,400 km (6,500 miles) at 12 knots, but, when they were submerged, their batteries would remain active a little less than a day at four knots.

The ultimate diesel-electric submarine evolved in the war was the German Type XXI, a 76-metre (250-foot), 1,600-ton craft that could attain 17.5 knots submerged for more than an hour, could travel at six knots underwater for two days, or could "creep" at slower speeds for four days. These submarines were fitted with snorkel devices, which made it unnecessary for them to surface fully to recharge their batteries after operating submerged. The Type XXI had an operating depth of 260 metres (850 feet), more than twice what was then normal, and was armed with four 33-mm (1.25-inch) guns and six forward torpedo tubes (23 torpedoes carried). These properties made all earlier submarines obsolete. Existing Allied antisubmarine forces would have had serious trouble coping with these craft had the war continued past the spring of 1945.

A final German war design of particular interest was the Walter turbine propulsion plant. The need for oxygen for combustion had previously prevented the use of steam turbines or diesels while the submarine was submerged and air was at a premium. Hellmuth Walter, a German scientist, developed a turbine propulsion system using oxygen generated by hydrogen peroxide to operate the turbine while submerged. A simplified submarine, the *V-80*, built in 1940 and propelled by a Walter turbine system, could attain speeds of more than 26 knots submerged for a short period of time. After many delays, the first Walter-propelled Type XVII combat submarines were completed and could reach 25 knots underwater for brief periods, and a submerged run of 20 knots for 5.5 hours was achieved on trials. But these submarines, like the Type XXI, were not ready for full-scale operations when the war ended.

A notable German submarine development of World War II was the *schnorchel* device (anglicized by the U.S. Navy to

U-BOATS

The term U-boat *is an English version of the German* U-boot, *for* Unterseeboot *("undersea boat"). Germany was the first country to employ submarines in war as substitutes for surface commerce raiders. At the outset of World War I, U-boats, though numbering only 38, achieved notable successes against British warships; the adoption of unrestricted U-boat warfare against merchant ships was largely responsible for the entry of the United States into the war. By the end of the war Germany had built 334 U-boats and had 226 under construction. The peak U-boat strength of 140 was reached in October 1917, but there were never more than about 60 at sea at one time. In 1914–18 the destruction—more than 10,000,000 tons—caused by the U-boats was especially remarkable in view of the small size (less than 1,000 tons), frailty, and vulnerability of the craft.*

The Armistice terms of 1918 required Germany to surrender all its U-boats, and the Treaty of Versailles forbade it to possess them in the future. In 1935, however, Adolf Hitler's Germany repudiated the treaty and forcefully negotiated the right to build U-boats. Britain was ill-prepared in 1939 for a resumption of unrestricted submarine warfare, and during the early months of World War II the U-boats, which at that time numbered only 57, again achieved great successes. The first phase, during which the U-boats generally operated singly, ended in March 1941, by which time many merchant ships were sailing in convoy, trained escort groups were becoming available, and aircraft were proving their effectiveness as anti-U-boat weapons. In the next phase the Germans, having acquired air and U-boat bases in Norway and western France, were able to reach much farther out into the Atlantic, and their U-boats began to operate in groups (called "wolf packs" by the British). One U-boat would shadow a convoy and summon others by radio, and then the group would attack, generally on the surface at night. These tactics succeeded until radar came to the aid of the escorts and convoys were given continuous sea and air escort all the way across the Atlantic in both directions. In March 1943, the Germans nearly succeeded in cutting Britain's Atlantic lifeline, but by May escort carriers and very-long-range reconnaissance bombers became available. After the U-boats lost 41 of their number during that month, they withdrew temporarily from the Atlantic.

In the next phase, U-boats were sent to remote waters where unescorted targets could still be found. Although at first they achieved considerable successes, especially in the Indian Ocean, the Allied strategy of striking at the U-boats' supply vessels and putting all possible shipping into convoys again proved successful. In the final phase the U-boats—then fitted with the snorkel ventilating tube, which permitted extended underwater travel and greatly reduced the effectiveness of radar—returned to the coastal waters around the British Isles, but they sank few ships and themselves suffered heavy losses.

In World War II Germany built 1,162 U-boats, of which 785 were destroyed and the remainder surrendered (or were scuttled to avoid surrender) at the capitulation.

"snorkel"). Its invention is credited to a Dutch officer, Lieut. Jan J. Wichers, who in 1933 advanced the idea of a breathing tube to supply fresh air to a submarine's diesel engines while it was running submerged. The Netherlands navy began using snorkels in 1936, and some fell into German hands in 1940. With the advent of radar to detect surfaced submarines, the Germans fitted hundreds of U-boats with snorkels to permit the operation of diesels at periscope depth (to recharge batteries for underwater propulsion) with less of a possibility of detection by Allied radar-equipped ships and aircraft.

In the Pacific war the Japanese employed a large number of submarines of various sizes and types, including aircraft-carrying submarines, midget submarines, and "human torpedoes" carried by larger submarines. The Japanese I-201 class was a high-speed submarine, of 79 metres (259 feet) and 1,291 tons displacement, that had diesel propulsion for 15 knots on the surface; while underwater, large batteries and electric motors could drive the vessel at a speed of 19 knots for almost one hour. Each boat had two 25-mm (1-inch) guns and four forward torpedo tubes and carried ten torpedoes.

The highly successful U.S. submarine campaign in the Pacific war was waged mainly with the Gato- and Balao-class submarines. These were approximately 311.5 feet (95 metres) long, displaced 1,525 tons, and had diesel-electric machinery for 20-knot surface and nine-knot underwater speeds. The principal difference between the two designs was the 300-foot (90-metre) operating depth for the Gato class and 400-foot (120-metre) depth for the Balao boats. Manned by 65 to 70, these submarines had one or two five-inch (125-mm) deck guns plus smaller antiaircraft weapons and 10 torpedo tubes (six forward, four aft) and carried 24 torpedoes.

Postwar Developments

After the war the Allies were quick to adopt advanced German submarine technology. The British built two peroxide turbine-propelled experimental submarines, but this concept lost favour because of the unstable properties of hydrogen peroxide and because of American success with nuclear propulsion. The Soviet Union began building modifications of the Type XXI submarine. Some 265 of these submarines, labeled Whiskey and Zulu class by North Atlantic Treaty Organization (NATO) observers, were completed between 1950 and 1958, more submarines than built by all of the world's other navies combined between 1945 and 1970. (In that period Soviet shipyards produced a total of 560 new submarines.)

The U.S. Navy studied German technology and converted 52 war-built submarines to the Guppy configuration (an acronym for "greater underwater propulsive power" with the "y" added for phonetics). These submarines had their deck guns removed and streamlined conning towers fitted; larger batteries and a snorkel were installed; four torpedoes and, in some craft, one of the four diesel engines were removed. The result was an underwater speed of 15 knots and increased underwater endurance.

Although the major powers switched to nuclear power after World War II, the great bulk of the world's navies have continued to buy—or in a few cases, build—submarines descended directly from the fast diesel-electric U-boats of the war. (Indeed, many of them have been designed and built in Germany.) Postwar diesel-electric submarines continue to be equipped with snorkels, but hunters have adopted improved radars that can detect even the small head of the snorkel, just as aircraft with more primitive radars could detect surfaced U-boats during World War II.

The main advances have been in weapons and sensors. Deck guns have been abandoned, in some cases for antiship missiles. Torpedoes, which can exceed 50 knots, either home onto their targets acoustically with self-contained sonar or are guided by electronic commands passed to them through a threadlike wire paid out behind the speeding projectile. In addition, many submarines are equipped with cruise missiles or antiship missiles for striking targets on land or on the sea surface. Submarine sonars, for detecting both surface ships and other submarines, are enormously improved, and on the most advanced submarines the familiar periscope is being replaced by so-called photonic masts, or optronic masts. These are sensor systems that, like the periscope, project upward to the surface from the submarine's sail; however, unlike the periscope, they relay optical, infrared, and radiowave information to the control room electronically, without the need for any hardware to pierce the submarine's hull. The masts are directed by a simple joystick in the control room, and the data can be displayed on screens located anywhere on the submarine.

Maximum submerged speed, meanwhile, has increased only somewhat (to more than 20 knots) over the German Type XXI, and endurance at top speed is no greater than at the end of World War II. Improvements in the design of conventional lead-acid batteries has somewhat increased endurance at low speed. Many modern submarines, for example, can remain submerged (at about three knots) for as long as a week to 10 days. This is an important improvement, since during so long a period sea conditions can easily arise that would allow a submarine to escape or force submarine hunters on the surface to disperse, but the development of "air-independent propulsion" (AIP) using fuel cells has brought even greater improvement. Some AIP-capable submarines, equipped with fuel cells that use stored hydrogen and oxygen to generate electricity, are said to be able to operate at low speeds underwater for as long as a month.

For these reasons, diesel-electric submarines are still furtive but effective platforms, operating very quietly and conserving their energy for the postattack escape. Because their electric motors are quieter than nuclear units (and can even be shut off for a time), they are sometimes proposed as antisubmarine ambushers that would silently await their prey in areas through which enemy submarines are known to pass. AIP offers the possibility of other roles, such as operating in polar seas for long periods under ice, tracking coastal shipping in antiterrorist operations, or inserting special operations forces onto foreign shores. Modern diesel-electric submarines, AIP-capable or not, are thus affordable weapons platforms for many navies around the world that wish to defend their own coastal areas against all potential enemies, even nuclear powers.

NUCLEAR PROPULSION

In 1954, with the commissioning of USS *Nautilus*, nuclear power became available. Since the nuclear reactor needed no oxygen at all, a single power plant could now suffice for both surface and submerged operation. Moreover, since a very small quantity of nuclear fuel (enriched uranium) provided power over a very long period, a nuclear submarine could operate completely submerged at high speed indefinitely.

This change was revolutionary. In the typical pre-nuclear submarine attack, the submarine approached the target on the surface to avoid draining the battery and submerged only just before coming within sight of the target. The submerged approach had to be made at very low speed, perhaps no more than two or three knots, again to avoid wasting battery power. The submarine commander had to husband his battery charge until after the attack, when he would have to use full underwater power (and a speed of perhaps seven to 10 knots) to evade the counterattack. Even then, a full battery charge would last only about one or two hours at top speed. This necessity of conserving battery power, which forced diesel-electric submarines to approach their targets as quietly and slowly as possible, meant that they could not engage most fast surface warships, such as aircraft carriers and battleships.

Nuclear submarines were in an altogether different class. Not only could they evade freely (that is, at top speed for indefinite periods) after attacking, they could also operate freely before attacking and keep up with fast surface ships. This principle was illustrated by the only instance of a nuclear submarine's firing of a weapon at a surface vessel in anger. During the Falkland Islands conflict in 1982, a British nuclear submarine, HMS *Conqueror*, followed the fast Argentine cruiser *General Belgrano* for more than 48 hours before closing in to sink it. That performance would have been entirely beyond the capability of any pre-nuclear submarine. For the first time, a submarine commander could maneuver freely underwater, without worrying that he was exhausting his vessel's batteries, and fast surface warships were vulnerable to submarine attack.

Initially, the major powers continued to build diesel-electric submarines alongside nuclear vessels, but some later gave in to the expense of maintaining two categories of submarine in parallel. After 1959 the U.S. Navy effectively ceased construction of nonnuclear submarines. The Royal Navy, which completed its first nuclear submarine, HMS *Dreadnought*, in 1963, followed a similar policy except for a brief period in the late 1980s and early 1990s, when it built the Upholder class of diesel-electric submarines. Following the end of the Cold War, the Royal Navy stopped the Upholder program at four boats, eventually decommissioning them and selling them to Canada, and returned to an all-nuclear submarine force. France completed its first nuclear submarine, *Le Redoutable*, in 1971 and effectively abandoned diesel-electric construction for its own navy in 1976, though it still builds conventional submarines for export. Although the Soviets continued to build diesel submarines, the bulk of their new construction shifted to nuclear power after their first nuclear submarines, of the November class, entered service in 1958. Since the dissolution of the Soviet Union in 1991, Russia has continued the policy of maintaining a mixed nuclear-conventional submarine force.

In 1968, the Chinese began to build nuclear submarines while continuing to build and purchase large numbers of nonnuclear submarines. India has followed roughly the same model, buying and building diesel-electric submarines but also, in 1998, beginning construction on its first nuclear vessel.

NUCLEAR POWER PLANTS

A nuclear reactor provides the heat that powers a steam turbine, which in turn drives a propeller. There are three main types of marine nuclear reactor: pressurized-water, natural-circulation, and liquid-metal.

Generally, uranium in a reactor produces heat by nuclear fission. In the reactor, the uranium is surrounded by a moderator, which is required to slow the reaction neutrons so that they will interact more efficiently with the uranium. In most reactors the moderator is water, which is also used to carry away the heat of reaction. This heated water is called the primary loop water. Pressurized to prevent it from boiling, it runs through a heat exchanger, in which the heat is passed to another, secondary, water circuit. The heat exchanger is essentially a boiler, and the secondary circuit, or loop, provides the steam that actually turns the turbine. So long as a sufficient seal is maintained, the water of the primary loop cannot contaminate the rest of the power plant.

In most cases the water in the primary loop is circulated by pump. Reactors can also be arranged so that differences in temperature—for example, between that portion of the reactor containing the reacting fuel and the rest of the reactor— force the water to circulate naturally. Typically, in these natural-circulation reactors cooled water from the heat exchanger is fed into the bottom of the reactor, and it rises through the fuel elements as they heat it.

The USS Seawolf *off the coast of Key West, Fla., 1958.* U.S. Navy Photograph

The liquid-metal-cooled reactor operates on the principle that molten metal can carry much more heat than water, so that a more compact turbine can be used. Against that advantage, molten metal can be made highly radioactive, so that leaks, which are dangerous enough in a pressurized-water plant, become much more so. Second, pumps in these reactors must be much more powerful, and the simplicity of using the same substance as moderator and heat sink is lost. Finally, there is always the possibility

that enough heat will be lost for the plant to seize up, the metal solidifying in the pipes, with catastrophic results.

Under the direction of Captain (later Admiral) Hyman Rickover, the U.S. Navy developed both pressurized-water and liquid-metal prototypes. It completed its first two nuclear submarines, the *Nautilus* and *Seawolf*, to test the two types, but problems (including leakage) in the *Seawolf* reactor led to the abandonment of the liquid-metal scheme. Later the navy also developed natural-circulation reactors. U.S. attack submarines (except for USS *Narwhal*, the natural-circulation prototype) are built with pressurized-water reactors, but the Ohio-class strategic submarines are powered by natural-circulation reactors. The latter are inherently quieter than pressurized-water 'units because they require no pumps, at least at low and moderate power.

The other nuclear navies have employed pressurized-water or natural-circulation reactors with one exception, the Soviet Union in its very fast Alfa-class attack submarines, which were built in the 1970s and '80s with liquid-metal reactors.

THE NUCLEAR NAVIES

The advent of the new nuclear submarines has had two great consequences. One is the rise of an altogether new kind of submarine, the strategic submarine. The other is a revolution in antisubmarine warfare, with attack submarines becoming the primary antisubmarine weapons. Attack submarines are armed with torpedoes and, in some cases, with antiship missiles. Strategic submarines may carry similar weapons, but their primary weapons are submarine-launched ballistic missiles (SLBMs), such as the U.S.-British Trident.

STRATEGIC SUBMARINES

Strategic submarines are valuable because they are so difficult to find and kill, and they have become even more important as long-range SLBMs have become more accurate. Accurate missiles can destroy missiles in fixed land sites; were all strategic missiles so based, the side firing first could hope to disarm its enemy. However, if a nuclear power had its missiles based at sea, such a first strike would become virtually impossible—barring some breakthrough in submarine detection. To the extent that preemptive attack is impractical, therefore, a force of strategic submarines has become an effective deterrent against enemy attack. For this reason, the United States, the Soviet Union (and its successor state, Russia), Great Britain, France, China, and India have all built submarines designed to be armed with SLBMs.

Strategic submarines actually predated the nuclear-propulsion era, in that during the 1950s both the U.S. and Soviet navies developed missile-carrying diesel-electric submarines. The U.S. submarines were armed with Regulus cruise missiles, and the Soviet ships carried SS-N-3 Shaddock cruise missiles and SS-N-4 Sark short-range SLBMs. (The "SS-N" designations were given by NATO to each series of surface-to-surface naval missiles produced by the Soviet Union and Russia.) However, these missiles had to be launched from the surface, and the submarines themselves could not remain submerged indefinitely. Strategic submarines did not become truly effective until nuclear power plants and dive-launched missiles enabled them to operate continuously without exposing themselves on the surface in any way.

The first modern strategic submarines were of the U.S. George Washington class, which became operational in 1959. These 5,900-ton, 382-foot (116-metre) vessels carried 16 Polaris missiles, which had a range of 1,200 nautical miles (2,200 km). In 1967 the first of the Soviet Union's 8,000-ton Yankee-class submarines were delivered, which carried 16 SS-N-6 missiles of 1,300-nautical-mile (2,400-km) range. These were followed a decade later by Delta-class vessels fitted with 16 SS-N-18 missiles. Each SS-N-18 had a range of 3,500 nautical miles (6,500 km). In 1982 the Soviet Union began to deploy its Typhoon class; at an estimated surface displacement of 25,000 tons and a length of 170 metres (560 feet), these were the largest submarines ever built. They have continued in the service of the Russian navy since the dissolution of the Soviet Union in 1991, carrying 20 R-39 SLBMs (NATO SS-N-20 Sturgeon), each of which can carry its warheads a distance of 4,500 nautical miles (8,300 km). As the Typhoon and Delta vessels have aged, Russia has proceeded with plans to introduce its new Borey class of submarines, the first of which was launched in 2007. The Borey submarines have been designed to carry the new Bulava (NATO SS-N-30) missiles, which have a range similar to that of the R-39.

Beginning in 1970, the United States fitted its Lafayette-class submarines with 16 Poseidon SLBMs, which could launch its warheads a distance of 2,500 nautical miles (4,600 km). To carry as many as 24 Trident missiles, improved versions of which could travel about 6,500 nautical miles (12,000 km), the U.S. Navy commissioned 18 Ohio-class submarines between 1981 and 1997 (though some of them have since been converted to non-SLBM use under the terms of arms control treaties). These vessels displace 16,600 tons at the surface and are about as long as the Soviet/Russian Typhoons.

Britain's first strategic submarines, of the Resolution class, entered service in 1967 with 16 Polaris missiles. Between 1994 and 1999 four Vanguard-class vessels, comparable to the U.S. Ohio vessels, entered service to carry as many as 16 Trident missiles each.

To supplement the Redoutable class of the 1970s, France built *L'Inflexible*. This 8,000-ton submarine, which entered service in 1985, carried 16 M-4 SLBMs, each with a range of 2,800 nautical miles (5,200 km). Between 1997 and 2010 four Triomphant-class submarines entered service; as replacements of *L'Inflexible* and the older Redoutable class, these are designed to carry 16 M45 or M51 SLBMs, which have ranges of 6,000 and 8,000 nautical miles (11,000 and 15,000 km), respectively.

In 1981 China launched its first Type 092 strategic submarine, which was based on an attack submarine derived from older Soviet designs. The Xia class, as it was called by NATO, was armed with 12 JL-1 missiles (NATO designation CSS-N-3), which had a range of 1,500 nautical

THE TRIDENT MISSILE

The Trident is an American-made submarine-launched ballistic missile (SLBM) that succeeded the Poseidon and Polaris missiles in the 1980s and '90s. It is the sole strategic-range nuclear weapon of the United Kingdom and constitutes the sea-based leg of the United States' nuclear forces.

Under development from the late 1960s, the Trident developed into two models. The first version, the Trident I, or C-4, was 34 feet (10.4 metres) long and 6 feet (1.8 metres) in diameter. It could deliver eight independently targetable 100-kiloton nuclear warheads to a range of 4,000 nautical miles (7,400 km). The Trident II, or D-5, is about 46 feet (14 metres) long and carries multiple independently targeted warheads. It has a maximum range of about 6,500 nautical miles (12,000 km).

The Trident warheads are launched by three solid-fueled booster stages and are dispersed toward their targets by a liquid-fueled "bus" in the missile's front end. With inertial guidance refined by stellar or satellite navigation, Tridents are more accurate than most land-based ballistic missiles. At the time of their deployment during the Cold War, their accuracy gave them the ability, unprecedented among SLBMs, to threaten hardened missile silos and command bunkers in the Soviet Union, and their extended range allowed their submarines to patrol almost anywhere in the Atlantic and Pacific oceans, making detection extremely difficult.

Beginning in 1979, Trident I missiles were fitted aboard older U.S. Poseidon-carrying submarines and newer Ohio-class vessels. The Ohio submarines were built with larger missile tubes designed to accommodate the newer Trident II beginning in 1990. Between 1994 and 1999 the United Kingdom commissioned its Vanguard submarines to carry the Trident II, which was fitted with warheads of British design. The British Trident IIs are reported to carry an average of three 100-kiloton warheads each, while the U.S. missiles are variously reported as carrying four, six, eight, or even more 475-kiloton warheads. The numbers of warheads are subject to budget constraints and arms-control treaties with Russia.

miles (2,800 km). The Type 092 program was followed in 2004 by the launching of the first vessel of the Type 094 program (called the Jin class by NATO). These submarines are designed to carry 12 JL-2 SLBMs (NATO designation CSS-N-5), with a range of 4,300 nautical miles (8,000 km).

In 2009 India launched the *Arihant*, its first strategic submarine, built in India with Russian technical assistance. The nuclear-powered vessel, developed over more than a decade in India's secret Advanced Technology Vessel program, is expected to go into service armed with India's K-15 SLBM, which has a range of 375 nautical miles (700 km). Future vessels are expected to be armed with the longer-range K-4 missile, capable of reaching 1,900 nautical miles (3,500 km).

ATTACK SUBMARINES

After the rise of nuclear-powered strategic submarines, it seemed that only other nuclear submarines would be able to maneuver in three dimensions and remain in contact long enough to destroy them. Surface ships were clearly handicapped because their sonars could not operate as freely as those of a submarine. That situation changed somewhat when surface warships began to tow passive sonar arrays at submarine-like depths and when ship- or helicopter-launched homing torpedoes acquired a fair chance of holding and killing their targets. Both submarines and surface ships, therefore, became effective antisubmarine weapons, but only submarines could operate near an enemy's bases, where hostile submarines would be easier to find, and only they could lie in ambush with little chance of being detected. For these reasons it was inevitable that navies with nuclear-powered strategic submarines would also build nuclear-powered attack submarines.

Almost all modern nuclear attack submarines are capable of two basic functions adopted during the Cold War—attack enemy surface ships and destroy enemy submarines. To these basic functions some have added other roles, the most important one being the ability to strike enemy installations on land. Other roles, also important in post-Cold War submarine navies, are minelaying, electronic intelligence gathering, and special operations support. A good example of this trend is four generations of U.S. nuclear attack submarines that spanned the Cold War and post-Cold War eras: the Sturgeon class, 37 vessels commissioned between 1967 and 1975; the Los Angeles class, 51 vessels commissioned between 1976 and 1996; the Seawolf class, 3 boats commissioned between 1997 and 2005; and the Virginia class, 18 projected vessels, of which the first was commissioned in 2004. The Sturgeon and Los Angeles submarines, designed at the height of the Cold War, originally carried not only conventional torpedoes for antisubmarine warfare but also rocket-launched nuclear depth bombs, known as SUBROCs. The Seawolf submarines, also Cold War designs (though commissioned after the collapse of the Soviet Union), were dedicated "sub hunters," capable of maintaining high speeds while making little sound and diving to exceptional depths. Too expensive to be justified since the end of the Cold War, they have been succeeded by the Virginia vessels, which are intended to serve a number of roles near shore as well as in midocean. All U.S. attack submarines are armed with conventional torpedoes as well as underwater-launched Harpoon missiles for attacking surface ships from as far away as 70 nautical miles (130 km). Since the 1980s they have been fitted with Tomahawk cruise missiles, which can be programmed to strike ships 250 nautical miles (450 km) away or, in a strategic variant, to hit land targets at ranges up to 1,300 nautical miles (2,500 km) with either a conventional or a nuclear warhead. In addition, many submarines either have been designed or retrofitted with special compartments or pods for launching and retrieving special operations personnel.

The Soviets tended to divide their attack submarines between antisubmarine and cruise-missile duties. The most prominent submarine-hunting submarines were of the three Victor classes. The Victor I vessels, which entered service beginning in 1968, introduced the "tear-drop" hull configuration to the underwater Soviet navy. These and the 6,000-ton Victor II and III classes of the following decades were fitted with rocket-launched torpedoes or nuclear depth bombs, giving them a battle range extending to 90 km (50 nautical miles).

Beginning in 1971, the SS-N-7 Starbright cruise missile, which could be launched underwater and could strike ships 65 km (35 nautical miles) away, was deployed in Soviet Charlie-class submarines. The SS-N-7 began a series of dive-launched antiship cruise missiles of increasing range, culminating in the SS-N-19 Shipwreck, a supersonic missile that could carry a nuclear warhead 630 km (340 nautical miles). Twenty-four of these weapons were carried aboard the gigantic 13,000-ton, 150-metre (500-foot) Oscar submarines, which entered service in 1980. Adding a land-attack role to Soviet attack submarines after 1987 was the SS-N-21 Sampson cruise missile, a weapon with a nuclear capability and range similar to those of the U.S. Tomahawk. These were carried by the Akula-class submarines, 7,500-ton, 111.7-metre (366-foot) vessels that continued to enter service with the Russian navy through the 1990s. In 2010 Russia launched its first Yasen-class submarine (called Graney by NATO), which carried the mixed armament of the Akula vessels—antisubmarine and antiship torpedoes and missiles as well as long-range cruise missiles.

The British Swiftsure class (6 vessels, commissioned 1974–81) and Trafalgar class (6 vessels, commissioned 1983–91) displaced between 4,000 and 4,500 tons at the surface and were about 87 metres (285 feet) long. They were originally armed only with torpedoes and dive-launched Harpoon missiles, consistent with their Cold War role of hunting and killing enemy submarines and surface ships. However, beginning in the 1990s some of them were fitted with Tomahawk cruise missiles, giving them a capability to attack land targets as well. The post-Cold War Astute class (a minimum of four vessels, the first being commissioned in 2010) has been designed from the beginning to carry cruise missiles.

In France the first nuclear attack submarine, the *Rubis*, was laid down in 1976 with antisubmarine torpedo and sonar systems inherited from the diesel-electric Agosta class. Beginning in 1984, the four vessels of this class were given improved sonar and silencing and were fitted with dive-launched Exocet antiship missiles. The Rubis vessels, the smallest nuclear attack submarines ever put into service, displaced about 2,400 tons at the surface and were about 71 metres (235 feet) long. They were followed in the early 1990s by two similar but slightly larger Amethyste-class submarines. In the late 1990s France brought its submarine posture into the post-Cold War era with plans for the Barracuda class, six submarines displacing some 4,000 tons at the surface and carrying land-attack cruise missiles and advanced electronic surveillance equipment as well as the usual torpedoes and antiship Exocets. Construction of the first Barracuda submarine began in 2007.

China began to plan for a nuclear attack submarine fleet in the 1950s. The first keel of the Type 091 vessel (known as the Han class to NATO), based partly on Soviet designs, was laid down in 1967, and the completed boat was commissioned in 1974. Four more Type 091 boats were commissioned over the next two decades. They were followed by the Type 093 class (NATO designation Shang), the first of which was commissioned in 2006. The Type 093 boats displace some 6,000 tons submerged and are about 110 metres (360 feet) long. Reflecting China's strategic goal of asserting its presence against other navies in waters adjacent to its coasts, Chinese nuclear attack submarines are mainly torpedo-equipped sub-hunters, though they can be fitted with antiship missiles as well.

DESIGN PRINCIPLES

Three major trends in nuclear attack submarine design emerged in the great Cold War confrontation between NATO and the Soviet Union. As exemplified in the submarine forces of the United States, Britain, and the Soviet Union, these three trends were increased speed, increased diving depth, and silencing.

SPEED

Increased speed required increased power. Since the resistance a submarine encounters is a function of its surface area, the ideal was to achieve greater power without increasing the volume or weight of the power plant and, therefore, the size of the submarine. A more powerful (and therefore noisier) engine could be silenced, but only by increasing the size of the submarine, which in turn would lower its speed. These complex trade-offs were illustrated by the Sturgeon and Los Angeles submarines. Reactor power approximately doubled between these two generations, but overall size increased enormously, from about 3,600 to 6,000 tons surfaced. The Soviets, meanwhile, achieved very high speed (about 40 knots, compared to slightly over 30 knots for fast Western submarines) in their Alfa class, but probably at the cost of a great deal of noise at high speed.

Speed was prized for several quite different reasons. At first, the U.S. and Soviet navies developed fast submarines primarily as antiship weapons. In the 1950s the Guppy-style hull design of USS *Nautilus* gave it a submerged speed of over 20 knots, which was fast enough to evade surface ships but not to counterattack them. To make up this deficit,

USS Albacore. U.S. Navy Photograph

U.S. submarines then under design were altered by adapting nuclear power to the tapered "tear-drop" hull of the experimental submarine *Albacore*. The resulting Skipjack class, which entered service in 1959, came up with a top speed in excess of 30 knots.

In a spectacular demonstration of the Soviets' fast attack capabilities, a Soviet nuclear submarine intercepted the nuclear aircraft carrier USS *Enterprise* in February 1968. The submarine was not quite as fast as the *Enterprise*, but it was fast enough to keep the carrier within weapon range while the carrier accelerated to top speed.

With the commencement of the Soviet fast nuclear program, the U.S. Navy shifted its emphasis to dual-purpose vessels capable of attacking submarines as well as surface ships. High speed, as achieved in the 1970s and '80s by the Los Angeles class, was then required to keep up with the fast surface targets that the Soviet submarines were expected to attack.

High sustained speed also made it possible for submarines to deploy more efficiently to distant patrol stations. Although nuclear submarines' fuel supplies were effectively unlimited, they were limited in their capacity for stores and could not expect to remain at sea for more than about 60 to 90 days. The more rapidly they could reach their patrol area, therefore, the more productive time they could spend there.

As in the case of nonnuclear submarines, higher speed was also valued for evasion after an attack. However, when that higher speed was bought at the cost of louder operation, submarines became easier to detect. Also, from the mid-1950s the main antisubmarine weapons were homing torpedoes, which became significantly faster than the submarines they sought, and nuclear depth bombs, which might be dropped effectively anywhere in the vicinity of a submarine. In all of these cases, sheer speed was no longer a guarantee of evasion, although it did make attack more difficult.

DEPTH

Deeper diving was valued for several reasons. As in the past, it could be combined with higher speed for better evasion. In addition, a deep-diving submarine could make better use of its own sonar, partly because it could operate in several quite different layers of the sea. This advantage was reflected in a change in U.S. submarine sonars that began about 1960. Previous submarine units had been

cylindrical, producing broad, fan-shaped beams that could determine target range and bearing but not target depth. The new sonars were spherical, producing narrow, pencil-shaped beams that could distinguish between targets at different depths. They could also make better use of sonar reflection off the sea bottom and surface to achieve greater range.

Finally, greater maximum operating depth became particularly important at high speed, when there was always a possibility that a submarine would accidentally tip down and descend below a safe operating depth before the downward motion could be corrected. It is no surprise, then, that the greatest reported diving depth (about 850 metres, or 2,800 feet) was associated with the highest reported maximum speed (about 43 knots), in the Soviet Alfa class. (Diving depth of most other modern attack submarines was reportedly between 300 and 450 metres, or 1,000 and 1,500 feet.)

Greater depth required a stronger (and heavier) hull, and increased power required a stronger power plant. Attempts to combine the two required a larger hull (to provide enough buoyancy); that in turn added underwater resistance, which cut the speed advantage gained from the more powerful engine. This tension between different requirements explains the characteristics of many modern submarines. For example, the Los Angeles class was said to have sacrificed some diving depth in order to achieve higher speed. In the Alfa class, weight was saved by adopting an expensive titanium-alloy hull and a very compact power plant.

SILENCING

Until the late 1950s, submarines were usually detected by active sonar; that is, by sound waves bounced off their hulls. Because these sound waves could also be detected by the hunted submarine, they gave it warning that it was in danger of attack. Also, because water can support only so much sonar energy, active sonar was limited in range. Beginning in the early 1950s, then, the U.S. and British navies began to investigate passive sonar, in which sensors detected noises emanating from the submarine itself. Early nuclear submarines were quite susceptible to such detection because their machinery was very noisy. In particular, the pumps required to circulate the coolant, which could not be turned off without melting the reactor core, could be heard at a considerable distance.

Beginning at that time, silencing became a major thrust in submarine design. The pumps of pressurized-water reactors were redesigned to be quieter, and in many submarines the machinery was carried clear of the hull on sound-absorbing mounts. All of this added to the size and weight of the machinery and to the expense of construction; it also added to the attraction of natural-circulation plants.

As a further step in silencing, hulls were coated with sound-absorbing material. Even relatively simple coatings could drastically reduce the effectiveness of homing torpedoes.

CHAPTER 4

NAVAL TACTICS

At all historical periods of their development, surface and underwater naval vessels have been the tools of strategy—that is, they have been practical means of reaching desired political or military goals. To reach those goals, surface ships and submarines have been employed in accordance with principles of naval tactics, which is the art and science of engaging in battle on, under, or over the sea.

FUNDAMENTALS

Tactics, being the activities of battle itself, are conceived and executed at the literal and metaphoric centre of war's violence. Tactical science is an orderly description of these activities, and tactical art is the skill required to carry them out in combat.

THE SEARCH FOR CONSTANTS

It should be said that, in order to achieve victory, willpower and courage must always accompany tactical art and science and often dominate the outcome of battle. These qualities are not tactics, but they are related to tactics in the way a sound decision is related to the resolution with which it is implemented. There is no finer example than Horatio Nelson. In the Battle of the Nile (Aug. 1-2, 1798), not only were Admiral Nelson's tactical decisions brilliant, but he had so imbued his captains with his thinking that, when they saw a chance for surprise by attacking the disengaged side of the French fleet, they were quick to seize it and gain a decisive advantage. Still, their decisions only established the basis of that great victory, for the French fought with desperation, and it took hard fighting by British tars, inspired by Nelson's charismatic leadership, to fulfill the promise of victory.

In a similar manner, new technology is not tactics, but it may have a decisive effect in both altering the face of battle and affecting its outcome. Navies put special emphasis on warships and aircraft. It is well said that on the ground men are served by their weapons while at sea weapons are served by men. Lest his readers be too enamoured of élan and fighting spirit, Rear Admiral Bradley Allen Fiske used a telling example in *The Navy as a Fighting Machine* (1916). He pointed out that in the American Civil War the Confederate ironclad *Virginia*, with 10 guns, handily defeated the Union sloops-of-war *Congress* and *Cumberland*, which carried a total of 74 guns. One day later the Union's *Monitor*, carrying two guns in a turret, fought the *Virginia* to a standstill. Courage and resolve were powerless against progress and armour.

The American naval strategist Alfred Thayer Mahan made perhaps too much of the influence on tactics of technological progress. In his seminal *The Influence of Sea Power upon History, 1660–1783* (1890), he wrote that, due to new fighting systems, "from time to time the structure of tactics has to be wholly torn down but the foundations of strategy so far remain, as though laid upon a rock." Mahan appreciated the utility of naval history for the discovery of strategic constants— that is, principles of strategy that have remained valid throughout technological change. Tacticians, on the other hand, are conscious of tactical constants as well, especially the following: the power of concentrated force (rarely in history has a naval tactician withheld a reserve); the special value of surprise; the abiding need for cohesion brought about by sound command and combat doctrine; the consummate goal of attacking effectively first; and the unique role played by timing and timeliness.

THE BATTLE OF THE NILE

The Battle of the Nile (also called the Battle of Aboukir Bay) was one of the greatest victories of the British admiral Horatio Nelson. It was fought on Aug. 1–2, 1798, between British and French fleets in Abū Qīr Bay, near Alexandria, Egypt, during the long period of war pitting revolutionary France against the royalist powers of Europe.

In 1798 the French general Napoleon Bonaparte had made plans for an invasion of Egypt in order to constrict Britain's trade routes and threaten its possession of India. The British government heard that a large French naval expedition was to sail from a French Mediterranean port under the command of Napoleon, and in response it ordered the Earl of St. Vincent, the commander in chief of the British fleet, to detach ships under Rear Adm. Sir Horatio Nelson to reconnoitre off Toulon and to watch French naval movements there. But Nelson's own ship was dismasted in a storm, and his group of frigates, now dispersed, returned to the British base at Gibraltar. Meanwhile, St. Vincent sent Nelson more ships, which joined Nelson on June 7, bringing his strength up to 14 ships of the line.

The French expedition eluded the British warships and sailed first for Malta, which the French seized from the British early in June. After spending a week at Malta, Napoleon sailed with his fleet for his main objective, Egypt. Meanwhile, Nelson had found Toulon empty and had correctly guessed the French objective. However, because he lacked frigates for reconnaissance, he missed the French fleet, reached Egypt first, found the port of Alexandria empty, and impetuously returned to Sicily, where his ships were resupplied. Determined to find the French fleet, he sailed to Egypt once more and on August 1 he sighted the main French fleet of 13 ships of the line and 4 frigates under Adm. François-Paul Brueys d'Aigailliers at anchor in Abū Qīr Bay, near the mouth of the Nile River.

Although there were but a few hours left until nightfall and Brueys' ships were in a strong defensive position, being securely ranged in a sandy bay that was flanked on one side by a shore battery on Abū Qīr Island, Nelson gave orders to attack at once. Half of the British warships were able to maneuver around the head of the French line of battle and thus got inside and behind their position, while the other half remained to seaward. With a light following wind, the English slowly worked down the French line, attacking each ship from two sides. During the fierce fighting, Nelson himself was wounded in the head. The climax came at about 10:00 PM, when Brueys' 120-gun flagship, which was by far the largest ship in the bay, blew up with most of the ship's company, including the admiral. The fighting continued for the rest of the night, with the end result that the British warships destroyed or captured all but two of Brueys' ships of the line. The British suffered about 900 casualties, the French about 10 times as many.

The Battle of the Nile had several important results. It isolated Napoleon's army in Egypt, thus ensuring its ultimate disintegration; it ensured that in due time Malta would be retaken from the French; and it both heightened British prestige and secured British control of the Mediterranean.

The Study of Trends

Naval officers also study history for its trends, because trends are the only clue as to how tactics are changing and are the best check against the fatal sin of preparing to fight the last war. The trend that has influenced all else in the conduct of naval battle is the increasing range and lethality of naval weapons. Paradoxically, greater lethality has not led a trend toward greater loss of life. The first reason is that, unlike ground combat, the principal aim at sea is to put the fighting machine, not the fighting man, out of action, and modern machines are (thus far) sensitive to damage. Second, it is a long-standing constant that naval battles, once joined, are fast-moving and decisive.

To sketch how the range of weapons has affected naval tactics, a simple structure that describes the processes of combat must be established. First is firepower delivery itself. Second is the scouting process, which gathers information by reconnaissance, surveillance, cryptanalysis, and other means and delivers it to the tactical commander. Third is command itself—or command and control (C^2) in modern parlance—which assimilates the information, decides which actions are called for, and directs forces to act accordingly.

Combat being the activities of force against force, there is a natural antithesis to all three processes described above. First, the effect of enemy firepower is reduced by shooting down the incoming aircraft or missile, by maneuvering to avoid a torpedo, and by ship survivability or "staying power"—that is, the ability to continue fighting after suffering damage. Second, when scouting was accomplished by ships or aircraft flung out ahead of a formation, information denial was accomplished by screening—that is, by flinging out an opposing line of ships and aircraft. Modern ways to confound the enemy's scouting effort are keeping radio silence and jamming his radars, both of which deny him information. Third, enemy C^2 can be confused by deceptive signals or decoy forces. It can also be crippled or delayed by electronically jamming enemy communications.

The six processes described above—namely, firepower delivery, scouting, C^2,

and the three countermeasures against them—as well as maneuver, are the raw materials of naval tactics. To achieve success, they are synthesized into a harmonious blend of action and counteraction. For example, a modern naval screen of ships or aircraft defends a formation both by destroying enemy aircraft or missiles and by denying tactical information. The screen itself may even be so central in importance that it becomes the focus of enemy attack, with destruction of the screen being tantamount to destruction of the force. Thus, the study of naval tactics has become more than the study of formations, firepower, and maneuvers. The increase in weapon range has been paralleled by scouting and the control of forces at longer and longer ranges; these in turn have opened up more avenues to gain information and confuse the enemy's picture by electronic means.

TACTICS IN THE MODERN ERA

The study of tactics has always emphasized actions between fleets that gain or challenge control of the sea lines of communications. That traditional emphasis is retained here, but since the 20th century three other types of combat at sea have demanded greater attention.

WAR FROM LAND TO SEA AND FROM SEA TO LAND

While navies have always had as their ultimate objective an influence over events on land, aircraft and missiles have extended the range and amplified the influence. Likewise, land-based systems have made their growing influence felt on warships and sea-lanes alike. Putting ground forces ashore from the sea by amphibious landing is an operation that has neither gained nor lost importance since the earliest galley warfare, but modern combined-arms tactics are quite different and require separate attention. A by-product of the extended range of modern weapons is the greater complexity of joint operations. The reorganization of many armed forces has been in large measure a response to the demand for well-coordinated operations.

NUCLEAR WEAPONS

The major powers of the world keep a considerable strategic deterrent force at sea in the form of submarine-launched ballistic missiles. The safeguarding or threatening of nuclear submarines has inspired a set of tactics unique in history. These tactics are among each nation's most closely guarded secrets and have never been used in anger, so that all knowledge of them is theoretical, based on mathematical computations, computer simulations, and constrained exercises at sea. This does not mean that such tactics, if ever used, will prove unsound. During the great transition from sail to steam and big gun, keen study by naval tacticians throughout the world developed the sound tactics that were finally practiced in World War I.

RAIDING

War against trade is the war of an inferior navy that cannot compete for command of the sea but that, instead, dispatches raiders to deny the enemy its free use. These tactics of sea denial are those of predator and prey, of hunter and evader, and are as unique from the force-on-force tactics of major sea battles as are guerrilla war tactics from those of decisive land battle.

HISTORICAL DEVELOPMENT

In the following examination of the history of naval tactics, a shift in importance between elements of combat will be apparent. In galley warfare, sheer power dominated the outcome, and maneuver of numerous small ships, much as on land, contributed to its concentration. In warfare under sail, great firepower could be concentrated in individual ships, and doctrine, formations, and signal flags were means of controlling the slow-moving, wind-constrained formations. With battleships, steam power gave freedom to maneuver in any direction, and the range of the big guns allowed a concentration of fire from the whole formation. The defensive element came to prominence, symbolized by armour. Tactical decisions had to be made before the enemy was in sight, so that scouting became more evident as a tactical ingredient. Control had to be exercised over much greater distances, which expanded the possibilities of exploiting the means of control, notably through radio direction finding and code breaking.

The growth in the tactical influence of scouting, anti-scouting, command and control, and countermeasures against command and control continued through the era of the aircraft carrier and into the era of the guided missile. These elements have become as important to tactical success at sea as firepower, consuming comparable thought and resources.

THE AGE OF GALLEY WARFARE

Galleys being relatively unseaworthy, war at sea among the ancients was always near land. Pictures of billowing sails notwithstanding, masts and canvas were stowed for battle, and oars were the means of propulsion. The most destructive weapon was a ram in the bow, which dictated a line abreast as the tactical formation. In the line abreast, two lines of opposing galleys approached each other head on, with the ram of each vessel unobstructed by the ships on either side. Momentum was the key to the ram's destructiveness, so that sprint speed—as much as seven or eight knots (nautical miles per hour, that is, eight to nine statute miles per hour or 13 to 15 km per hour)—was as important as maneuver. Multiple banks of oars afforded speed, and the geometry of their arrangement fascinated naval architect-historians of later eras.

Major battles comprised hundreds of ships on a side. Battles occurred because of the threat of invasion, so that many armed men were present. These participated as archers or boarders. Rome developed grappling hooks and the *corvus* (a long boarding plank spiked at the end) to secure the victim ship while disciplined legionnaires fought their way on board.

Scouting the enemy formation was a subordinate issue, although contemporary descriptions indicated that formations and maneuvers, showing ingenuity and cunning, played a large part in the outcomes. Since battles were nearly impossible in foul weather, good visibility permitted the deployment of the lines abreast, often in two echelons, much as the commander intended. Descriptions of the battles (and the period was rich in them) were usually couched in the terms of land warfare—such as the routing of a flank, or an attempt to crush by encirclement. Galley tactics were so similar to land tactics that a reserve was actually held back—a practice that ever afterward was regarded in navies as a mistake. An inference cannot be drawn that a commander had tight control of his ships in action, however, and the correct image of a galley battle would be that of a wild melee, with oars smashed, hulls crushed, armour-clad soldiers drowned, losses enormous, and battles decisive with lasting consequences.

The ultimate battle under oar was at Lepanto on Oct. 7, 1571. Fought between a combined fleet of the Mediterranean's Christian nations and the vaunted Turkish navy, this battle was reported in great tactical detail. More than 200 Christian oared vessels met 270 of the Turks' in the Gulf of Patras on the Ionian

Sea. By this time, three to five guns were fitted in the bows of galleys, and harque-buses were fired by Spanish soldiers. But, as was usual in galley warfare, the outcome was decided by boarding and hand-to-hand fighting with sword and pike. The Christian fleet under Don John of Austria prevailed in a bitterly contested donnybrook; losses to the Turks were placed at 30,000 killed, against 8,000 among the victors.

THE AGE OF FIGHTING SAIL

By the middle of the 17th century guns arrayed along the sides of fighting ships were the decisive weapon. Heavy guns required a gun deck and a short, sturdy hull, which were at odds with the galley's requirements of lightness and length. Thus, the shift to sail was a victory of fighting strength over maneuver. Tactically, sailing navies became victims of the wind's whim, but strategically they benefited from nearly limitless range and, compared to the frail galleys, greatly improved seakeeping.

The column, or line ahead, became the logical tactical formation for bringing the most guns to bear. With all the ships of a battle line following one another, their guns could face the enemy line without obstruction. The three Anglo-Dutch Wars of 1652–74 saw the first closely studied battles of sail and gun. In them the column was as much a means for command and control as it was for concentration of fighting force, for as long as a fleet maintained station in line ahead,

each ship separated by a scant 200 or 300 metres (219 to 328 yards), cohesion was assured, maneuvers were coordinated, and any malingering by reluctant captains was obvious.

The line was not a formation that permitted the concentration of fire, however, for naval guns in a rolling platform were effectively accurate at only about one-quarter of a mile (0.4 km), and the range for penetrability of shot was even less. In effect, engagements were decided within pistol shot, a battle line being a thin ribbon of death, miles long but scarcely 300 metres (328 yards) wide. When the English fought the Dutch in the 17th century, this was not considered a problem, because the tactics of both sides called for closing with the other aggressively. But in the 18th century their French opponents felt that their strategic interests lay in avoiding battle at close quarters, and in the Anglo-French wars the Royal Navy endured a long period of indecisive actions handicapped by a tactical doctrine so rigidly interpreted by courts-martial as to have become tactical dogma. These *Fighting Instructions*, though soundly conceived when first issued in 1653, were unsuited to this new opponent, for the implementing system of signals was unimaginative and constraining. Indeed, the two most admired tactical writers of the day, Paul Hoste and Sébastien François Bigot de Morogues, were French.

Toward the end of the 18th century, the British admiral Richard Kempenfelt began to unshackle the Royal Navy with a better system of signaling. The new freedom of maneuver came finally and forever to be embodied in the tactical genius and personal inspiration of Horatio Nelson, whose matchless victories at the battles of the Nile, Copenhagen (April 2, 1801), and Trafalgar (Oct. 21, 1805) drew the enduring admiration of naval tacticians.

Tactical study during this era concentrated on maneuver. "Breaking the line" of the enemy fleet was one aim, because this broke the enemy's tactical cohesion and made it possible to overwhelm individual ships by bringing greatly superior force to bear on each of them in turn. Popular aims were raking (firing a broadside the length of an enemy ship from across the bow or stern) or doubling (concentrating force by putting ships on both sides of the enemy line, as Nelson did at Abū Qīr Bay). The most reliable way to concentrate gunfire was to build it into ships vertically by stacking gun decks one over the other. Later tacticians demonstrated analytically what every fighting seaman of the seafaring era knew instinctively: with equal competency exhibited on both sides, not only would a two-decked frigate beat a lighter, one-decked corvette, and a three-decker beat a frigate, but the loser would come away having done very little damage to his bigger opponent. Whence came the big "ship of the line," a three-decked ship that could stand in the line of battle and beat down smaller opponents while surviving to fight again.

THE AGE OF STEAM AND BIG GUN

Tactics and technology complement each other, and there is no better period in history for studying their interrelationship than the shift from sail to steam in the 19th century. The shell gun (raised to naval attention during the Crimean War by the Battle of Sinope, Nov. 30, 1853) compelled navies to adopt the iron sheathing of hulls. This pointed the way to all-metal hulls (iron, then steel), which in turn both permitted and demanded as a response the installation of rifled, breech-loaded guns of major calibre. Concurrently, iron boilers and screw propellers made steam propulsion practical and gave great new freedom of maneuver. Navies were unfettered tactically from the wind, but only at the strategic price of having to remain within steaming range of coaling stations.

The sweeping consequences of these and other technological innovations lacked the crucible of war in which to test them, for it was an era of Pax Britannica, with the maritime peace kept by the Royal Navy. The *Monitor* and the *Virginia* (at the battle of Hampton Roads, March 8–9, 1862) marked the short-lived ascendancy of armour and the defense. This led to a brief revival of the ram and to some very speculative tactical concepts that looked outrageous in later days.

But the superiority of defense at sea did not last long. The tactical–technical turning point came from the observation of a few battles in East Asia around the turn of the century and from an often overlooked bit of military technology. The battles were those of the Yalu (Sept. 17, 1894), the Yellow Sea (Aug. 10 and 14, 1904), and Tsushima (May 27–29, 1905), in which the gun regained primacy to such an extent that the Russian vice admiral Stepan Osipovich Makarov could confidently write, "A good gun causes victory, armour only postpones defeat." The new technology was fire control, which enabled major-calibre rounds to be placed on target at five, then 10, and ultimately 15 nautical miles (9.3, 18.5, and 27.8 km).

By World War I the tactical issues were settled. First, big guns would dominate, a burly battleship firing a battery of them in broadside. Second, although armour could "postpone defeat," it was all but powerless against torpedoes; therefore, a destroyer screen was essential to protect the fleet. Third, a fleet cruised in compact formation but quickly deployed in column to fight. Since the opposing fleets would close with each other at a relative 40 knots, a scouting line had to be thrown out well in front to report enemy movements by wireless. Despite the elephantine appearance of a line of battleships, there would not be a moment to lose when the enemy was sighted and no margin for error.

A column of battleships was not like a column of sailing ships. With greater range and improved fire control, gunfire from most of the ships on each side could reach most of the ships on the opposite side, making concentration of firepower by a whole fleet feasible and expected. The advantage was worked out mathematically in what were called the "N-square law" and the "square law of attrition": success would build on itself, so that any small advantage at the outset of an engagement would compound in favour of the superior force. With long-range gunnery, the advantage accrued fleet-wide, not merely ship by ship as in the days of fighting sail.

A positional advantage could be added to this firepower advantage if the fleet "crossed the T" of the enemy, that is, if its own column crossed in front of the enemy column at a right angle and with the ships at the head of the enemy column within range of its guns. From this position at the top of the T, all the guns of the fleet could fire upon the head of the enemy column, while only the first enemy ships could return fire. This was the raking position sought by an individual sailing ship writ large, for at battleship gunnery ranges the whole force could concentrate successively on each enemy ship as it approached. It was reckoned that in fair weather and good visibility a fleet could destroy an enemy in the capped position in 20 minutes; or, if an enemy of equal strength could be surprised with unanswered fire within effective range for as little as five minutes, he would be demolished with little harm to the victor. There would be no leisurely approach, no chance to recover from a missed maneuver or a wrong turn. In fact, in practice the very swiftness of decision worked against maneuvering to cross the T. Much was made of the successful use of this tactic by the Japanese admiral Tōgō Heihachirō against the much slower Russians at Tsushima, but commanders at sea understood that the fast pace of battle worked against a T-crossing except by accident or surprise.

With one salient exception, there were no unforeseen tactics in World War I. The exception was the ease with which a fleet could be surprised at sea. The Battle of Jutland (May 31, 1916) was fought in great confusion, owing to a fog of smoke from the stacks and guns of 250 ships as well as the sloppy work of the commanders of the two scouting forces. The German commander, Reinhard Scheer, twice had his T capped for lack of visibility; for the same reason, the British commander, Sir John Jellicoe, twice was unable to exploit this, the ideal tactical position.

The lesser engagements of the war were also marked by surprise, but from another source. At one time or another, both the Germans and British broke each other's codes. Special intelligence and attempts to entrap a weaker enemy were rife throughout the war, leading to surprise in each of the battles in the North Sea: Helgoland Bight (Aug. 28, 1914), Dogger Bank (Jan. 24, 1915), and Jutland itself.

THE AGE OF THE AIRCRAFT CARRIER

Early in World War II the primary instrument for delivering naval combat power became the aircraft carrier. The reason was range: aircraft could deliver a concerted attack at 200 nautical miles (370.4 km) or more, whereas battleships could do so only at 20 nautical miles (37 km) or less. The foremost tactical question during the transition in the 1920s and '30s was whether aircraft could lift enough destruction to supersede the battleship. Into the 1930s skeptics were correct that aircraft could not. But by the end of that decade, engines were carrying adequate payloads, dive-bomber and torpedo-plane designs had matured, carrier arresting gear and associated flight-deck handling facilities were up to their tasks, and proficient strike tactics had been well practiced. U.S. and Japanese naval aviators were pacesetters in these developments.

There was a subordinate tactical question as well: could the enemy be found at the outer limits of aircraft range? The ability to attack fixed targets such as the Panama Canal or Pearl Harbor, and to achieve surprise in doing so, had been amply demonstrated in naval exercises as well as in battle, but finding, reporting, and closing on ships at sea was a greater challenge. Without detracting from the courage and skill of aviators, it may be said that effective scouting was the dominant tactical problem of carrier warfare and had utmost influence on the outcomes of the crucial carrier battles of the Pacific Theatre in 1942: the Coral Sea (May 4–8), Midway (June 3–6), the Eastern Solomons (August 23–25), and the Santa Cruz Islands (October 26). In those closely matched battles the quality of U.S. and Japanese aviators and their planes was virtually on a par. When the United States won, it did so by superior scouting and screening, owing in large measure to air-search radar and to the advantage of having broken the Japanese code.

The command and control structure polished by the U.S. Navy during the war was the third vital component, after scouting and the delivery of firepower. The tangible manifestation of modern C² was the Combat Information Center, which centralized radar information and voice radio communications. By 1944 the tactical doctrine of coordinating fighter air defenses, along with the now much strengthened antiaircraft firepower on ships of the fleet, was so effective that in the Battle of the Philippine Sea (June 19–21, 1944) more than 90 percent of 450 Japanese aircraft were wiped out in a fruitless attack on Adm. Raymond Spruance's 5th Fleet.

The new tactical formation was circular, with carriers in the centre defended by an antiaircraft and antisubmarine screen composed of their own aircraft plus battleships, cruisers, and destroyers. For offensive purposes, a circle allowed a rapid simultaneous turn by all ships in a task group in order to launch and recover aircraft. For antiaircraft defense, the circle was shrunk in diameter as tightly as possible so that each screening ship, by defending itself, helped defend its neighbour.

The new battle paradigm called for a pulse of combat power to be delivered in a shock attack by one or more air wings. Despite every intention, though, air strikes against alerted defenses were rarely delivered as compactly as practiced, nor were they as decisive tactically as naval aviators had expected. In the five big carrier battles, one attacking air wing took out an average of only one enemy carrier. (Viewed strategically, this average, along with losses of aircraft of around 50 percent per battle, was enough to govern the pattern of the Pacific war.) Since it took more than two hours to launch, marshal, and deliver an air strike, it was difficult to attack before an enemy counterstrike was in the air. Successful command at sea depended as never before on effective scouting and communication, because in order to win a decisive battle, in World War II as in all of naval history, it was necessary to attack effectively first.

Dominant though it was, carrier-based air power did not control the seas at night. With a modicum of success, the high-quality ships of Germany exploited the hours of darkness, especially during the winter months and in northern waters. In the bitterly contested campaign for Guadalcanal in the fall of 1942, guns ruled supreme at night and very nearly tipped the balance in favour of Japan. Expecting to be outnumbered as a result of the Five-Power Naval Limitation Treaty of 1922, the Imperial Japanese Navy had practiced night tactics assiduously in order, as they supposed, to whittle down the U.S. battle line during its slow march west across the Pacific. Having developed the matchless Long Lance torpedo, they installed it liberally in light cruisers and destroyers and developed tactics that would hurl a barrage of the long-range weapons in the direction of the enemy line—at the same time taking care not to expose the beams of their own ships to a counterstroke. Standard U.S. doctrine, on the other hand, called for fighting in column, employing guns as the primary weapon; the advantages that should have accrued to the Americans at night from superior radar were largely squandered. Between August 1942 and July 1943, in the cruiser–destroyer battles of Savo Island, Cape Esperance, Tassafaronga, Kula Gulf, and Kolombangara, Japanese night tactics prevailed. Not until mid-1943, with tactics attributed to Capt. (later Adm.) Arleigh Burke that exploited the radar advantage in full, did the U.S. Navy redress the balance.

Still, naval aircraft were the weapons of decision. Although the duels of the great carrier fleets received more attention, air strikes from sea to shore were as crucial in securing control of the seas. Strikes by the British at Taranto, Italy (Nov. 11, 1940), by the Japanese at Pearl Harbor (Dec. 7, 1941), and by the Americans in the South Pacific at Rabaul (Nov. 5 and 11, 1943) and Truk (Feb. 17–18, 1944) were as important to that end as were the more sensational fleet engagements.

Also, in 1944 and 1945 the U.S. 3rd and 5th fleets, 27 fast carriers strong, took the war successfully against entire complexes of airfields in Formosa (now Taiwan), the Philippines, and Japan itself. A traditional tactical maxim, "Ships do not fight forts," was suspended for the duration of the war.

In the closing days of the war in the Pacific, the Battle of Okinawa served to indicate the nature of future combat at sea. By that time the U.S. Navy had reduced the Japanese Navy to impotence, and manned aircraft could not penetrate the sure American defenses. Nevertheless, during the three-month campaign for Okinawa (April–June 1945) the U.S. Navy lost 26 ships and suffered damage to 164 more—this time to Japanese kamikazes (suicide pilots) flying out of airfields in Japan. The pilots who flew these one-way missions were delivering, in effect, human guided missiles. Kamikazes showed that missiles could, on sufficient occasion, get through otherwise impenetrable defenses. The missile-guidance technology exhibited in the late stages of the war in Europe indicated that missiles would be the kamikazes of the future. And the atomic bomb offered the ugly threat of "one hit, one kill" at sea.

THE PEARL HARBOR ATTACK

The aerial attack on the U.S. naval base at Pearl Harbor, Hawaii, by the Japanese Imperial Navy on Dec. 7, 1941, came as a complete surprise to the American defenders, but in fact it climaxed a decade of worsening relations between the United States and Japan. Japan's invasion of China in 1937, its subsequent alliance with the Axis powers (Germany and Italy) in 1940, and its occupation of French Indochina prompted the United States to respond in July 1941 by freezing Japanese assets in the United States and declaring an embargo on petroleum shipments and other vital war materials to Japan. By late 1941 the United States had severed practically all commercial and financial relations with Japan. Though Japan continued to negotiate with the United States up to the day of the Pearl Harbor attack, the government of Prime Minister Tōjō Hideki decided on war.

Adm. Yamamoto Isoroku, the commander in chief of Japan's Combined Fleet, had planned the attack against the U.S. Pacific Fleet with great care. On November 26 a Japanese fleet, under Vice Adm. Nagumo Chuichi and including 6 aircraft carriers, 2 battleships, 3 cruisers, and 11 destroyers, sailed to a point some 440 km (275 miles) north of Hawaii. From there, about 360 planes in total were launched.

The first Japanese dive bomber appeared over Pearl Harbor at 7:55 AM (local time). It was part of a first wave of nearly 200 aircraft, including torpedo planes, bombers, and fighters. Reconnaissance at Pearl Harbor had been lax; an Army private who noticed this large flight of planes on his radar screen was told to ignore them, since a flight of B-17 bombers from the United States was expected at any moment. The anchored ships in the harbour made perfect targets for the Japanese bombers, and since it was Sunday morning (a time chosen by the Japanese for maximum surprise) they were not fully manned. Similarly, the U.S. military aircraft were lined up on the airfields of the Naval Air Station on Ford Island and adjoining Wheeler and Hickam Fields to guard against sabotage, and many were destroyed on the ground by Japanese strafing. Most of the damage to the battleships was inflicted in the first 30 minutes of the assault. The Arizona was completely destroyed and the Oklahoma capsized. The California,

A U.S. battleship sinks during the Pearl Harbor attack. National Archives, Washington, D.C.

Explosions rock the U.S. naval base at Pearl Harbor, Hawaii, during the Japanese surprise air attack on Dec. 7, 1941. National Archives

Nevada, *and* West Virginia *sank in shallow water. Three other battleships, three cruisers, three destroyers, and other vessels were also damaged. More than 180 aircraft were destroyed. U.S. military casualties totaled more than 3,400, including more than 2,300 killed. The Japanese lost from 29 to 60 planes, five midget submarines, perhaps one or two fleet submarines, and fewer than 100 men.*

The Pearl Harbor attack severely crippled U.S. naval and air strength in the Pacific. However, the three aircraft carriers attached to the Pacific Fleet were not at Pearl Harbor at the time and thus escaped. Of the eight battleships, all but the Arizona *and* Oklahoma *were eventually repaired and returned to service, and the Japanese failed to destroy the important oil storage facilities on the island. The "date which will live in infamy," as U.S. Pres. Franklin D. Roosevelt termed it, unified the U.S. public and swept away any earlier support for neutrality. On December 8 Congress declared war on Japan.*

THE AGE OF THE GUIDED MISSILE

At the end of World War II the supremacy of the U.S. Navy was as pronounced as that of the Royal Navy in the 19th century. With no enemy battle fleet to fight, it staked out the classic role of dominant navies throughout history—projecting its influence over land. Carrier-based aircraft, nuclear missile-carrying submarines, and amphibious-assault units extended that influence greatly. While the U.S. Navy served to link the North Atlantic Treaty Organization (NATO) across the Atlantic, its carrier-centred battle fleet stood ready to deliver sea power over the land. The principal opposing navy, that of the Soviet Union, was configured to challenge NATO's sea link and to confront U.S. aircraft carriers. The result was a new, asymmetrical tactical environment: a surface fleet facing a "fleet" composed mainly of submarines and land-based aircraft.

On a smaller scale than the U.S.-Soviet naval competition, the Falkland Islands War between the United Kingdom and Argentina in 1982 exhibited the tactical environment of sea-based forces fighting land-based forces in the guided-missile era. In this, the only extended naval campaign after World War II, were observed several modern influences on naval combat. First, submarines were formidable weapons, not only in the sinking of an obsolescent pre-World War II cruiser (the *General Belgrano*, formerly the USS *Phoenix*) by a nuclear-powered attack submarine (HMS *Conqueror*) but, less

obviously, in the harrying of the whole British fleet by one Argentine diesel-electric submarine. Second, the nature, if not the full extent, of the threat of modern air-launched antiship missiles was seen in two Argentine attacks, first against the destroyer HMS *Sheffield* and then, after penetrating fleet defenses, the supply ship *Atlantic Conveyor*. Also, a land-to-sea missile struck and damaged the destroyer HMS *Glamorgan*, presaging more strikes from land in future maritime wars. Third, the British relearned lessons of damage control and ship survivability, while the Argentines found that aircraft armed only with unguided bombs were outclassed by ships with surface-to-air missiles. Fourth, and perhaps most fundamental, both sides saw the crippling effect of inadequate scouting, for both were without first-line sea-based air surveillance. Both had to manage with makeshift sources, such as picket submarines and commercial aircraft, for conducting reconnaissance.

Despite the opposition, the British put forces ashore, maintained sufficient control of the airspace, and kept open the very long lines of supply, and this enabled them to retake the islands. A hasty prediction, made by some modern tacticians, that surface warships would be driven from the seas by modern missiles did not prove true. Indeed, in the Falklands conflict, the recorded history of sea battles was reaffirmed. By their very nature, sea battles, once joined, still tended to be fast, deadly, and decisive. The commander of a fleet, always the most expensive component of an armed force, might, as Winston Churchill said of Jellicoe at Jutland, lose his ships and the war in an afternoon.

In response to growing weapon range, the collection and delivery of tactical information continued to grow in importance and consumed more manpower and facilities. Radar and electronic intelligence satellites, over-the-horizon radars, large surveillance aircraft, and electronic signal collectors of utmost sophistication were all manifestations of this trend. These scouting devices had their antitheses in electronic jammers and countermeasures—in effect, antiscouting systems.

In theory, modern communications have permitted the coordinated delivery of missiles or air strikes at great ranges from vessels in dispersed formations, and the three components of naval combat power—firepower, scouting, and C^2—can be highly dispersed. The major navies of the world, however, have continued to build aircraft carriers and cruisers, indicating a reliance on concentrated battle fleets and on strong defenses rather than dispersal to avoid destruction. The tactical value of concentrated as opposed to distributed power will ultimately depend on whether the historical trend observed above—that is, the growing range and lethality of naval weapons—continues. Battleships delivered salvos of gunfire in a continuous stream of destructive power, and the tactical effect was the N-square law of accumulating advantage. An aircraft carrier delivered a pulse of striking power that, if successful, destroyed about its own weight of the enemy. The classic naval tactic of attacking effectively first was vital. The question of the guided-missile age is whether one ship armed with missiles can sink more than one of the enemy, in spite of the enemy's defenses and ability to absorb punishment. If that is now the case, attacking first will be everything. Missiles that outrange the enemy's will be valuable, but even more valuable will be a compatible scouting system that detects and tracks the missiles close enough to their moving targets for the missiles' terminal guidance systems to lock onto them.

The swift naval engagements of the Arab-Israeli War of October 1973 are enlightening. In that war Syrian and Egyptian Osa- and Komar-class gunboats were armed with Russian-made SS-N-2 missiles, which outranged the Gabriel missiles carried by the Israeli Saar boats. Both fleets were small in numbers and size, but speedy. Based on relative missile range and the obvious sufficiency of firepower on both sides, the Arab boats should have struck first and won handily. The Israeli navy, however, had recognized its disadvantage and had developed tactics that emphasized better scouting and C^2 as well as the use of chaff to deflect and neutralize the homing mechanisms of incoming missiles. This superior combination won decisively for them against both opponents. Therefore it could not be concluded that the advantage on paper of highly destructive and potentially decisive long-range missiles would win unless it was coupled with good sensors, modern C² systems, expert command, and sound training.

Guerrilla War at Sea: The Submarine

When submarines first went to sea early in the 20th century, they were immediately recognized as an extraordinary threat to surface ships. By World War II they were so effective against warships that they sank nearly as much aircraft carrier tonnage as was sunk by aircraft. Postwar attack submarines, nuclear-powered and armed with missiles and more advanced torpedoes, now pose an even greater threat to surface warships.

In both world wars, submarines were also a serious threat to merchant shipping. In World War II, German U-boats nearly severed the lifelines to Great Britain, U.S. submarines successfully isolated Japan by nearly wiping out its merchant fleet, and, in the Mediterranean, British and Axis submarines vied in attempts to cut their opponents' communication with North Africa.

Barring a brief period in 1942–43, when U-boats operated successfully in so-called wolf packs, submarines have always been solo performers, relying for successful attack on concealment and surprise rather than concentration of force. These tactics, quite different from fleet actions, are akin to guerrilla war at sea. The submarine stalks its prey while the target—a warship, merchant ship, or convoy—seeks clues as to its presence in order to take evasive action. Simultaneously, antisubmarine forces—destroyers, maritime patrol aircraft, or helicopters—are predators and submarines the prey. The tactical competition between the two is all search and screening, deadly hide-and-seek, for when the submarine closes, its target can do naught but try to escape the blow, and when antisubmarine forces localize a submarine, no help will come and it will either have to fight like a cornered beast or go silent and try to slip away.

If submarines were able to protect sea lanes from attack, including air attack, then they would be serious candidates to succeed the aircraft carrier as the capital ship of the missile era. But as soloists their role has remained that of sea denial, not sea control, that of spoilers rather than champions of sea power. They are the latest in a long line of raiders of the deep, carrying on a tradition of isolation and stealth that began in the 16th century, when the English privateers Francis Drake and John Hawkins seized treasure ships at sea and raided Caribbean possessions in the teeth of the Spanish navy. Later, in the American Civil War, Confederate raiders such as Raphael Semmes in the *Alabama* harried Northern shipping despite the overwhelming superiority of the Union Navy.

To the modern mind, a convoy has become a group of merchant ships protected against submarines. But, beginning in the age of fighting sail, there was a long tradition of protecting convoys against surface raiders, called "cruisers."

In *Some Principles of Maritime Strategy* (1911), Sir Julian S. Corbett sorted out the separate roles of the battle fleet and the cruisers: the former established control of the seas by its concentrated presence or in a climactic battle; the latter either struck at lines of communication or attempted to fend off other raiders by operating alone or in small detachments. Corbett also traced the influence of long-range radio communication and predicted that this development would allow navies to bring such a swift concentration of superior power that the utility of surface raiders would come to an end. That he was right was proved by the fate of such surface raiders of World War II as the German battleship *Bismarck*, which was sunk by an overwhelming combination of bombs, naval guns, and torpedoes.

Corbett fully appreciated the major role submarines would play against capital ships, but he did not grasp the extent to which submarines would become the cruisers of the future. Indeed, submarines have become the biggest threat to commerce, ahead of mines and aircraft. In addition, they are at or near the top of the list of effective killers of submarines. Guerrilla war is therefore the apt term for submarine warfare. The battle tactics are dispersion, surprise, strikes where the enemy is weak and unprepared, disappearance into the vastness of the ocean, and a continuing erosion of enemy morale and dilution of his resources.

CHAPTER 5

WARPLANES IN THE PROPELLER AGE

ircraft have been an important part of military power since World War II (1939–45), but even before World War I (1914–18)—indeed almost from the very invention of fixed-wing flight before 1910—they were recognized as fundamentally changing the conduct of war. During the World War I and World War II period, warplanes were powered by piston engines turning one or more propellers. This configuration limited the capabilities of military aircraft to well below those seen today, but it did not prevent airplanes from being formidable platforms that could deliver munitions, troops, or cargo over distances and at speeds that previously had been unthinkable.

EARLY HISTORY

When the first practical aircraft were produced, in the form of hot-air and hydrogen balloons in 1783, they were adopted quickly for military duties. In 1793 the French National Convention authorized formation of a military tethered-balloon organization, and a company of "Aérostiers" was formed on April 2, 1794. Two months later the first military reconnaissance from such a balloon was made before the city of Maubeuge. Until the Aérostiers were disbanded in 1799, their reports contributed to the success of French armies in many battles and sieges. Similar reconnaissance balloons were used later by other armies, notably by both armies during the American Civil War and by the British in Africa from 1884 to 1901.

True military aviation began with the perfection of the navigable airship in the late 19th century and the airplane in the first decade

Hydrogen gas generator being used to inflate an observation balloon during the American Civil War, 1862. U.S. Department of Defense; Brady Collection

of the 20th century. The brothers Wilbur and Orville Wright, who made the first powered, sustained, and controlled flights in an airplane on Dec. 17, 1903, believed such an aircraft would be useful mainly for military reconnaissance. When they received the first contract for a military airplane from the U.S. government in February 1908, it called for an aircraft capable of carrying two persons at a speed of at least 40 miles (65 km) per hour for a distance of 125 miles (200 km). The aircraft they delivered in June 1909 was listed as "Airplane No. 1, Heavier-than-air Division, United States aerial fleet."

The most formidable aircraft of the years before World War I were airships rather than airplanes. Airships were large self-propelled craft consisting of a rigid fabric-covered metal frame within which were gas bags containing a lighter-than-air gas such as hydrogen. The most ambitious examples of this type of craft were the huge airships designed and built in Germany by Ferdinand, Count von Zeppelin. A typical zeppelin could carry five 50-kg (110-pound) high-explosive bombs and 20 2.5-kg (5.5-pound) incendiary bombs at a time when most military airplanes were without any form of weapons, being intended only for reconnaissance.

Experiments with arming airplanes were made spasmodically after 1910, when August Euler took out a German patent on a machine-gun installation. Bombing techniques evolved simultaneously. Dummy bombs were dropped on a target in the form of a ship by the American designer Glenn Curtiss on June 30, 1910. This test was followed by the dropping of a real bomb and the devising of the first bombsight. In England the Royal Flying Corps (RFC) fitted some of its aircraft with bomb carriers, which consisted of a kind of pipe rack beside the observer's cockpit in which small bombs were retained by a pin. The pin was pulled out over the target by tugging on a string. It was primitive but it worked. The Naval Wing of the RFC subsequently attempted to drop torpedoes from Short and Sopwith seaplanes, with some success, and efforts were soon under way to develop means to launch and recover such craft on shipboard. In 1910–11 a Curtiss biplane had been flown from and onto wooden platforms erected over the decks of anchored U.S. Navy cruisers, and in May 1912 a pilot of the Naval Wing, RFC, flew a Short S.27 biplane from HMS *Hibernia* while the ship was steaming at 10.5 knots (nautical miles per hour—i.e., 12 statute miles per hour, or 20 km per hour). The following year the old cruiser *Hermes* was fitted with a short deck from which seaplanes took off on wheeled trolleys that were fitted under their floats and dropped away as the machines became airborne.

Thus, by 1914 reconnaissance, bomber, and carrier-based aircraft all were evolving, and some had been used in combat. The first use of an airplane in war was on Oct. 23, 1911, during the Italo-Turkish War, when an Italian pilot made a one-hour reconnaissance flight over enemy positions near Tripoli, Libya, in a Blériot XI monoplane. The first bombing raid came nine days later, when a pilot dropped four grenades on Turkish positions. The first reconnaissance photographs of enemy positions were taken on Feb. 24–25, 1912, in the same conflict.

WORLD WAR I

At the start of World War I the land and sea forces of both sides used the aircraft put at their disposal primarily for reconnaissance, and air fighting began as the exchange of shots from small arms between enemy airmen meeting one another in the course of reconnoitering. Fighter aircraft armed with machine guns, however, made their appearance in 1915. Tactical bombing and the bombing of enemy air bases were also gradually introduced at this time. Contact patrolling, with aircraft giving immediate support to infantry, was developed in 1916.

Strategic bombing, on the other hand, was initiated early enough: British aircraft from Dunkirk bombed Cologne, Düsseldorf, and Friedrichshafen in the autumn of 1914, their main objective being the sheds of the German dirigible airships, or zeppelins; and raids by German airplanes or seaplanes on English towns in December 1914 heralded a great zeppelin offensive sustained with increasing intensity from January 1915 to September 1916 (London was first bombed during the night of May 31–June 1, 1915). Subsequent raids by German Gotha bombers made the British think more seriously about strategic bombing and about the need for an air force independent of the other fighting services. The Royal Air Force (RAF), the world's first separate air service, was brought into active existence by a series of measures taken between October 1917 and June 1918.

AIRSHIPS

At the start of the war, the German armed forces had 10 zeppelins and three smaller airships, but this impressive offensive capability was largely offset by the highly explosive nature of the hydrogen gas that gave the zeppelins their lifting power. After losing three zeppelins in daylight raids over heavily defended areas in the first month of the war, the army abandoned airship operations, but the navy, with its battle fleet blockaded in port by the Royal Navy, mounted a night bombing offensive—the first aerial strategic bombardment campaign in history.

The finest of the zeppelins was the LZ-70; this craft was 220 metres (720 feet) long, was able to fly above 4,900 metres (16,000 feet), and had a range of 12,000 km (7,500 miles). The LZ-70 was shot down late in the war, however,

and large rigid (metal-framed) airships were never again employed as combat aircraft. Smaller, nonrigid airships were used throughout World War I by the British for antisubmarine patrol, convoy escort, and coastal reconnaissance, achieving a remarkable record of protecting coastal convoys from German submarines. They were revived by the U.S. Navy during World War II for the same use.

Unpowered, captive balloons also were used extensively for observation and artillery spotting in World War I, but by World War II they had become so vulnerable that they were used only as unmanned antiaircraft barrage balloons. Anchored to the ground or ships by cables, they compelled attacking enemy aircraft to fly high to avoid the cables; they also brought down many German pilotless V-1 "buzz bombs" over England in 1944–45.

RECONNAISSANCE AIRCRAFT

At the outbreak of World War I, heavier-than-air craft were used only for visual reconnaissance, since their feeble engines could carry little more than a pilot and, in some cases, an observer aloft. They soon proved their worth in this mission, however, and RFC aviators provided reconnaissance that enabled the British and French armies to counterattack in the decisive Battle of the Marne on Sept. 6–12, 1914, turning back the invading Germans just short of Paris.

More powerful engines and better aircraft designs soon made possible specialized reconnaissance aircraft that could fly at high altitudes to avoid interception. The Germans, for example, had Rumpler two-seaters in service by 1917 that could operate as high as 7,300 metres (24,000 feet). Radios were carried aloft to permit aerial observers to spot and adjust artillery fire, at first with transmitters only and then, as radios became lighter, with receivers for two-way communication.

FIGHTERS

The importance of aerial reconnaissance and artillery spotting (particularly the latter) made it clear that the belligerent able to deny the enemy use of airspaces above the battlefield would enjoy enormous advantages. This realization led to the emergence of fighters as a distinct category of aircraft. In the early days of the war, pilots and observers blazed away at enemy aircraft with pistols, rifles, and even shotguns, but to little effect. Machine guns were the obvious solution. In 1913 the Vickers company in Britain had exhibited a two-seat biplane of pusher configuration (i.e., with the propeller behind the engine) that was armed with a machine gun fired by an observer who sat ahead of the pilot in a tublike crew compartment. A development of this machine, the Vickers F.B.5 Gunbus, entered service in early 1915 as the first production aircraft designed from the outset with air-to-air armament. The French armed similarly configured Voisin pushers with machine guns (one had shot down a German aircraft as early as Oct. 5, 1914), but, burdened with the extra weight of observer and gun, such aircraft were slow and unmaneuverable, and their successes were mostly the result of accidental encounters. Light single-seat aircraft of tractor configuration (i.e., with the propeller at the nose) had much better performance, but efforts to arm them with machine guns firing at an angle to avoid hitting the propeller produced little success.

The solution to the problem emerged in the spring of 1915 in the form of an interrupter gear, or gun-synchronizing device, designed by the French engineer Raymond Saulnier. This regulated a machine gun's fire so as to enable the bullets to pass between the blades of the spinning propeller. The interrupter itself was not new: a German patent had been taken out on such a device by the Swiss engineer Franz Schneider before the war. The real breakthrough was made by Roland Garros, a famous sporting pilot before the war and a friend of Saulnier, who perceived that a machine gun fitted with such a device and mounted rigidly atop the fuselage could be aimed accurately simply by pointing the airplane in the desired direction. Though the French machine gun had a tendency to "hang fire," so that steel deflector plates had to be fitted onto the rear of the propeller blades to prevent their being shot off, Saulnier quickly perfected his device and fitted it to Garros's Morane L monoplane. With this machine, Garros shot down three German aircraft on April 1, 13, and 18. Then, on April 19, Garros himself force-landed with a ruptured fuel line and was taken prisoner. His efforts to burn his aircraft failed, and the secrets of Saulnier's interrupter gear were laid bare. The Germans reacted quickly, putting the designer Anthony Fokker to work on a similar device. With Saulnier's gear as his inspiration (and perhaps drawing on earlier German work), Fokker swiftly came up with an efficient interrupter gear, which he fitted onto a monoplane of his own design—ironically, a copy of a French Morane. The result was the Fokker Eindecker ("monoplane"), which entered service in July 1915 and reigned supreme in the air over the Western Front until the following October—a period known among Allied aviators as the "Fokker Scourge."

The Eindecker's mastery was ended by new versions of the French Nieuport with a machine gun mounted above the top wing, allowing it to fire clear of the propeller arc, and by British D.H.2 and F.E.2b pushers with nose-mounted guns. Though a superb flying machine, the Nieuport was limited by its light armament, while the two British machines had taken the aerodynamically inefficient pusher configuration to its limit and were soon outclassed. Thereafter, the pace of fighter development began to be set by improvements in engine design—a phenomenon that was to persist well into the jet age.

Most Allied fighters at that time were powered by rotary radial engines

(i.e., with the cylinders, arranged radially about the crankcase like the spokes of a wheel, rotating around a stationary crankshaft). These engines were relatively powerful in relation to their weight, but their large frontal areas produced a great deal of drag, and the gyroscopic forces induced by their whirling mass posed serious aircraft-control problems. In mid-1916 Germany took the lead in fighter design on the basis of its superb Daimler and Benz water-cooled in-line engines, such as those that powered the streamlined Albatros D.I, D.II, and D.III series of fighters. These were faster than their Allied opponents and, most important, could carry two machine guns without sacrificing performance. The Albatros D.I pioneered a fighter configuration that was to prevail into the 1930s: a compact single-seat, externally braced tractor biplane armed with two synchronized machine guns mounted ahead of the pilot on the upper fuselage decking and aimed with a simple ring-and-bead sight. Albatros fighters gave British airmen a terrible drubbing above the Arras battlefield during the "Bloody April" of 1917, but a new generation of French and British fighters with more powerful engines soon tilted the balance toward the Allies. Prominent among these were the French Spad fighters and the British S.E.5, both powered by the Spanish-designed and French-built Hispano-Suiza watercooled V-8, as well as the British Sopwith Camel and new versions of the French Nieuport, powered by improved rotary radial engines.

THE RED BARON

Manfred, Freiherr (baron) von Richthofen, was born on May 2, 1892, in Breslau, Ger. (now Wrocław, Pol.). Members of a prosperous family, Richthofen and his younger brother Lothar followed their father into military careers. In 1912 Richthofen became a lieutenant in the 1st Uhlan Cavalry Regiment of the Prussian Army. As a member of this regiment, he fought in Russia after the outbreak of World War I and then participated in the invasion of Belgium and France.

When trench warfare settled in and the cavalry became sidelined, Richthofen joined the infantry. In 1915 he transferred to the Imperial Air Service and in September 1916 entered combat as a fighter pilot. He became commander of Fighter Wing I (Jagdgeschwader 1), which, because of its frequent moves by rail and its fancifully decorated planes, came to be known as "Richthofen's Flying Circus." Flying his trademark red-painted plane (at first an Albatros D.III biplane, later and more famously a Fokker DR.I triplane), Richthofen became known as der rote Freiherr ("the red baron") or der rote Kampfflieger ("the Red Fighter Pilot"). He personally was credited with shooting down 80 enemy aircraft. Germany's leading ace was killed on April 21, 1918, at Vaux-sur-Somme, France, when his plane was caught in a barrage of enemy ground fire from Australian units during a battle near Amiens. According to another account, the Red Baron was shot down by Captain A. Roy Brown, a Canadian in the Royal Air Force. His eventual successor as commander of the fighter group was Hermann Göring, future head of the German air force during World War II.

Manfred, Freiherr von Richthofen. Encyclopædia Britannica, Inc.

Though Germany fell decisively behind France and Britain in aircraft production in 1917, and thus lost the war in the air, perhaps the definitive single-seat fighter of World War I was the Fokker D.VII of 1918. Typically powered by a 160-horsepower Mercedes engine, the D.VII was a fabric-covered biplane that differed from others in having a sturdy fuselage structure of welded steel tubing. Armed with two machine guns, it had a top speed of 188 km (117 miles) per hour. Even more powerful engines made two-seat fighters possible. The best of these was the British Bristol F.2b, powered by the 220-horsepower water-cooled Rolls-Royce Falcon, a V-12 engine that gave the Bristol a top speed of almost 120 miles (200 km) per hour. The F.2b was armed with a synchronized machine gun for the pilot and two flexible machine guns for the observer.

GROUND ATTACK

The Allies fielded specialized aircraft for ground attack only at the very end of the war. Notable among these was the Sopwith Salamander, a development of the Sopwith Camel with an armoured cockpit and two machine guns firing downward through the floor at a fixed angle to rake enemy trenches while flying low over them. The Germans produced a number of specialized two-seat aircraft for this purpose—notably the Halberstadt CL.III of 1917, which was armed with a forward-firing synchronized machine gun as well as a flexible gun and racks of grenades for the observer. At the Battle of Cambrai in November and December 1917, the Germans sent large formations of such aircraft over the British trenches and into the rear areas with devastating effect. By the end of the war, they were using numbers of armoured all-metal Junkers J-1 ground-attack aircraft, one of the most advanced machines to see combat during the war.

BOMBERS

Since they had to carry heavy disposable loads over long distances in order to be effective, specialized bombers were slower to develop. The first bombing raids to achieve significant success (and the first to cross national boundaries) were mounted against the Zeppelin works at Friedrichshafen from Belgian bases by airmen of the Royal Naval Air Service (RNAS) on Oct. 8 and Nov. 21, 1914. However, their spectacular success owed more to the highly flammable nature of the zeppelins themselves than to the destructive power of the 20-pound (9-kg) bombs used. These raids prompted the Admiralty to commission the development of the first specialized heavy night bomber, the Handley Page H.P. O/100, which flew for the first time in December 1915. Meanwhile, other air forces began building and putting into service strategic day bombers. Among the first were French Voisins. The type L was used in early 1915 to carry about 60 kg (130 pounds) of small bombs that simply lay in the bottom of the cockpit until the time came for the observer to drop them overboard. Later models had more powerful engines and were equipped alternatively as attack aircraft, carrying up to 300 kg (660 pounds) of bombs or having a 37-mm (1.5-inch) gun mounted in the nose. None flew faster than 135 km (85 miles) per hour, so the Voisins operated mainly under cover of darkness in the last year of the war.

Italy too was quick to appreciate the value of bombing attacks on enemy targets. Its big three-engined, twin-tailboom Capronis were among the finest bombers of World War I. Even larger were the Russian Ilya Muromets bombers of the tsar's Squadron of Flying Ships. Designed by Igor Sikorsky, now remembered mainly as a helicopter pioneer, these biplanes spanned about 30 metres (100 feet) and were descended from his "Russky Vityaz" of May 1913, the world's first successful four-engined airplane. About 80 were built, and they made 400 raids on German targets with the loss of only one plane. The best-known German strategic bombers of World War I were twin-engined Gotha "pusher" biplanes, which made several daylight raids on London in formation in the summer of 1917 before reverting to night operations. The German air force also operated a family of giant four-engined metal bombers known as Riesenflugzeug, or R-planes. Typical of these was the Staaken R.VI number R.25, which was powered by four 260-horsepower Mercedes engines. This had a takeoff weight of 11,372 kg (25,269 pounds), which included a crew of seven and a bomb load of up to 1,800 kg (4,000 pounds).

Naval Aviation

Equally significant progress was made in naval flying in World War I. Three distinct categories of combat aircraft emerged: long-range overwater reconnaissance and antisubmarine aircraft operating from shore bases, shorter-range floatplane reconnaissance and fighter aircraft, and ship-borne aircraft. Long-range flying boats (so called because their fuselages were shaped like the hull of a boat) were used extensively by the British. These pioneered the technique of searching for submarines with methodical, mathematically developed search patterns. The German navy made extensive use of reconnaissance and fighter floatplanes from Belgian coastal bases to counter Allied air patrols and coastal naval operations. Some of these, notably Hansa-Brandenburg machines designed by Ernst Heinkel, rivaled their land-based equivalents in performance.

The most efficient of the long-range coastal-based airplanes were large twin-engined flying boats designed by Glenn Curtiss and others. Despite their bulk, these aircraft were sufficiently fast and maneuverable to engage enemy zeppelins and aircraft in combat. Curtiss's flying boats were the only aircraft of U.S. design to see frontline combat service in World War I.

Carrier-based air power also advanced rapidly. In early 1916 the first landplanes (British Sopwith Pups) were flown off the 200-foot (60-metre) decks of primitive carriers that had been

American aeronautic pioneer Glenn Hammond Curtiss piloted his Model E flying boat over Keuka Lake, near Hammondsport, N.Y., in 1912. Library of Congress, Washington, D.C. (neg. no. LC-DIG-ggbain-11555)

converted from merchant ships, and on Aug. 2, 1917, a pilot landed a Pup on the takeoff deck of HMS *Furious* while the ship was under way. The concept of the true aircraft carrier had been born.

Britain went on to develop more formidable naval aircraft, and in October 1918 a squadron of Sopwith Cuckoos, each able to carry an 18-inch (460-mm) torpedo, was embarked on HMS *Argus*. The war ended before the squadron could go into action, but the RNAS had already used torpedoes dropped from Short

seaplanes to sink enemy ships in the Mediterranean, and the Cuckoo, with its modest top speed of 103 miles (166 km) per hour and endurance of four hours, heralded the eventual demise of the battleship in the face of air-power dominance at sea.

AIR TRANSPORT AND TRAINING

Military air transport showed little development in 1914–18. Aircraft were used on occasion to drop supplies to cut-off or besieged forces, but the methods were primitive in the extreme: bags of food, medical supplies, or munitions were dropped from bomb racks or simply heaved over the side.

Conversely, training made enormous strides during the war. At the RFC School of Special Flying at Gosport, Eng., Maj. Robert Smith-Barry introduced a curriculum based on a balanced combination of academic classroom training and dual flight instruction. Philosophically, Smith-Barry's system was based not on avoiding potentially dangerous maneuvers—as had been the case theretofore—but on exposing the student to them in a controlled manner so that he could learn to recover from them, thereby gaining confidence and skill. Technologically, it was based on the Avro 504J, a specialized training aircraft with dual controls, good handling characteristics, adequate power, and in-flight communication between instructor and student by means of an acoustic system of soft rubber tubing—the so-called Gosport tube. For the first time, military pilots flew into action as masters of their airplanes. The Gosport system of training was eventually adopted at training schools throughout the world, remaining the dominant method of civil and military flight instruction into the jet age.

INTERWAR DEVELOPMENTS

In the two decades between the end of World War I and the start of World War II, military aviation underwent a complete transformation. The typical combat aircraft of 1918 was a fabric-covered externally braced biplane with fixed landing gear and open cockpits. Few aero engines developed as much as 250 horsepower, and top speeds of 200 km (120 miles) per hour were exceptional. By 1939 the first-line combat aircraft of the major powers were all-metal monoplanes with retractable landing gear. Powered by engines that developed 1,000 horsepower or more and that were supercharged to permit flight at altitudes above 9,000 metres (30,000 feet), fighters were capable of exceeding 560 km (350 miles) per hour, and some bombers flew faster than 400 km (250 miles) per hour. Gyroscopically driven flight instruments and electrical cockpit lighting permitted flying at night and in adverse weather. Crews were seated in enclosed cockpits, were provided with oxygen for breathing at high altitudes, and could converse with other aircraft and ground stations by voice radio. Parachutes, worn by a few German fighter pilots in the last days of World War I, were standard equipment.

Most of these changes occurred after 1930. The end of World War I left the victorious Allies with huge inventories of military aircraft, and this combined with economic strictures and a lack of threat to retard the development of military aviation in the 1920s. Provisions of the Treaty of Versailles prohibiting developments in military aviation had the same effect in Germany. Nevertheless, advances in key technologies, notably high-performance aero engines, continued. The U.S.

government, for instance, sponsored a systematic program of aerodynamic research under the aegis of the National Advisory Committee for Aeronautics (NACA), which was to yield enormous dividends in aircraft performance through drag-reduction, engine-cooling, and airfoil technologies. Still, the most significant technical advance in the 1920s was the abandonment of wooden structures in favour of metal frames (still fabric-covered) to provide the strength needed to cope with increasingly power-ful engines and to resist harsh climates around the world.

CIVILIAN DESIGN IMPROVEMENTS

When more drastic changes came, they emerged not from military requirements but from civilian air racing, particularly the international seaplane contests for the coveted Schneider Trophy. Until the appearance of variable-pitch propellers in the 1930s, the speed of landplanes was limited by the lengths of existing runways, since the flat pitch of high-speed propellers produced poor takeoff acceleration. Seaplanes, with an unlim-ited takeoff run, were not so constrained, and the Schneider races, contested by national teams with government backing, were particularly influential in push-ing speeds upward. During the 1920s the Curtiss company built a remarkable series of high-speed racing biplanes for the U.S. Army Air Corps and Navy. These were powered by the innovative D-12, a 12-cylinder liquid-cooled engine, also

of Curtiss design, that set international standards for speed and streamlining. One of the Curtiss planes, an R3C-2 piloted by Lieut. James Doolittle, won the 1925 Schneider race with a speed of 232.5 miles (374.1 km) per hour—in sharp contrast to the winning speed of 145.62 miles (234.3 km) per hour in 1922, before the Curtiss machines took part in the event. The influence of the Curtiss engine extended to Europe when British manufacturer C.R. Fairey, impressed with the streamlining made possible by the D-12, acquired license rights to build the engine and designed a two-seat light bomber around it. The Fairey Fox, which entered service in 1926, advanced the speed of RAF bombers by 50 miles (80 km) per hour and was faster than con-temporary fighters. Nor were British engine manufacturers idle; when the U.S. Army and Navy standardized on air-cooled radial engines in the 1920s, Curtiss ceased developing liquid-cooled engines, but British engine designers, partly inspired by the D-12, embarked on a path that was to produce the superlative Rolls-Royce Merlin.

The year that Doolittle won the Schneider Trophy, an even more revo-lutionary design appeared—the S.4 seaplane designed by R.J. Mitchell of the British Supermarine Company. A wooden monoplane with unbraced wings, the S.4 set new standards for streamlining, but it crashed from wing flutter before it could demonstrate its potential. Nevertheless, it was the progenitor of a series of monoplanes that won the trophy three

The U.S. Navy racing team posing in front of its Curtiss R₃C-2 seaplane at the 1926 Schneider Trophy Competition, Norfolk, VA. Rare Book and Special Collections Division/Library of Congress, Washington, D.C. (digital. id. cph 3b52232)

times, giving Britain permanent possession in 1931. The last of these, the S.6B, powered by a liquid-cooled Rolls-Royce racing engine with in-line cylinders, later raised the world speed record to more than 400 miles (640 km) per hour. The S.6B's tapered fuselage and broad, thin, elliptical wings were clearly evident in Mitchell's later and most famous design, the Spitfire.

In the United States the Thompson Trophy, awarded to the winner of unlimited-power closed-circuit competitions at the National Air Races, was won in 1929 for the first time by a monoplane, the Travel Air "R" designed by Walter Beech. Powered by the Wright Cyclone, a 400-horsepower radial engine with a streamlined NACA cowling that contributed 40 miles (65 km) to its maximum speed of 235 miles (375 km) per hour, the "R" handily defeated the far more powerful Curtiss biplanes flown by the army and navy. Embarrassed, the military withdrew from racing—and the army soon ordered its first monoplane fighter, the Boeing P-26. In 1935 the industrialist Howard Hughes set a world landplane speed record of 352 miles (563 km) per hour in a racer designed to his own specifications and powered by a 1,000-horsepower twin-row radial engine built by Pratt & Whitney. The Hughes H-1 was a low-wing monoplane built with unbraced wings with a "stressed-skin" metal covering that bore stress loads and thereby permitted a reduction in weight of the internal structure. These features, along with a flush-riveted, butt-joined aluminum fuselage, an enclosed cockpit, and power-driven retractable landing gear folding flush into the wing, anticipated the configuration, appearance, and performance of the fighters of World War II.

FIGHTERS

By the 1930s the advantages of monoplanes with unbraced wings and retractable landing gear were evident, and fighters of this description began to appear. The first of these to see operational service was the Soviet I-16, designed by Nikolay Polikarpov. The I-16 first flew in 1933 and enjoyed considerable success against German and Italian biplanes in the Spanish Civil War of 1936–39. It was powered by a radial engine derived from the Wright Cyclone and had manually

retracted landing gear and an open cockpit. Its armament of four 7.62-mm (.3-inch) machine guns, two in the wings and two in the engine cowling, was heavy for the time.

As the I-16 entered combat in Spain, two important British fighters were under development: the Supermarine Spitfire, a cleanly elegant fighter of stressed-skin aluminum construction, and the Hawker Hurricane, a more traditional design with a structural frame of welded steel tubes and a fabric covering over the rear fuselage. Both were powered by a Rolls-Royce Merlin engine of some 1,200 horsepower, and both carried an unprecedented armament of no fewer than eight .303-inch (7.7-mm) Browning machine guns, mounted in the wings outboard of the propeller arc so that no interrupter gear was needed. Meanwhile, in Germany the nascent Luftwaffe (air force) was taking delivery of the first versions of the Bf 109, designed by Willy Messerschmitt for the Bayerische Flugzeugwerke ("Bavarian Aircraft Factory"). Like the Spitfire, the Bf 109 was a low-wing monoplane of all-metal stressed-skin construction. Early versions, fitted with fixed-pitch propellers, fought on a par with the I-16 in Spain, but later versions, powered by a Daimler-Benz engine that was equivalent to the Merlin and fitted with variable-pitch propellers for optimal performance at low and high altitudes, totally outclassed the Soviet fighter.

BOMBERS

Bombers evolved in parallel with fighters, changing to high-strength metal construction in the late 1920s and to monoplane design, which brought higher speeds, in the early 1930s. In 1931 the Boeing Aircraft Company produced the B-9 bomber. Anticipating all-metal fighters, the B-9 was the first operational combat aircraft with all-metal cantilever monoplane design, semiretractable undercarriage, and variable-pitch propellers. Two 600-horsepower engines gave it a speed of 188 miles (302 km) per hour, representing a 50 percent improvement over the biplane bombers then in service, without any reduction in bombload. Within months of its first flight, the B-9 was overshadowed completely by the Martin B-10 of 1932, which brought the biggest single advance in bomber design since the Handley Page night bomber of World War I. To the innovations of the B-9 it added enclosed cockpits and an internal bay for its 2,260-pound (1,020-kg) bombload. Maximum speed went up to 213 miles (341 km) per hour, making the B-10 faster than the fighters of its day. Following this success, in 1935 Boeing built a four-engined craft known as the Model 299, which became the prototype of the B-17 Flying Fortress. This famous plane was based on the concept that a bomber could penetrate to any target in daylight as long as it had sufficient defensive armament to battle past fighter opposition. Gun turrets for defensive machine guns had already been pioneered by Machines Motrices in France, and a license-built version of their turret had appeared on the British Boulton Paul Overstrand bomber in 1934. Meanwhile, the U.S. Army Air Corps claimed that its highly secret Norden bombsight provided such accuracy that "a bomb could be placed in a pickle barrel from 20,000 feet."

An important type of bomber to emerge in the interwar period was the dive bomber, designed to release its bombs at a low point of a steep dive. Accuracy was maintained by the use of air brakes, which were flaps that could be extended outward to slow the dive by increasing the aircraft's drag. The dive bomber as a distinct type of aircraft was a product of tests undertaken during the 1920s by the U.S. Navy.

GENERAL BILLY MITCHELL

William ("Billy") Mitchell was a U.S. Army officer who early advocated a separate U.S. air force and greater preparedness in military aviation. He was court-martialed for his outspoken views and did not live to see the fulfillment during World War II of many of his prophecies: strategic bombing, mass airborne operations, and the eclipse of the battleship by the bomb-carrying airplane.

Mitchell was born of American parents in Nice, France, on Dec. 29, 1879, and grew up in Milwaukee, Wis. After enlisting as a private in the 1st Wisconsin Infantry during the Spanish-American War (1898), he served in Cuba and the Philippines, and in 1901 he was commissioned a first lieutenant in the regular army. He served in various duties, was promoted to captain in 1903, and was assigned to the aviation section of the Signal Corps in 1915. He learned to fly the following year, when he was also promoted to major.

Mitchell was already in Europe as an observer when the United States entered World War I. As the war progressed, he proved to be a highly effective air commander. In June 1917 he was named air officer of the American Expeditionary Forces, with the rank of lieutenant colonel. By May 1918 he was a colonel and air officer of the I Corps, a combat post more to his liking. He was the first American airman to fly over enemy lines, and throughout the war he was regularly in the air. In September 1918 he commanded a mass bombing by a French-U.S. air armada of almost 1,500 planes—the largest concentration of air power up to that time.

After the war Mitchell was appointed assistant chief of the Air Service. He became an outspoken proponent of an independent air force and continued working on improvements in aircraft and their use. He claimed that the airplane had rendered the battleship obsolete and, over the vociferous protests of the Navy Department, carried his point in 1921 and 1923 by sinking several captured and overage battleships from the air. Mitchell was persistently critical of the low state of preparedness of the tiny Air Service and of the poor quality of its equipment, but his harrying of his superiors won him only a transfer to the minor post of air officer of the VIII Corps area at San Antonio, Texas, and reversion to the rank of colonel in April 1925. He continued, however, to use the press to fight his case.

The climax of Mitchell's campaign came in September 1925, when the loss of the navy dirigible Shenandoah in a storm inspired him to publicly accuse the War and Navy departments of "incompetency, criminal negligence, and almost treasonable administration of the national defense." He was, as he expected, immediately court-martialed, and, after he made the trial a platform for his views, he was convicted in December of insubordination. Sentenced to suspension from rank and pay for five years, he resigned from the army on Feb. 1, 1926, and retired to a farm near Middleburg, Va.

Mitchell continued to promote air power and to warn against the danger of being outstripped by other countries, particularly Japan. He hypothesized a possible attack by Japanese aircraft launched from great carrier ships and directed at the Hawaiian Islands. He died on Feb. 19, 1936, in New York. Subsequent events proved the validity of many of his prophesies, and many of his ideas were adopted by the Army Air Forces during World War II. The utter decisiveness that he claimed for air power never materialized, however. In 1946 the U.S. Congress authorized a special medal in his honour; it was presented to his son in 1948 by Gen. Carl Spaatz, chief of staff of the newly created U.S. Air Force.

These demonstrated the advantages of bombing the lightly armoured upper decks of warships and resulted in the appearance of the first real dive bomber, the Curtiss F8C Helldiver, in 1929. Impressed by a Helldiver demonstration, the Luftwaffe, whose doctrine stressed the direct support of ground forces, requested a more advanced aircraft with similar capabilities. The result was the Ju 87 "Stuka" (for *Sturzkampfflieger*, or "dive bomber"), which gained a fearsome reputation for destructiveness during the Spanish Civil War.

CARRIER AIRCRAFT

By the 1930s, ship-based aircraft were fitted under the tail with arrester hooks that engaged cables strung across the landing deck in order to bring them to a halt after landing. Folding wings then enabled them to be taken by elevator to below-deck hangars. Japanese and U.S. aircraft carriers had mixed complements of single-seat fighters, dive bombers, and torpedo planes; the Royal Navy pursued a less-successful course, developing two-seat reconnaissance fighters such as the Fairey Fulmar, which were outperformed by their land-based equivalents.

WORLD WAR II

It was in World War II that the design improvements of the 1930s were put to the test and showed beyond any doubt that warfare had changed forever. Since that conflict, war in the third (vertical) dimension has had an importance beyond the skies; what happens in the skies also influences what happens on the ground or on the surface of the sea.

FIGHTERS

Air superiority was crucial to the outcome of most of the decisive campaigns of World War II, and here the performance of single-seat fighters was generally the critical factor. First-class fighters required extremely powerful aero engines suitable for compact, low-drag installation, and in this respect Britain, Germany, and the United States were in a class by themselves. The only significant exception was the Japanese Mitsubishi A6M carrier fighter, known as the Zero, which was designed by Horikoshi Jiro. The Zero was so remarkably strong and light that it achieved first-class performance with a second-class engine—though at the cost of being vulnerable to battle damage.

The outstanding fighters of the early war years (1939–41) were the Supermarine Spitfire, the Bayerische Flugzeugwerke Bf 109 (known to the wartime Allies as the Me 109), the Zero, the Hawker Hurricane, and the Grumman F4F Wildcat (this last a U.S. Navy fighter powered by a supercharged twin-row radial engine by Pratt & Whitney). The Lockheed P-38 Lightning, a novel twin-boom interceptor designed before the war by Clarence ("Kelly") Johnson, had exceptional performance, but until 1943 it was available only in small numbers. The main U.S.

Lockheed P-38 Lightning. U.S. Air Force Photograph

Army Air Forces fighters of the early war, the Curtiss P-40 Warhawk and the Bell P-39 Airacobra, were badly outclassed by the Bf 109 and the Zero as a result of production decisions that deprived their high-performance Allison engines of scarce turbosuperchargers, assigning them instead to bombers. The best Soviet fighters were similarly outclassed: the MiG-3, from the MiG design bureau of Artem Mikoyan and Mikhail Gurevich, was fast, but it had marginal handling characteristics, and the performance of Semyon Lavochkin's LaGG-3 was ruined by a disastrously heavy airframe.

The Spitfire and the Hurricane were determined opponents of the Bf 109 during the Battle of Britain, the first battle fought entirely in the air. The German fighter was armed with two 7.62-mm (.3-inch) machine guns in the cowling and two wing-mounted cannon firing 20-mm (.75-inch) exploding shells. The aerial cannon, perfected by the Germans during the interwar period, was intended to ensure the greatest possible destruction against metal-skinned aircraft in the short periods during which a target could be kept in the gunsights at rapidly increasing speeds. The Bf 109 was superior

Focke-Wulf Fw 190, German fighter plane of World War II. U.S. Air Force Photograph

in fighter-to-fighter combat, while the massed batteries of .303-inch (7.7-mm) machine guns in the British fighters were highly effective in destroying bombers. Aiming was accomplished by gyroscopic lead-computing gunsights that projected the aim point onto a transparent screen in front of the pilot.

More powerful and heavily armed versions of the Spitfire and the Bf 109 were tactically viable through the end of the war, but they were hampered by a short radius of action (the farthest distance to which they could fly, engage in combat, and return to base). In 1942–43 fighters began to enter service fitted with newer and more powerful engines and designed on the basis of the most recent aerodynamic data. Notable among these were the German Focke-Wulf Fw 190, designed by Kurt Tank, and the U.S. Republic P-47 Thunderbolt, Grumman F6F Hellcat, and North American P-51 Mustang. All were heavily

P-47 Thunderbolt, U.S. fighter-bomber of World War II. U.S. Air Force

armed, the Fw 190 with as many as two 7.6-mm (.3-inch) machine guns and four 20-mm (.75-inch) cannon, the P-47 with eight .50-inch (12.7-mm) machine guns, and the F6F and P-51 with six .50-inch (12.7-mm) machine guns. The Fw 190, the P-47, and the F6F had distinctively bulky fuselages widened to accommodate their twin-row radial engines, while the slimmer P-51, designed in 1940 by J.H. ("Dutch") Kindleberger under a British contract, was fitted with in-line engines and incorporated the latest drag-reduction and airfoil data provided by NACA. Powered by the Rolls-Royce Merlin, the P-51 became the outstanding high-altitude escort fighter of the war. It was at least competitive with contemporary versions of the Spitfire, the Bf 109, and the Fw 190 in speed, rate of climb, and maneuverability, but it had a more spacious fuselage, a more efficient wing, and, fitted with droppable fuel tanks, a far greater radius of action of more than

U.S. Navy F6F Hellcat. U.S. Navy Photograph

1,000 miles (1,600 km). During 1943 the Soviet Red Air Force also gained technical parity with the Luftwaffe with its radial-engined Lavochkin La-5 and La-7 and the in-line-powered Yakovlev Yak-3 and Yak-9.

By war's end, piston-engined fighter technology had reached its peak in later versions of the Fw 190, powered by in-line Jumo engines by Junkers, and in the Hawker Tempest, powered by the massive 2,200-horsepower, 24-cylinder in-line Napier Sabre. Armed with four 20-mm (.75-inch) cannon and able to attain speeds in excess of 435 miles (700 km) per hour, the Tempest was the fastest piston-engined fighter ever to see service.

During the Battle of Britain, the RAF converted twin-engined bombers such as the Bristol Blenheim into night fighters by installing offensive ordnance and radar, but these had little success, since they were no faster than their prey. On the other hand, Messerschmitt's Me 110, a disastrous failure as a twin-engined two-seat day fighter, became highly successful at night fighting, as did similarly modified Ju 88 bombers. The RAF later used radar-equipped versions of the de Havilland Mosquito to protect its bombers during the battle for the night skies over Germany in 1943–45.

THE SPITFIRE

The Supermarine Spitfire was the most widely produced and strategically important British single-seat fighter of World War II. Renowned for winning victory laurels in the Battle of Britain (1940–41) along with the Hawker Hurricane, the Spitfire served in every theatre of the war and was produced in more variants than any other British aircraft.

The Spitfire was designed by Reginald Mitchell of Supermarine Ltd., in response to a 1934 Air Ministry specification calling for a high-performance fighter with an armament of eight wing-mounted 0.303-inch (7.7-mm) machine guns. The airplane was a direct descendant of a series of floatplanes designed by Mitchell to compete for the coveted Schneider Trophy in the 1920s. Designed around a 1,000-horsepower, 12-cylinder, liquid-cooled Rolls-Royce PV-12 engine (later dubbed the Merlin), the Spitfire first flew in March 1935. It had superb performance and flight characteristics, and deliveries to operational Royal Air Force (RAF) squadrons commenced in the summer of 1938. A more radical design than the Hurricane, the Spitfire had a stressed-skin aluminum structure and a graceful elliptical wing with a thin airfoil that, in combination with the Merlin's efficient two-stage supercharger, gave it exceptional performance at high altitudes.

The version of the Spitfire that fought in the Battle of Britain was powered by a Merlin engine of 1,030 horsepower. The plane had a wingspan of 36 feet 10 inches (11.2 metres), was 29 feet 11 inches (9.1 metres) long, and reached a maximum speed of 360 miles (580 km) per hour and a ceiling of 34,000 feet (10,400 metres). Faster than its formidable German opponent the Bf 109 at altitudes above 15,000 feet (4,600 metres) and just as maneuverable, Spitfires were sent by preference to engage German fighters while the slower Hurricanes went for the bombers. More Hurricanes than Spitfires served in the Battle of Britain, and they were credited with more "kills," but it can be argued that the Spitfire's superior high-altitude performance provided the margin of victory.

By war's end the Spitfire had been produced in more than 20 fighter versions alone, powered by Merlins of up to 1,760 horsepower. Spitfires were used in the defense of Malta, in North Africa and Italy, and, fitted with tail hooks and strengthened tail sections, as Seafires from Royal Navy aircraft carriers from June 1942. Spitfires helped to provide air superiority over the Sicily, Italy, and Normandy beachheads and served in the Far East from the spring of 1943. One of the Spitfire's most important contributions to Allied victory was as a photo-reconnaissance aircraft from early 1941. Superior high-altitude performance rendered it all but immune from interception, and the fuel tanks that replaced wing-mounted machine guns and ammunition bays gave it sufficient range to probe western Germany from British bases.

In late 1943 Spitfires powered by Rolls-Royce Griffon engines developing as much as 2,050 horsepower began entering service. Capable of top speeds of 440 miles (710 km) per hour and ceilings of 40,000 feet (12,200 metres), these were used to shoot down V-1 "buzz bombs." When production ceased in 1947, 20,334 Spitfires of all versions had been produced, 2,053 of them Griffon-powered versions. Fighter versions of the Spitfire were dropped from RAF service during the early 1950s, while photo-reconnaissance Spitfires continued in service until 1954.

GROUND ATTACK

The most effective attack aircraft of the war was the Soviet Ilyushin Il-2 Stormovik. Heavily armoured for protection against ground fire and defended by a gunner in the rear of the two-seat cabin, the Il-2 could fly at up to 450 km (280 miles) per hour at tree-top level and was able to attack ground targets with cannons, bombs, and rockets. It was the first close-support type to employ rockets in vast quantities and had a great influence on the adoption of such weapons by other Allied forces. Though not designed for ground attack, the American P-47 Thunderbolt proved to be especially resistant to battle damage and thus a highly effective ground-attack aircraft as well. Another important ground-attack aircraft was Britain's Hawker Typhoon, originally intended to be a high-altitude fighter but limited to low altitudes by its thick wing. Armed with rockets and 20-mm (.75-inch) cannon, it specialized in attacking trains, tanks, and other moving ground targets.

BOMBERS

The Junkers Ju 87 Stuka dive bomber was used to great effect during the invasions of Poland, France, and the Low Countries in 1939–40, but its slow speed rendered it vulnerable to fighter attack. The Germans' principal bombers of the Battle of Britain were the twin-engined Heinkel He 111, the Dornier Do 17, and Ju 88. The Ju 88 was fast, with a top speed of 450 km (280 miles) per hour, but it carried a modest bombload; the other German bombers had mediocre performance and were lightly armed by British or American standards. The later Do 217 had a range of 2,400 km (1,500 miles) and could carry a bombload of 4,000 kg (8,800 pounds), but it was built only in small numbers. The Germans never built a successful four-engined bomber.

Combat experience showed that the heavily armed British and U.S. bombers were more vulnerable to fighter attack than expected. This was dramatically revealed on Dec. 18, 1939, when a formation of Vickers Wellingtons—one of the most battle-worthy bombers of the day, with a powered four-gun Boulton Paul tail turret—was decimated over the Heligoland Bight by cannon-armed German fighters. In time this led to the adoption of self-sealing fuel tanks, armour protection for crews, and even heavier defensive armament, but the British responded immediately by abandoning daylight bombing except under special circumstances. Bombing at night reduced vulnerability to fighters, but finding and hitting targets proved difficult: nothing smaller than a city could be effectively attacked, and, as operational analysis revealed in 1941–42, ordinary crews had trouble doing even that. The problem was solved partly by using specially trained

Lancaster heavy bomber, the most successful bomber flown by the Royal Air Force during World War II. Andrea Featherby

"Pathfinder" crews to mark targets with flares and partly by electronic navigation aids. During the Battle of Britain, the Germans used electronic beams to guide bombers to their targets at night, and the British later developed onboard radars, such as the H_2S blind bombing system, that could produce maplike pictures of terrain beneath the aircraft through clouds or in darkness. From 1943, powerful four-engined bombers such as the Handley Page Halifax and the Avro Lancaster, carrying H_2S radar and heavy armament, kept RAF bomber losses within barely acceptable limits.

An independent British development was the de Havilland Mosquito. Constructed entirely of wood, powered by two Rolls-Royce Merlin engines, and carrying a crew of two and no defensive armament, this extraordinarily fast aircraft remained effectively immune to interception until the appearance of jet fighters, and it could reach Berlin with a 4,000-pound (1,800-kg) bomb. It was perhaps the most successful multimission aircraft ever made, serving with distinction as a low-level day bomber, radar-equipped night fighter, and long-range photoreconnaissance aircraft.

The U.S. Army Air Forces armed later versions of their Boeing B-17 Flying Fortresses and Consolidated-Vultee B-24 Liberators with 12 or more .50-inch (12.7-mm) machine guns, eight of them in twin-gun power-driven turrets in nose, tail, ventral, and belly positions. Still, losses were high, reaching unacceptable numbers in raids against the Schweinfurt ball-bearing works on Aug. 17 and Oct. 14, 1943. Daylight bombing had to be curtailed until the arrival of P-38, P-47, and P-51 escort fighters equipped with drop tanks to provide the necessary range. For high-altitude attacks from 25,000 feet (7,500 metres), the B-17 could carry 4,000 pounds (1,800 kg) of bombs at 215 miles (345 km) per hour with a radius of action of some 800 miles (1,300 km). The B-24 carried more bombs and was slightly faster, but it could not fly as high and was more vulnerable to enemy fire. British heavy bombers carried larger bombloads—the Lancaster could carry 7,000 pounds (3,150 kg) with a radius of action of nearly 1,000 miles (1,600 km) or a bombload of 14,000 pounds (6,300 kg) over

a radius of 500 miles (800 km)—but only at medium altitudes of less than 20,000 feet (6,000 metres). The heaviest bomber of World War II was the Boeing B-29 Superfortress, which entered service in 1944 with a fully pressurized crew compartment (previously used only on experimental aircraft) and as many as 12 .50-inch (12.7-mm) machine guns mounted in pairs in remotely-controlled turrets. Although these features were intended to optimize the B-29 for very high-altitude missions at 35,000 feet (10,500 metres), it was most effectively used when, stripped of almost all its heavy defensive armament, it carried bombloads as heavy as 12,000 pounds (5,400 kg) in low-altitude firebombing attacks against Tokyo and other Japanese cities from bases 2,000 miles (3,200 km) away in the Mariana Islands. Specially modified B-29s dropped atomic bombs on Hiroshima and Nagasaki.

NAVAL AVIATION

During World War II, carrier-based attack aircraft replaced the big guns of capital ships as the dominant offensive weapon of naval warfare. This was first demonstrated by the destruction of Italian battleships at Taranto by Fairey Swordfish torpedo biplanes on the night of Nov. 11–12, 1940; by the Japanese attack on Pearl Harbor on Dec. 7, 1941; and by the decisive Battle of Midway (June 3–6, 1942), in which surface vessels never exchanged gunfire while U.S.

Two U.S. Navy Avengers, one (background) in the fighter-bomber configuration of World War II and the other (foreground) carrying a radar pod for postwar antisubmarine duty. U.S. Navy Photograph

aircraft destroyed four Japanese aircraft carriers for the loss of only one of their own. In addition to such fighters as the F6F, the Zero, and modified Spitfires and Hurricanes, notable carrier aircraft of the war included dive bombers such as the U.S. Douglas SBD Dauntless and the Japanese Aichi 99 as well as torpedo planes such as the Grumman TBF Avenger and the Nakajima B5N.

Land-based torpedo planes were also effective, as shown in attacks on the British battleships *Repulse* and *Prince of Wales* by twin-engined Japanese Mitsubishi G3M and G4M bombers off Malaya on Dec. 10, 1941.

KAMIKAZE

Kamikaze is a term for suicidal attacks carried out by Japanese pilots in World War II; they deliberately crashed their planes into enemy targets, usually ships. The term also denotes the aircraft used in such attacks. The practice first appeared in the Battle of Leyte Gulf, October 1944, and continued to the end of the war. The word kamikaze *in Japanese means "divine wind," a reference to a typhoon that fortuitously dispersed a Mongol invasion fleet threatening Japan from the west in 1281. Most kamikaze planes were ordinary Zero fighters or light bombers, usually loaded with bombs and extra gasoline tanks before being flown into their targets.*

Later in the war a piloted missile was developed for kamikaze use that was called the Ohka ("Cherry Blossom") by the Japanese but was given the nickname Baka by the Allies, from the Japanese word for "fool." The pilot had no means of getting out once the missile was fastened to the aircraft that would launch it. Dropped usually from an altitude of over 7,500 metres (25,000 feet) and more than 80 km (50 miles) from its target, the missile would glide to about 5 km (3 miles) from its target before the pilot turned on its three rocket engines, accelerating the craft to more than 1,000 km (600 miles) per hour in its final dive. The explosive charge built into the nose weighed more than a ton.

Kamikaze attacks sank 34 ships and damaged hundreds of others during the war. At Okinawa they inflicted the greatest losses ever suffered by the U.S. Navy in a single battle, killing almost 5,000 men. Usually the most successful defense against kamikaze attack was to station picket destroyers around capital ships and direct the destroyers' antiaircraft batteries against the kamikazes as they approached the larger vessels. By the end of the war, there were no more skilled kamikaze volunteers, and the tactic became no more effective than traditional dive bombing.

RECONNAISSANCE

For military staffs contemplating offensive operations, aerial photography became the most important source of detailed information on enemy dispositions. British reconnaissance aircraft were especially capable. Modified versions of the Spitfire and the Mosquito, stripped of armament and fitted with extra fuel tanks, proved essentially immune to interception at high altitudes. Stripped-down versions of the P-38 and the P-51, called the F-4 and the F-5, were also effective photoreconnaissance platforms, the latter excelling at high-resolution coverage from low altitudes.

TRAINING

Japan and Germany entered World War II with exceptionally well-trained aviators, but their provisions for training replacements were inadequate. The

British Commonwealth and the United States gained a vital advantage over the Axis by establishing large, well-organized air-crew training programs. Outstanding training aircraft included the British de Havilland Tiger Moth, the U.S. Stearman PT-19, and the German Bücker Bü 133 Jungmeister—all biplanes. Only the United States built specialized single-engined trainers with such features characteristic of operational craft as retractable landing gear and variable-pitch propellers. Notable among these was the North American AT-6.

AIR TRANSPORT

Major advances in air transport were made during the war. Mass drops of parachute troops had been pioneered by the Soviet Union in the 1930s, but the Luftwaffe first used the technique operationally, notably during the invasion of Crete, in which 15,000 airborne and parachute troops were

U.S. Army Air Forces C-54 Skymaster, a military version of the Douglas DC-4 airliner. The four-engined C-54 was produced from 1942 to 1947 and provided truly intercontinental transport for the U.S. military during World War II, the Korean War, the Berlin blockade and airlift, and other theatres of operation. U.S. Air Force Photo

landed onto that island by 700 transport aircraft and 80 gliders. The troop-carrying glider was one of the developments of World War II that had no continuing place in postwar air forces, but the transport airplane was only at the beginning of its useful life. The Germans built transports such as the Ju 52 only in small quantities, but the twin-engined Douglas C-47 Skytrain, which had revolutionized American commercial aviation in the mid-1930s as the DC-3, was produced in huge numbers and was the backbone of tactical air transport in every Allied theatre of the war. One of the few transports with a large side door suitable for dropping paratroopers, the C-47 was also the mainstay of British and American airborne operations. Douglas also manufactured the four-engined C-54 Skymaster, which entered service in 1943–44 as the first land-based transport with intercontinental flight capabilities. The C-54 was particularly important in the vast distances of the Pacific-Asian theatre of operations.

HELICOPTERS

In the years before World War II, both the U.S. Army and the RAF had experimented with autogiros; these were craft that employed a propeller for forward motion and a freely rotating unmotorized rotor for lift. Autogiros proved too expensive and mechanically complex and were supplanted by conventional light aircraft. Meanwhile, during the late 1930s Igor Sikorsky in the United States and Anton Flettner and Heinrich Focke in Germany had perfected helicopter designs with serious military potential. The Sikorsky R-4, powered by a single lifting rotor and an antitorque tail rotor, was used for local rescue duties at U.S. air bases in the Pacific and was also used in several combat rescues in Burma. The German navy used a handful of Flettner Fl 282s, powered by two noncoaxial, contrarotating lifting rotors, for ship-based artillery spotting and visual reconnaissance.

CHAPTER 6

WARPLANES IN THE JET AGE

Beginning in the 1920s, steady advances in aircraft performance had been produced by improved structures and drag-reduction technologies and by more powerful, supercharged engines, but by the early 1930s it had become apparent to a handful of farsighted engineers that speeds would soon be possible that would exceed the capabilities of reciprocating engines and propellers. The reasons for this were not at first widely appreciated. At velocities approaching Mach 1, or the speed of sound (about 1,190 km [745 miles] per hour at sea level and about 1,055 km [660 miles] per hour at 11,000 metres [36,000 feet]), aerodynamic drag increases sharply. Moreover, in the transonic range (between about Mach 0.8 and Mach 1.2), air flowing over aerodynamic surfaces stops behaving like an incompressible fluid and forms shock waves. These in turn create sharp local discontinuities in airflow and pressure, creating problems not only of drag but of control as well. Because propeller blades, describing a spiraling path, move through the air at higher local velocities than the rest of the aircraft, they enter this turbulent transonic regime first. For this reason, there is an inflexible upper limit on the speeds that can be attained by propeller-driven aircraft. Such complex interactions in the transonic regime—and not the predictable shock-wave effects of supersonic flight, which ballisticians had understood since the late 19th century—presented special problems that were not solved until the 1950s. In the meantime, a few pioneers attacked the problem directly by conceiving a novel power plant, the jet engine.

FIGHTERS

While still a cadet at the Royal Air Force College, Cranwell, in 1928, Frank Whittle advanced the idea of replacing the piston engine and propeller with a gas turbine, and in the following year he conceived the turbojet, which linked a compressor, a combustion chamber, and a turbine in the same duct. In ignorance of Whittle's work, three German engineers independently arrived at the same concept: Hans von Ohain in 1933; Herbert Wagner, chief structural engineer for Junkers, in 1934; and government aerodynamicist Helmut Schelp in 1937. Whittle had a running bench model by the spring of 1937, but backing from industrialist Ernst Heinkel gave von Ohain the lead. The He 178, the first jet-powered aircraft, flew on Aug. 27, 1939, nearly two years before its British equivalent, the Gloster E.28/39, on May 15, 1941. Through an involved chain of events in which Schelp's intervention was pivotal, Wagner's efforts led to the Junkers Jumo 004 engine. This became the most widely produced jet engine of World War II and the first operational axial-flow turbojet, one in which the air flows straight through the engine. By contrast, the Whittle and Heinkel jets used centrifugal flow, in which the air is thrown radially outward during compression. Centrifugal flow offers advantages of lightness, compactness, and efficiency—but at the cost of greater frontal area, which increases drag, and lower compression ratios, which limit maximum power. Many early jet fighters were powered by centrifugal-flow turbojets, but, as speeds increased, axial flow became dominant.

SUBSONIC FLIGHT

Though Whittle was first off the mark, the Germans advanced their programs with persistence and ingenuity. The Messerschmitt Me 262, powered by two Jumo engines and with wings swept back 18.5°, was capable of 845 km (525 miles) per hour. Armed with four 30-mm (1.2-inch) cannon and unguided rockets, it was an effective bomber destroyer, but it entered service too late to have a major effect on the war. The Gloster Meteor entered service on July 27, 1944, about two months before the Me 262; though it was less capable than the German fighter, it was effective in intercepting V-1 "buzz bombs." Desperate to combat Allied bombers, the Germans also turned to rocket propulsion, fielding the tailless Me 163 Komet in the final months of the war. Powered by a hydrogen peroxide rocket designed by Hellmuth Walter, the Komet had spectacular performance, but its short range and ineffective cannon armament made it an operational failure. In addition, the propellants were unstable and often exploded on landing.

Meanwhile, the U.S. aviation industry entered the jet race with the receipt by General Electric of a Whittle engine in 1941. The first U.S. jet, the Bell P-59A Airacomet, made its first flight the following year. It was slower than contemporary piston-engined fighters, but in 1943–44 a small team under Lockheed designer Clarence ("Kelly") Johnson developed the P-80 Shooting Star. The P-80 and its British contemporary, the de Havilland Vampire, were the first successful fighters powered by a single turbojet.

The jets of World War II inaugurated the first generation of jet fighters, in which turbojet propulsion was applied to existing airframe technology and aerodynamics. (Indeed, some early postwar jets—notably, the Soviets' Yakovlev Yak-15 and Yak-23 and the Swedish Saab 21R—were simply reengined propeller-driven fighters.) These aircraft generally outperformed their piston-engined contemporaries by virtue of the greater thrust that their jets provided at high speeds, but they suffered from serious deficiencies in range and handling characteristics owing to the high fuel consumption and slow acceleration of early turbojets. More fundamentally, they were limited to subsonic speeds because the relatively thick airfoils of the day were prone to the compressibility problems of transonic flight—especially at high altitudes, where the higher speeds required to produce lift in thin atmosphere brought aircraft more quickly to transonic speed. For this reason, first-generation jets performed best at low altitudes.

Other first-generation fighters included the U.S. McDonnell FH Phantom and the British Hawker Sea Hawk (the first jet carrier fighters), the McDonnell F2H Banshee, and the French Dassault Ouragan. These single-seat day fighters were in service by 1950, while first-generation all weather fighters, burdened with radar and a second crew member, entered service through the late 1950s.

TRANSONIC FLIGHT

As the first generation of jet fighters entered service, many aerodynamicists and engineers believed supersonic flight a practical impossibility, owing to transonic drag rise or compressibility, which threatened to tear an aircraft apart. Nevertheless, on Oct. 14, 1947, U.S. Air Force Capt. Charles Yeager, flying a rocket-powered Bell X-1 launched from the bomb bay of a B-29 Superfortress bomber, became the first human to exceed the speed of sound. Designed exclusively for research, the X-1 had thin, unswept wings and a fuselage modeled after a .50-inch (12.7-mm) bullet. Yeager's flight marked the dawn of the supersonic era, but it was only part of a broad wave of testing and experimentation that had begun during World War II. Germany had experimented then with swept-back and delta-shaped wings, which delayed transonic drag rise, and after extensive testing these configurations were widely adopted in the postwar years. At the same time, the development of slats, slotted flaps, and other sophisticated high-lift devices for landing and takeoff enabled designers to use smaller wings, which in turn allowed them to achieve higher speeds. Turbojets became more powerful, and in the late 1950s afterburning, or reheat, was introduced. This permitted large temporary thrust increases by the spraying of fuel into hot exhaust gases in the tailpipe—in effect turning the turbojet into a ramjet.

As these developments took hold, a second generation of fighters appeared that were capable of operating in the transonic regime. These aircraft had thinner lifting and control surfaces than first-generation jets, and most had swept-back wings. Aerodynamic refinements and more powerful, quicker-accelerating engines gave them better flight characteristics, particularly at high altitudes, and some could exceed the Mach in a shallow dive. In addition, airborne radars became more compact and reliable, and radar-ranging gunsights began to replace the optically ranging sights used in World War II. Air-to-air missiles, using radar guidance and infrared homing, became smaller and more capable. Outstanding fighters of this generation were the U.S. North American F-86 Sabre and its opponent in the Korean War (1950–53), the Soviet MiG-15. The F-86 introduced the all-flying tail (later a standard feature on high-performance jets), in which the entire horizontal stabilizer deflects as a unit to control pitch, yielding greater control and avoiding the compressibility problems associated with hinged surfaces. This and a radar-ranging gunsight helped the F-86 achieve a favourable kill ratio over the MiG-15, despite the Soviet fighter's greater speed, higher service ceiling, and heavier armament. Other jets of this generation were Britain's superlative Hawker Hunter, the MiG-17, and the diminutive British-designed Folland Gnat. The latter two, introduced in the mid-1950s, later became successful low-altitude dogfighters—the Gnat against

The MiG-15

The MiG-15 was the first "all-new" Soviet jet aircraft, one whose design did not simply add a jet engine onto an older piston-engine airframe. Employing swept-back wings, a tail fin, and horizontal stabilizers to reduce drag as the plane approached the speed of sound, it clearly exploited aerodynamic principles learned from German engineering at the close of World War II.

The MiG-15 was built by the Mikoyan-Gurevich design bureau and was powered by a centrifugal-flow engine that had been licensed from the British company Rolls-Royce and then upgraded by the Soviet manufacturer Klimov. The fighter was first flown in 1947, and deliveries to the military began in 1948. Designed as a bomber interceptor, the single-seat MiG-15 carried a formidable armament of two 23-mm (.9-inch) guns and one 37-mm (1.5-inch) gun firing exploding shells.

In November 1950 the appearance over North Korea of MiG-15s, bearing Chinese markings though flown by Soviet pilots, marked a major turning point in the Korean War and indeed in all of aerial warfare. Shocked by the speed, climbing ability, and high operating ceiling of the Soviet fighter, the United States hurried delivery to Korea of the new F-86 Sabre, which managed to reestablish U.S. air supremacy in part because of a superior pilot-training system instituted by the U.S. Air Force. Nevertheless, the MiG-15 virtually ended daylight bombing runs by huge, slow, World War II-era B-29 Superfortresses, and Soviet pilots continued to engage in combat with U.S. and allied planes even as they trained Chinese and North Koreans to fly in the new jet age.

More than 15,000 MiG-15s were built, including those produced in Soviet-bloc countries.

Pakistani F-86s in the Indo-Pakistani conflict of 1965 and the MiG-17 against U.S. aircraft in the Vietnam War (1965–73).

SUPERSONIC FLIGHT

A third generation of fighters, designed around more powerful, afterburning

U.S. Air Force F-102A Delta Dagger. U.S. Air Force Photograph

engines and capable of level supersonic flight, began to enter service in the mid-1950s. This generation included the first fighters intended from the outset to carry guided air-to-air missiles and the first supersonic all-weather fighters. Some were only marginally supersonic, notably the U.S. Convair F-102 Delta Dagger, an all-weather interceptor that was the first operational "pure" delta fighter without a separate horizontal stabilizer. Other aircraft included the Grumman F11F Tigercat, the first supersonic carrier-based fighter; the North American F-100 Super Sabre; the Dassault Mystère B-2; the Saab 35, with a unique double-delta configuration; and the MiG-19.

To this point, jet fighters had been designed primarily for air-to-air combat, while older aircraft and designs falling short of expectations were adapted to ground attack and reconnaissance. Since land-based surface attack was to be carried out by bombers, the first operational jets of fighter size and weight designed to attack surface targets were based on aircraft

U.S. Air Force F-100 Super Sabre. U.S. Air Force Photograph

carriers. These paralleled the third generation of fighters, but they were not supersonic. One example was the British Blackburn Buccaneer, capable of exceptional range at low altitudes and high subsonic speeds. The Douglas A-4 Skyhawk, entering service in 1956, sacrificed speed for ordnance-delivery capability. One of the most structurally efficient aircraft ever built, it carried the burden of U.S. Navy attacks on ground targets in North Vietnam and was often used by Israeli pilots in the Middle Eastern conflicts. The A-4 Skyhawk was still in use with the Kuwaiti air force during the Persian Gulf War (1990–91), an astonishingly long service life. The Grumman A-6 Intruder, which entered service in the 1960s, was another subsonic carrier-based aircraft. The first genuine night/all-weather low-altitude attack aircraft, it was highly successful over North Vietnam and continued to be in service until the late 1990s. The

Three U.S. Navy A4D Skyhawk carrier-based jet aircraft carrying Bullpup air-to-surface missiles, 1959. U.S. Navy Photograph

A U.S. Navy A6-A Intruder touching down and then taking off again from the deck of the USS Forrestal, 1963. U.S. Navy Photograph

electronic warfare version, the EA-6B Prowler, was projected to remain in service well into the 21st century.

MACH 2

A fourth generation of fighters began to appear in the 1960s, capable of maximum speeds ranging from about Mach 1.5 to 2.3. Top speeds varied with the intended mission, and increasing engine power, aerodynamic sophistication, and

more compact and capable radars and avionics began to blur the differences between two-seat all-weather fighters and single-seat air-superiority fighters and interceptors. By this time military designers had become convinced that air-to-air missiles had made dogfighting obsolete, so many interceptors were built without guns. This generation included the first land-based jet fighters designed with surface attack as a secondary or primary mission—a

U.S. Air Force F-4 Phantom fighter jet on a test flight near Nellis Air Force Base, Nevada, 1962. U.S. Air Force Photograph

development driven by the appearance of surface-to-air missiles such as the Soviet SA-2, which denied bombers medium- and high-altitude penetration. Precursor to this generation was the Lockheed F-104 Starfighter, designed by a team under Kelly Johnson and first flown in 1954. Capable of speeds well above Mach 2, this interceptor was built with short and extremely thin wings to reduce the generation of shock waves. However, light armament, limited avionics, and poor maneuverability made it an ineffective air-to-air fighter, and only with the installation of up to date bombing and navigation systems in the 1960s did it become a useful low-level attacker.

The truly outstanding fighters were the U.S. McDonnell F-4 Phantom II and the MiG-21. A large twin-engined two-seater, the F-4 was originally a carrier-based interceptor armed only with air-to-air missiles, but it was so successful that the U.S. Air Force adopted it as its primary fighter. When combat in Vietnam showed that gun armament was still valuable for close-range dogfighting, later versions of the F-4 were fitted with an internally mounted 20-mm (.75-inch) rotary cannon. The MiG-21 was a small delta-wing, single-seat aircraft designed as a specialized daylight interceptor, but it soon proved amenable to modification for a broad

U.S. Air Force F-105D Thunderchief fighter-bomber. U.S. Air Force Photograph

range of missions and became the most widely produced jet fighter ever. It was a formidable threat to U.S. airmen over North Vietnam and to Israeli pilots over the Sinai Peninsula and Golan Heights in 1973.

Also outstanding was the Republic F-105 Thunderchief, one of the largest single-engined fighters ever built. Designed to carry a nuclear bomb internally as a low-altitude penetrator and therefore exceptionally fast at low altitudes, the F-105, with heavy loads of conventional bombs under the wings, carried out the brunt of U.S. Air Force attacks against North Vietnam. Also

noteworthy in this generation were the British Electric Lightning, one of the first Mach-2 interceptors to enter service and one of the fastest at high altitudes; the Soviets' twin-engined all-weather Yak-28 Firebar; the Convair F-106 Delta Dart, a single-seat air-defense interceptor with superior speed and maneuverability; the Dassault Mirage III, the first successful pure delta in the air-to-air role and an enormous export success; the Soviet Sukhoi Su-21 Flagon, a tailed-delta single-seat all-weather interceptor; and the Vought F-8 Crusader, an outstanding carrier-based dogfighter over Vietnam.

U.S. Air Force Convair F-106A Delta Dart, 1965. U.S. Air Force Photograph

MULTIMISSION

By the 1970s steady improvements in engine performance, aerodynamics, avionics, and aircraft structures had resulted in a trend toward multimission fighters. Also, as engine acceleration characteristics improved dramatically and radars, fire-control systems, and air-to-air missiles became more compact and capable, the performance of aircraft themselves became less important than the capabilities of their missiles and sensors. It was now clear that, even with supersonic aircraft, almost all aerial combat occurred at transonic and subsonic speeds. Thenceforth, speed and operating ceiling were traded off against sustained maneuvering energy, sensor capabilities, mixed ordnance of guns and missiles, range, takeoff and landing qualities, multimission capability, political goals, and—above all—cost. A dramatic manifestation of the complexity of this new design equation was the Hawker Harrier, the first vertical/short takeoff and landing (V/STOL) fighter. Transonic and short-ranged but able to dispense with runways, the Harrier became operational

The F-15

The F-15 Eagle is a twin-engine jet fighter produced by the McDonnell Douglas Corporation that has been the premier air-to-air fighter of the United States Air Force since the 1970s and is expected to stay in service until at least 2030. Based on a design proposed in 1969 for an air-superiority fighter to replace the F-4 Phantom II, it has also been built in fighter-bomber versions. F-15s were delivered to the U.S. Air Force between 1974 and 1994; they have also been sold to Israel and Saudi Arabia and to U.S. allies in Asia, and they have been assembled under contract in Japan.

The F-15 has a wingspan of 42 feet 9.75 inches (13.05 m) and a length of 63 feet 9 inches (19.43 m). It is powered by two Pratt & Whitney or General Electric turbofan engines, which with afterburning can generate from 23,000 to 29,000 pounds of thrust, accelerating the aircraft to more than twice the speed of sound. Despite its large size, the F-15 has a high thrust-to-weight ratio as well as low wing loading (a low weight-to-wing area ratio), giving the fighter superior

U.S. Air Force F-15 Eagle fighter over Iraq. TSGT Jack Braden, USAF

acceleration and maneuverability. The single-seat air-superiority version is armed with a 20-mm (.79-inch) rotary cannon and an array of short-range and medium-range air-to-air mis-

siles. Flown in combat by U.S. and Israeli pilots, F-15s have shot down scores of enemy planes over Lebanon, Syria, Bosnia, and Iraq without suffering a single loss.

In the F-15E fighter-bomber version, known as the Strike Eagle, a weapons system officer seated behind the pilot controls the delivery of a number of guided missiles and bombs. The Strike Eagle carried out much of the nighttime precision bombing of Iraqi installations during the Persian Gulf War of 1990–91 and at the opening of the Iraq War in 2003, and it struck targets during the intervention in Libya in 2011. It has also provided close-air support for ground troops in the Afghanistan War.

U.S. Air Force F-15E Strike Eagle fighter-bomber over Afghanistan, 2006. Master Sgt. Lance Cheung/U.S. Department of Defense

with the RAF in 1967 and over the following decades was fitted with avionics of growing capabilities. The Royal Navy's Sea Harrier version distinguished itself in the 1982 Falkland Islands War both against Argentine ground positions and in dogfights with A-4s and Mirage IIIs.

The new generation of fighters was characterized by Mach 2+ performance where necessary, multimission capability, and sophisticated all-weather avionics. Many aircraft of this generation employed variable-geometry wings, permitting the amount of sweep to be changed in flight to obtain optimal performance for a given speed. Important aircraft in this generation included, roughly in order of operational appearance, the following: the MiG-25 Foxbat, a large single-seat interceptor and reconnaissance aircraft with a service ceiling of 80,000 feet (24,400 metres) and a top speed on the order of Mach 2.8 but with limited maneuverability and low-altitude performance; the MiG-23 Flogger, a variable-wing interceptor able to acquire and engage with missiles below it in altitude; the MiG-27 Flogger, a ground-attack derivative of the MiG-23; the Saab 37 Viggen, designed for short takeoff with a main delta wing aft and small delta wings with flaps forward; the fixed-wing Sepecat Jaguar, developed by a French-British consortium in ground-attack and interceptor versions; the Grumman F-14 Tomcat, a highly maneuverable twin-engined, two-seat variable-geometry interceptor armed with long-range missiles for the defense of U.S. aircraft-carrier fleets; the Dassault-Breguet Mirage F1, designed for multimission capability and export potential; the McDonnell Douglas F-15 Eagle, a single-seat, twin-engined fixed-geometry air-force fighter designed for maximum sustained maneuvering energy (a concept developed by U.S. Air Force Col. John Boyd) and the first possessor of a genuine "look-down/shoot-down" capability, which was the product of pulse-Doppler radars that could detect fast-moving targets against cluttered radar reflections from the ground; the Panavia Tornado, a compact variable-geometry aircraft developed jointly by West Germany, Italy, and Great Britain in no fewer than four versions, ranging from two-seat all-weather, low-altitude

attack to single-seat air-superiority; the U.S. General Dynamics F-16 Fighting Falcon, a high-performance single-seat multirole aircraft with impressive air-to-ground capability; the MiG-29 Fulcrum, a single-seat, twin-engined fixed-geometry interceptor with a look-down/shoot-down capability; the MiG-31 Foxhound interceptor, apparently derived from the MiG-25 but with less speed and greater air-to-air capability; and the McDonnell Douglas F/A-18 Hornet, a single-seat carrier-based aircraft designed for ground attack but also possessing excellent air-to-air capability.

BOMBERS

Jet propulsion presented the possibility—long sought among military planners—of building bombers that would be able to carry large bomb loads and still fly fast and high enough to elude pursuit planes and avoid antiaircraft weapons on the ground. This capability has never truly materialized, though during the jet age bombers have been built in many configurations. In general, bombers have sought immunity either by flying at high altitudes (at the highest reach of enemy defenses) or at very low altitudes (below the long-range vision of enemy warning systems).

High-Altitude Craft

The Luftwaffe fielded the first operational jet bomber, the Arado Ar 234, in the waning months of World War II, but

U.S. Air Force B-58 Hustler, a supersonic high-altitude bomber of the early 1960s. U.S. Air Force Photograph

it had minimal impact. The jet bombers of the immediate postwar years enjoyed only indifferent success, mostly serving to test engineering and operational concepts and being produced in small numbers. By the mid-1950s, however, first the Americans and then the British and the Soviets began to field highly capable jet bombers. The first of these to be produced in large numbers was the swept-wing, six-engined Boeing B-47 Stratojet, deployed in 1950 and used by the U.S. Strategic Air Command as a long-range nuclear weapons carrier. It was followed in 1955 by the eight-engined Boeing B-52 Stratofortress. This huge bomber, 160 feet 10.9 inches (49 metres) long and with a wing span

of 185 feet (56 metres), remained the principal long-range nuclear weapons carrier of the United States for 30 years. During the Vietnam War it dropped conventional bombs on both tactical and strategic missions, and in the 1980s it received a new lease on life by being fitted with air-launched cruise missiles, which permitted it to threaten targets from beyond the range of air-defense systems.

The British "V-bombers," introduced in the 1950s, comprised the Vickers Valiant, the Handley Page Victor, and the Avro Vulcan. These served as the backbone of Britain's nuclear deterrent until superseded by Polaris-missile-equipped nuclear submarines in the 1970s. The

THE B-52

Designed by the Boeing Company in 1948, first flown in 1952, and first delivered for military service in 1955, the B-52 Stratofortress immediately became the principal long-range heavy bomber of the U.S. Air Force during the Cold War. Though originally intended to be an atomic-bomb carrier capable of reaching the Soviet Union, it has proved adaptable to a number of missions, and some B-52s are expected to remain in service well into the 21st century. The B-52 has a wingspan of 185 feet (56 metres) and a length of 160 feet 10.9 inches (49 metres). It is powered by eight jet engines mounted under the wings in four twin pods. The plane's maximum speed at 55,000 feet (17,000 metres) is Mach 0.9 (595 miles per hour, or 960 km/hr); at only a few hundred feet above the ground, it can fly at Mach 0.5 (375 miles per hour, or 600 km/hr). It originally carried a crew of six, its sole defensive armament being a remotely controlled gun turret in the tail. In 1991 the gun was eliminated and the crew reduced to five.

Between 1952 and 1962, Boeing built 744 B-52s in a total of eight versions, designated A through H. The B-52A was primarily a test version; it was the B-52B that entered service in the U.S. Strategic Air Command as a long-range nuclear bomber. The C through F versions, their range extended by larger fuel capacity and in-flight refueling equipment, were adapted to carry tons of conventional bombs in their bomb bay and on pylons under the wings. Beginning in 1965, B-52Ds and Fs flying from bases on Guam and Okinawa and in Thailand carried out highly destructive bombing campaigns over North and South Vietnam. The B-52G, also used to attack North Vietnam, was given even greater fuel capacity and was equipped to launch a number of

A U.S. Air Force KC-135 Stratotanker refueling a B-52 bomber. U.S. Air Force Photograph

air-to-surface and antiship missiles. The B-52H switched from turbojet engines to more efficient turbofans. In the 1980s the G and H were equipped to carry air-launched cruise missiles with both nuclear and conventional warheads. In 1991, during the Persian Gulf War, B-52Gs were flown from Diego Garcia in the Indian Ocean but also from as far away as the mainland United States to strike targets in Iraq. After 1994 the B52H was the only version remaining in service. It was used to launch cruise missiles and drop bombs against Iraq and Yugoslavia in the 1990s and over Afghanistan in 2001.

The huge airframe of the B-52 earned it the nickname "Big Ugly Fat Fellow" (BUFF), but it also allowed the plane to be retrofitted with highly sophisticated navigational, weapons-control, and electronic countermeasures systems. Over the years, the bomber has frequently served as a "mother ship" for air-launching experimental aircraft, such as the X-15.

Vulcan, the first jet bomber to use the delta-wing configuration, remained in service long enough to drop conventional bombs in the Falkland Islands War.

The first Soviet jet bombers with strategic potential were the twin-engined Tupolev Tu-16 Badger (deployed in 1954) and the larger and less-successful four-engined Myasishchev M-4 Bison (deployed in 1956). In 1956 the Soviets also fielded the only turboprop strategic bomber to see service, the Tu-95 Bear, a large swept-wing aircraft powered by four huge turboprop engines with contrarotating propellers. The Tu-95 proved to have excellent performance. Like the B-52, it was adapted to maritime and cruise missile patrol after it had become obsolete as a strategic bomber, and it too continued service into the 21st century.

The aircraft mentioned above were capable of only subsonic speeds. The first operational supersonic bomber was the delta-winged Convair B-58 Hustler of the United States, placed in active service in 1960. This bomber carried its nuclear weapon and most of its fuel in a huge jettisonable pod beneath the fuselage.

LOW-LEVEL PENETRATION

The B-58 had a service life of only three years, because in the early 1960s it became apparent that surface-to-air missiles could shoot down aircraft even at previously safe altitudes of over 50,000 feet (15,240 metres). In response, bombers sought protection from early-warning radar by flying at low levels, and a new generation of high-performance bombers came into service that took complete advantage of the propulsion, aerodynamic, and electronic advances of the postwar era. The first of these was the U.S. General Dynamics F-111, the first operational aircraft to use a variable-sweep wing. Variable geometry was originally intended to allow the F-111 to combine the missions of low-altitude bomber and high-altitude fleet-defense fighter, but the fighter version was eventually abandoned. After a poor showing in Indochina in 1968, the F-111 became a successful high-speed, low-altitude, all-weather penetrator. As such, it joined with considerable effect in the final stages of the U.S. aerial offensive on North Vietnam, and it was assigned to the North Atlantic Treaty Organization (NATO) as a tactical-range nuclear weapons carrier. The F-111 also played an important role in the Persian Gulf War (1990–91). The Soviet Su-24 Fencer was similar to the F-111.

Larger strategic bombers using variable geometry to achieve high performance at low altitudes included the Soviet Tu-22 Backfire, the U.S. Rockwell International B-1, and the Tu-160 Blackjack. These bombers, supplementing the older purely subsonic aircraft, formed an important part of the U.S. and Soviet nuclear forces after their deployment in 1975, 1985, and 1988, respectively. In common with all first-line combat aircraft, they were equipped with sophisticated electronic countermeasure (ECM) equipment designed to jam or deceive enemy radars. They could deliver free-fall conventional or nuclear bombs, air-to-surface missiles, and cruise missiles. The B-1B Lancer, the operational version of the B-1, could achieve supersonic flight only in short bursts at high altitude, while the Soviet bombers were capable of supersonic "dash" at low level and could fly at twice the speed of sound at high altitude.

STEALTH

Stealth is any technology intended to make vehicles or other objects nearly invisible to enemy radar or other electronic detection. It has been applied to many military platforms, including submarines and surface ships, but its most prominent application has been to military aircraft. Specific details concerning stealth technology are jealously guarded by all military powers, but some general information is known. The United States is the principal developer of stealth aircraft, and what is known about the U.S. craft serves to illustrate the technology.

THE FIRST OPERATIONAL CRAFT

The existence of a Stealth program, designed to produce aircraft that were effectively immune to radar detection at normal combat ranges, was announced by the U.S. government in 1980. The first aircraft employing this technology, the single-seat Lockheed F-117A Nighthawk ground-attack fighter, became operational in 1983. The second was the Northrop B-2 Spirit strategic bomber, which first flew in 1989. Both aircraft had unconventional shapes that were designed primarily to reduce radar reflection. The B-2 was of a flying-wing design that made it only slightly longer than a fighter yet gave it a wingspan approaching that of the B-52, while the F-117A had a short pyramid-shaped fuselage and sharply swept wings.

THE B-2

Developed in the 1980s as the Advanced Technology Bomber, the B-2 Spirit was delivered to the U.S. Air Force starting in 1993. Built and maintained by Northrop Grumman Corporation, the "flying wing" was originally intended to be able to penetrate the sophisticated air defenses of the Soviet Union, deliver nuclear weapons to strategically important targets, and return to bases in the continental United States. It is the most expensive aircraft in the world, with a price of more than $1 billion per plane. The original plan was to produce 132 of the bombers. However, during the 1990s, with the Cold War at an end, production was reduced to 20 operational bombers and one experimental plane. The chief role of the B-2 was changed to conventional weapons delivery, though the bomber retains a nuclear capability. The operational bombers were assigned to Whiteman Air Force Base in Missouri, though they have also flown from bases overseas—for example, at Guam or Diego Garcia. B-2 bombers struck targets in Serbia in 1999, Afghanistan in 2001, Iraq in 2003, and Libya in 2011.

B-2 Spirit stealth jet bomber. Northrop Grumman served as the prime contractor for the four-engine, subsonic, flying-wing aircraft, which entered operational service with the U.S. Air Force in 1993. U.S. Air Force; photo, Master Sgt. Kevin J. Gruenwald

STEALTH TECHNOLOGY

Ever since radar-directed defenses began taking a toll of bomber formations in World War II, aircraft designers and military aviators had sought ways to avoid radar detection. Many materials of the early jet age were known to absorb radar energy rather than reflect it, but they were heavy and not strong enough for structural use. It was not until after the 1960s and '70s, with the development of such materials as carbon-fibre composites and high-strength plastics (which possessed structural strength as well as being transparent or translucent to radar), that radar signature reduction for piloted combat aircraft became possible.

Reducing radar signature also required controlling shape, particularly by avoiding right angles, sharp curves, and large surfaces. In order to direct radar energy in the least-revealing directions, the external shape of a stealth aircraft was either a series of complex large-radius, curved surfaces (as on the B-2) or a large number of small, flat, carefully oriented planes (as on the F-117A). Fuel and ordnance were carried internally, and engine intakes and exhausts were set flush or low to the surface. To avoid interception of radar emissions, stealth aircraft had to rely on inertial guidance or other nonemitting navigational systems. Other possibilities included laser radar, which scanned the ground ahead of the craft with a thin, almost undetectable laser beam.

To escape detection in the infra-red spectrum, first-generation stealth aircraft were not equipped with large, heat-producing afterburner engines. This rendered them incapable of supersonic flight. Also, the shapes and structures optimal for stealth aircraft were often at odds with aerodynamic and operational requirements. Since all weaponry had to be carried internally, ordnance loads were less than those for equivalent conventional aircraft, and sophisticated artificial stabilization and control systems were needed to give stealth aircraft satisfactory flying characteristics. Unlike the fighter, the B-2 had no vertical fin stabilizers but instead relied on flaps on the trailing edge of its notched wing to control roll, pitch, and yaw.

A second-generation stealth aircraft, the U.S. Air Force F-22 Raptor, which first flew in 1997, is capable of "supercruise," reaching supersonic speeds without afterburning.

TRANSPORT

The success of the C-47 and C-54 in World War II inspired the development of specialized military freighters with nose- and tail-loading features, roller conveyors on the floor, and built-in winches. These permitted the quick loading of vehicles and large equipment as well as their air-dropping by parachute. Military transports ranged from small V/STOL liaison aircraft and modified versions of civilian transports

U.S. Air Force C-130 Hercules transport aircraft, 1961. U.S. Air Force Photograph

to huge craft such as the Lockheed C-5 Galaxy, designed in the 1960s to carry two tanks, 16 three-quarter-ton trucks, or 245 troops. After its introduction in 1969, the C-5 was the largest aircraft in the world for almost two decades, until it was surpassed by the Soviet Antonov An-225. With a cargo bay 6.4 metres wide, 4.4 metres high, and 42 metres long (21 by 14.5 by 140 feet), the An-225 was designed to carry a payload of as much as 250,000 kg (551,000 pounds).

In a special category is the tilt-rotor aircraft, which can take off and land vertically like a helicopter or rotate its engines and fly like a fixed-wing turboprop airplane. This technology is employed by the V-22 Osprey, jointly produced by Bell Helicopter Textron and Boeing as a military assault transport for the U.S.

Marines. First flown in prototype in 1989 and delivered to the U.S. Marine Corps and Air Force in 2007, the Osprey can achieve speeds in excess of 500 km (310 miles) per hour.

RECONNAISSANCE

Reconnaissance aircraft in the jet age have gone far beyond the camera-equipped planes of the World War II era. Reconnaissance aircraft today carry electromagnetic countermeasure devices and rely heavily on electronic and infrared sensors to supplement their cameras. Their tasks are to locate and photograph targets, using radar and conventional photographic techniques, and to probe enemy electronic defense systems to discover and evaluate the types of radio and radar equipment that are in use. They have done this by offshore patrols just outside territorial limits and, more rarely, by overflights.

The best-known American jets used for overflights during the Cold War were two Lockheed aircraft—the U-2, first flown in the mid-1950s, and the SR-71 Blackbird, which came into service in the mid-1960s. The U-2, built of aluminum and limited to subsonic flight, could cruise above 70,000 feet (21,000 metres) for very long periods. The SR-71 had a titanium airframe to resist the heat generated by flying at Mach 3; this aircraft could operate above 80,000 feet (24,000 metres). The SR-71 was finally retired in the 1990s, the difficult, dangerous, and expensive job of manned overflights having been taken over by orbiting spy satellites.

Offshore patrolling of foreign coasts continues to be practiced in the post-Cold War era, frequently making use of the long-distance capabilities of the turboprop engine. For instance, Russia has long put the huge airframe Tupolev Tu-95 bomber to work in coastal reconnaissance, and since 1969 the U.S. Navy has employed its EP-3 Aries, a modification of the Lockheed P-3 Orion antisubmarine patrol plane, in the same capacity.

AIRBORNE EARLY WARNING

Carrier-based early-warning aircraft have a large radar to detect aircraft or ships; some can also control interceptor fighters defending the fleet. This kind of airborne warning and control system (AWACS) airplane also appears in land-based air forces to detect low-flying enemy raiders and direct interceptors toward them. The first aircraft of this type was a Soviet turboprop, the Tu-126 Moss, which was succeeded in the 1980s by the jet-powered Ilyushin Il-76 Mainstay. These craft, like the U.S. E-3 Sentry (a converted Boeing 707), carry a large saucer-shaped radar on the fuselage. The E-3 provides AWACS service for NATO and has been sold to the United Kingdom, France, and Saudi Arabia.

HELICOPTERS

The helicopter had its first significant impact on military operations during the Korean War, but it came of age in Vietnam. Helicopters fielded air-mobile infantry units, evacuated casualties, hauled artillery and ammunition, rescued downed aviators, and served as ground-attack craft. Helicopters became serious operational machines only after American manufacturers fitted them with gas-turbine engines, which were much less sensitive than piston engines to high temperatures and low atmospheric density, had far greater power-to-weight ratios, and occupied considerably less space.

ASSAULT AND ATTACK HELICOPTERS

The mainstay of U.S. Army assault units in Vietnam was the Bell UH-1 Iroquois, popularly known as the Huey. As early as 1962, army aviators were adding turret-mounted automatic 40-mm (1.50-inch) grenade launchers, skid-mounted rocket pads, and remotely trainable 7.62-mm (.3-inch) machine guns. These experiments, which proved effective in supporting helicopter assault operations, led to the AH-1G HueyCobra, deployed in 1967 as the first purpose-built helicopter gunship. With its pilot seated behind and above the gunner, the HueyCobra pioneered the tandem stepped-up cockpit configuration of future attack helicopters.

After the Vietnam War the lead in gunship design passed to the Soviet Union, which, in the Afghan War of the 1980s, fielded the Mil Mi-24 Hind, the fastest and possibly most capable helicopter gunship of its time. A primary role of the Hind was to attack armoured vehicles; to this end it mounted guided antitank missiles on stub wings projecting from the fuselage. In addition to the two-man cockpit configuration of the HueyCobra, it had a small passenger and cargo bay that gave it a limited troop-transport capability. Later the Soviets produced the Mi-28 Havoc, a refinement of the Hind that, with no passenger bay, was purely a gunship.

The successor to the HueyCobra was the McDonnell Douglas AH-64 Apache, a heavily armoured antiarmour helicopter with less speed and range than the Hind but with sophisticated navigation, ECM, and fire-control systems. The Apache has been operational since 1986 and has proved highly effective in several conflicts, including the Persian Gulf War, the Iraq War, and the Afghanistan War.

NAVAL HELICOPTERS

Helicopters have been adapted extensively to antisubmarine roles, given the capability of "dipping" sonar sensors into the water to locate their targets and launching self-homing torpedoes to destroy them. Ship-borne helicopters also serve as firing platforms for antiship missiles and are used to carry warning and surveillance radars, typically sharing information with their mother ships. By firing heat-producing or chaff flares to confuse infrared and radar homing systems, naval helicopters can serve as decoys for antiship missiles.

UNMANNED AERIAL VEHICLES (UAVS)

UAVs are aircraft that are guided autonomously, by remote control, or by both means and that carry some combination of sensors, electronic receivers and transmitters, and offensive ordnance. They are used for strategic and operational reconnaissance and for battlefield surveillance, and they can also intervene on the battlefield—either indirectly, by designating targets for precision-guided munitions dropped or fired from manned systems, or directly, by dropping or firing these munitions themselves.

General Atomics MQ-9 Reaper, a U.S. Air Force reconnaissance unmanned aerial vehicle, landing at Joint Base Balad, Iraq, 2008. Tech. Sgt. Erik Gudmundson/U.S. Air Force

EARLY TARGET DRONES AND RPVS

The earliest UAVs were known as remotely piloted vehicles (RPVs) or drones. Drones were small radio-controlled aircraft first used during World War II as targets for fighters and antiaircraft guns. They fell into two categories: small, inexpensive, and often expendable vehicles used for training; and, from the 1950s, larger and more sophisticated systems recovered by radio-controlled landing or parachute. The vehicles were typically fitted with reflectors to simulate the radar return of

enemy aircraft, and it soon occurred to planners that they might also be used as decoys to help bombers penetrate enemy defenses. (High-performance drones are still developed—for example, to test systems designed to shoot down antiship cruise missiles.)

It also occurred to planners that RPVs could be used for photographic and electronic reconnaissance. One result of this idea was the AQM-34 Firebee, a modification of a standard U.S. target drone built in various versions since about 1951 by the Ryan Aeronautical Company. First flown in 1962, the reconnaissance Firebee saw extensive service in Southeast Asia during the Vietnam War. It was also used over North Korea and, until rapprochement in 1969, over the People's Republic of China. A swept-wing, turbojet-powered subsonic vehicle about one-third the size of a jet fighter, the AQM-34 penetrated heavily defended areas at low altitudes with impunity by virtue of its small radar cross section, and it brought back strikingly clear imagery. Firebees fitted with receivers to detect electronic countermeasures returned intelligence about Soviet-built surface-to-air missiles that enabled American engineers to design appropriate detection and jamming equipment.

MODERN ELECTRONICS

AQM-34s operated with the limitations of 1960s technology: they carried film cameras, were launched from underwing pylons on a C-130 Hercules transport plane, and were recovered by parachute—snagged from the air by a harness hung from a helicopter. The full advantages of UAVs were to remain unexploited on a large scale until the 1980s, when reliable miniaturized avionics combined with developments in sensors and precision-guided munitions to increase the capabilities of these vehicles dramatically. One critical development was small high-resolution television cameras carried in gimbaled turrets beneath a UAV's fuselage and remotely controlled via a reliable digital downlink and uplink. Often, the vehicles also carried a laser designator for

Ryan AQM-34 Firebee, a remotely piloted vehicle used for combat reconnaissance in Southeast Asia during the Vietnam War; at the National Museum of the United States Air Force, Wright-Patterson Air Force Base, Dayton, Ohio. National Museum of the U.S. Air Force

homing munitions. Global positioning system (GPS) sensors provided precise location information for both the UAVs and their guided munitions.

Employing these new technologies, the United States has fielded strategic-range UAVs, using communications satellites to relay control signals and sensor readouts between UAVs and control centres over global distances. For instance, in 2003 Ryan (which had been purchased by Teledyne, Inc., in 1968 and by Northrop Grumman Corp. in 1999) produced the first of a series of RQ-4 Global Hawk UAVs. The Global Hawk is capable of carrying a wide array of optical, infrared, and radar sensors and takes off from and lands on a runway. Its service ceiling of 65,000 feet (20,000 metres), its relatively small size, and the reach of its sensors render it effectively immune

Northrop Grumman RQ-4 Global Hawk, a strategic-range unmanned aerial vehicle used by the U.S Air Force to relay intelligence, surveillance, and reconnaissance data to fighting units on the ground. Courtesy Photo/U.S. Air Force

to surface-based defensive systems. Prototype Global Hawks were pressed into wartime use over Afghanistan in 2002 and over Iraq as early as 2003. They are currently the most important strategic-range UAVs in service.

USE IN WAR

The advantages of strategic UAVs notwithstanding, the emergent technologies described here were first exploited in war by Israeli battlefield UAVs. The first of these was the Tadiran Mastiff, a twin-boom aircraft introduced in 1975 that resembled a large model airplane weighing just over 90 kg (200 pounds) with a boxy fuselage and a pusher propeller driven by a small piston engine. It could be catapulted from a truck-mounted ramp, launched by rocket booster, or operated from a runway. The Mastiff and the larger but similar Scout, produced by Israeli Aircraft Industries (IAI), proved effective in identifying and locating surface-to-air missiles and marking them for destruction during hostilities in Lebanon in 1982. The U.S. Marine Corps procured the Mastiff, and

General Atomics MQ-1 Predator, a reconnaissance unmanned aerial vehicle of the U.S. Air Force, 2006. Dave Cibley—214th Reconnaissance Group/U.S. Air Force

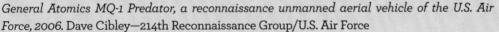

it followed up this vehicle with the IAI-designed and U.S.-built RQ-2 Pioneer, a slightly larger vehicle with secure up- and downlink. The Pioneer, fielded in 1986, was used by the Marine Corps and Navy in the Persian Gulf War of 1990–91. Meanwhile, the U.S. Army promoted the development of a similar but still larger UAV, the Israeli-designed RQ-5 Hunter, which had a gross weight of 1,600 pounds (720 kg) and was propelled by both pusher and tractor propellers. Although not pro-cured in quantity, Hunters served in the 2003 invasion of Iraq.

Following the lead of Israel, the United States has aggressively devel-oped UAVs. The most important UAV in operational use is the General Atomics MQ-1 Predator, powered by a piston engine driving a pusher propeller. The Predator entered service in 1995 and, after initial problems, developed into a capable surveillance craft carrying a wide variety of optical, infrared, electronic, and radar sensors. The first operational use of armed UAVs involved Predators carrying antitank missiles and operated by the Central Intelligence Agency during the 2001 invasion of Afghanistan. However, Predators are operated mainly by the U.S. Air Force, often to locate and mark tar-gets for heavily armed fighter-bombers or gunships. Supplementing the MQ-1 is General Atomics' MQ-9 Reaper, a larger

AeroVironment RQ-11 Raven, an unmanned aerial vehicle used for battlefield surveillance, being hand-launched by a U.S. soldier, Patika province, Iraq, 2006. Sgt. 1st Class Michael Guillory/U.S. Army

version of the Predator powered by a turboprop engine. The Reaper can carry some 3,000 pounds (1,360 kg) of ordnance and external fuel and has a significantly higher service ceiling than the Predator. It entered operations over Afghanistan in the autumn of 2007. Predators and Reapers have been purchased by allies of the United States, notably the United Kingdom.

All major military powers and even some militia groups employ battlefield surveillance UAVs to extend the view of ground and naval forces and to enhance the reach and accuracy of their supporting fire. For example, in its conflict with Israel, the Lebanese group Hezbollah has used the Iranian-built Ababil ("Swallow"), a vehicle with a wingspan of 3.25 metres (10 feet 8 inches) that is powered by a pusher propeller and launched either from a truck-mounted pneumatic launcher or by a booster rocket. Tactical surveillance craft range in sophistication from vehicles that, like the Ababil, loiter over battlefields acquiring and designating targets to hand-launched "mini-UAVs" carrying a single visible- or infrared-spectrum television camera. An early example of the latter is the U.S. AeroVironment FQM-151 Pointer, a UAV weighing less than 10 pounds (4.5 kg) and resembling a powered model sail-plane. The Pointer first saw service with the U.S. Marine Corps in the Persian Gulf War. It is being replaced by the Puma, a development of the Pointer with more-advanced sensors, by the RQ-11 Raven, a scaled-down version of the Puma, and by the Wasp, a tiny vehicle weighing about 1 pound (less than half a kilogram) with a wingspan of 2 feet 4.5 inches (72 cm); the last is being issued to air force ground combat control teams as well as marines down to the platoon level.

ADVANCED UAVS

Hovering UAVs have entered service— for example, the U.S. Honeywell RQ-16

Northrop Grumman MQ-8 Fire Scout, a hovering unmanned aerial vehicle, approaching a U.S. Navy amphibious transport dock ship, 2006. Kurt Lengfield/U.S. Navy Photo

T-Hawk, a ducted-fan vehicle weighing 18.5 pounds (8 kg), fielded in 2007 and used to locate improvised explosive devices, and the Russian Kamov Ka-137, a 280-kg (620-pound) helicopter powered by coaxial contrarotating blades and carrying a television camera for border patrol. The much larger Northrop Grumman MQ-8 Fire Scout, a 3,150-pound (1,420-kg) single-rotor craft resembling an unmanned helicopter, has been operational with the U.S. Navy since 2009; it was first used in anti-drug smuggling operations off the coasts of the United States.

In 1997 the U.S. Defense Advanced Research Projects Agency (DARPA) began to fund feasibility studies of extremely small "micro UAVs" no larger than 6 inches (15 cm). These studies (and similar studies conducted since 2003 in Israel) have produced a bewildering variety of designs powered by electric motors or tiny gas turbines the size of a watch battery, but no publicly acknowledged use has yet been found for them.

The next wave of UAV development is likely to be so-called uninhabited combat air vehicles (UCAVs). If the experimental Boeing X-45 and Northrop Grumman X-47 are representative of these vehicles, they will resemble small B-2 Spirit stealth bombers and will vary in size from one-third to one-sixth the gross weight of a single-seat fighter-bomber. They will most likely supplement or even replace piloted fighter-bombers in the attack role in high-threat environments. Finally, large, extremely light solar-powered "endurance UAVs" have been flown in order to test the feasibility of communications and surveillance vehicles that would stay on station at high altitude for months or even years at a time.

CHAPTER 7

AIR TACTICS

Air tactics are the art and science of aerial warfare, that is, the conducting of military operations by airplanes, helicopters, or other manned craft that are propelled aloft. Aerial warfare may be conducted against other aircraft, against targets on the ground, and against targets on the water or beneath it. Air tactics are almost entirely a creation of the 20th and 21st centuries, in which they have become a primary branch of military operations.

THROUGH WORLD WAR I

Powered aircraft were first used in war in 1911, by the Italians against the Turks near Tripoli, but it was not until the Great War of 1914–18 that their use became widespread. At first, aircraft were unarmed and employed for reconnaissance, serving basically as extensions of the eyes of the ground commander. Soon, however, the need to deny such reconnaissance to the enemy led to air-to-air combat in which each side tried to gain superiority in the air. Fighter planes were armed with fixed, forward-firing machine guns that allowed the pilot to aim his entire aircraft at the enemy, and the effective range of these weapons (no more than about 200 yards [182.9 metres]) meant that the first aerial combat took place at very short range.

By the second year of the war fighter tactics emerged on all sides emphasizing basic concepts that, with modification, remained applicable through the jet age. First was the surprise attack; from the very beginning of aerial warfare in World War I, "jumping" or "bouncing" unsuspecting victims accounted for more kills than did the spectacular aerobatics of dogfighting. Because a pilot's only warning system was the naked eye, attacking fighters, whenever possible, approached from the rear or dove out of the sun, where they could not be seen. The German ace Max Immelmann, in exploiting the superior abilities of his Fokker Eindeker to climb and dive quickly, helped expand aerial combat from the horizontal into the vertical dimension. Immelmann developed what became known as the Immelmann turn, in which an attacking fighter dove past the enemy craft, pulled sharply up into a vertical climb until it was above the target again, then turned hard to the side and down so that it could dive a second time. Fighters operated at least in pairs, flying 50 to 60 yards (45.7 to 54.8 m) apart, so that the wingman could protect the leader's rear. Flying speed averaged 100 miles (160 km) per hour, and communication was by hand signaling, rocking the wings, and firing coloured flares.

The next role to emerge for military aircraft was ground attack, in which planes, by strafing with machine guns and dropping rudimentary bombs, aided an advance on the ground, helped cover a retreat, or simply harassed the enemy. By the late stages of the war, ground-attack aircraft had forced almost all large-scale troop movements to be carried out at night or in bad weather.

By war's end a fourth vision of air power arose—that of an independent air force attacking the enemy far from the front lines, the purpose being to destroy essential elements of the enemy's war capability by bombing factories, transportation and supply networks, and even centres of government. This role, never effectively implemented in World War I, was spurred largely by the German air attacks on London. Carried out at first by zeppelin airships, the bombing was later done by aircraft such as the Gotha bomber, which, by flying at night and often as high as 20,000 feet (6,096 m) (forcing the crew to breathe bottled oxygen through a tube in the mouth), operated beyond the ceiling of many defensive fighters.

Thus, the basic roles that aircraft would play in modern war were presaged in World War I: reconnaissance, air superiority, tactical ground support, and strategic bombing.

THROUGH WORLD WAR II

The all-metal monoplane represented a huge increase in performance and firepower over the aircraft of World War I, and the effects were first seen in fighter tactics.

AIR SUPERIORITY

Airspeeds of the new fighters jumped to more than 400 miles per hour (643.7 km per hour), and some planes could operate at altitudes of 30,000 feet (9,144 m). Wing-mounted machine guns and aerial cannon were lethal at 600 yards (549 m), and pilots communicated with one another and the ground via the radio telephone. These developments—especially the greater speeds—led Germans participating in the

Spanish Civil War (1936–39) to fly their Bf 109 fighters in loose, line-abreast *Rotten*, or pairs, about 200 yards (183 m) apart. Two of these *Rotten* formed a *Schwarm*, and this flexible formation—called "finger-four" by English-speaking airmen—was eventually adopted by all the major air forces in World War II. An exception was the U.S. Navy, whose fighter pilots developed a system called the "Thach weave," whereby two fighters would cover one another from attack from the rear. This proved highly successful against the Japanese.

Attacking out of the sun was still favoured, both because it preserved the element of surprise and because diving added speed. An alert defending fighter pilot, however, might use his attacker's speed to his own advantage by executing a maneuver called a rudder reversal, in which he would turn and do a snap roll, suddenly reducing his forward motion so that the speeding attacker would overshoot and find the intended victim on his tail. Tight maneuvers such as the rudder reversal were most effective when attempted with such agile fighters as the British Spitfire and the Japanese Zero. Fighters such as the Bf 109 and the U.S. P-47 Thunderbolt, which were noted for their speed, best escaped by diving hard and pulling back up when the attacker had been shaken.

A diving maneuver called the split-S, half-roll, or *Abschwung* was frequently executed against bombers. Heavily armed fighters such as the British Hurricane or the German Fw-190, instead of approaching from the side or from below and to the rear, would attack head-on, firing until the last moment and then rolling just under the big planes and breaking hard toward the ground. The object was to break up the bomber formations so that individual ships could be set upon and destroyed.

Defensive fighter squadrons were directed by radar control stations on the ground to the vicinity of the bombers, at which point the pilots would rely once more upon the naked eye. This was adequate for day fighting, when enemy bombers could be seen miles away, but at night the pilots had to get within a few hundred yards (a few hundred metres) before spotting a bomber's silhouette against the sky or against the conflagration on the ground. For this reason, night fighting was ineffective until radar was installed in the planes themselves. This beginning of the age of electronic warfare required a novel teamwork between pilot and navigator, and it was best carried out in two-seat aircraft such as the British Beaufighter and Mosquito and the German Ju-88 and Bf-110. Some of these long-range, twin-engined night fighters also served as "intruders," slipping into enemy bomber formations, following them home, and shooting them down over their own airfields.

GROUND ATTACK

The German Air Force, or Luftwaffe, was configured primarily to fly in support of ground forces, and, in the Spanish Civil War and the first years of World War II, the Ju-87 Stuka dive-bomber was its principal ground-attack craft. In a typical Stuka attack, several planes would circle above the target, then one plane after another would peel off to dive almost vertically before releasing its bombs, pulling up, and returning to the circle to dive again. In the Pacific Theatre, carrier-based dive-bombers such as the U.S. Dauntless and Helldiver and the Japanese Type 99 "Val" applied this maneuver to naval warfare. Dropping straight down from a cruising altitude of about 15,000 feet (4,572 m) and releasing their bombs from below 2,000 feet (610 m), these planes destroyed or damaged many battleships and aircraft carriers. During the assault phase of amphibious landings, U.S. dive-bombers helped compensate for the flat trajectories of naval guns in disabling Japanese shore defenses. Because dive-bombers generally had top speeds in level flight of less than 300 miles per hour (482.8 km per hour), they were most effective where air superiority had been secured by fighters such as the Zero or the U.S. F6F Hellcat. Spitfire pilots of the RAF made such short work of unescorted Stukas that they referred to these one-sided dogfights as "Stuka parties."

Ground attack was most devastating when conducted by fighter-bombers, which were often converted air-superiority fighters. Taking advantage of their speed, British Spitfires and Mosquitos and U.S. P-51 Mustangs and P-38 Lightnings, flying very low to avoid radar detection, bombed and strafed countless airfields and infantry columns. Pilots of the P-51, after escorting bombers into Germany, often freely attacked ground targets while racing back to England at treetop level. In North Africa

in 1942–43, the Royal Air Force (RAF) perfected close-air support by concentrating its air power under a centralized control that was exercised jointly by the senior ground and air commanders in the theatre of operations. This system, by concentrating maximum force at decisive points as the desert campaigns unfolded, achieved a flexibility of employment that later emerged as the central tenet of air power.

STRATEGIC BOMBING

World War II saw massive bombing of military targets and major cities. The big, slow-moving bombers operated in formations (sometimes numbering 1,000 or more) that were intended not to evade enemy defenses but to beat them back or simply swamp them with numbers.

The key to bombing during the day was to provide an escort of fighters adequate to turn back defending fighters. (Antiaircraft artillery was of little hazard to bombers flying above 30,000 feet (9,144 m), though few early World War II bombers would fly this high, the B-17 being the exception.) During the Battle of Britain (July–September 1940), a typical formation of German He-111, Ju-88, and Do-17 bombers would cross the English Channel at about 15,000 feet (4,572 m). Close escort would be provided by Bf-109s and Bf-110s weaving in and out of the formation. The Germans quickly learned that the twin-engined Bf-110s could not hold their own against the humbler Spitfires and Hurricanes and removed them from frontline daylight service. More effective were fighter sweeps, in which

Bf-109s would leave the bombers and attack distant airfields before the defending fighters could get off the ground. But the Luftwaffe, in one of the major miscalculations of the aerial war, usually confined its fast, deadly fighters to close escort of the bomber formations.

The U.S. Army Air Force learned the value of fighter sweeps in its long-range daylight bombing of Germany, but not before placing what proved to be excessive faith in the capacity of its B-17 Flying Fortress and B-24 Liberator bombers to defend themselves with their own heavy armament. In late 1942 and early 1943 these bombers began to fly in what became known as the "combat box" formation, devised by Colonel (later General) Curtis E. LeMay. In such a formation, a single combat wing of about 48 bombers would be divided into three groups, with the lead group flying at 20,000 feet (6,096 m) and the others trailing in echelon at intervals of 500 to 1,000 yards (457 to 914 m) and at slightly higher altitudes. Within each group would be three squadrons, composed of two elements of three aircraft each, and the bombers would be staggered in such a way as to give their guns as free a field of fire as possible to cover themselves and their fellows.

The defensive formation was sorely tested in 1943, when, flying beyond the radius of the fighter escorts then available (less than 200 miles [322 km]), U.S. bombers suffered losses too severe to be borne regularly. Activity over Germany was curtailed until the widespread adoption in late 1943 and early 1944 of droppable external fuel tanks that enabled P-38, P-47, and, particularly, P-51 fighters to fly escort the 1,000 miles (1,609 km) to Berlin. With enough fighters to allow one escort for every bomber, some were cut loose to sweep the airspace hundreds of miles away. In this way, the Luftwaffe was finally overwhelmed.

Night bombing relieved bombers of the fighter threat (at least until effective radar was installed in planes), but it presented difficulties in finding and hitting targets. With visual navigation impossible except on the clearest moonlit nights, electronic aids became vital. In the blitz of London and other cities, the Luftwaffe used a system called *Knickebein*, in which bombers followed one radio beam broadcast from ground stations on the Continent until that beam was intersected by another beam at a point over the target. Lead bombers dropped incendiary bombs, which set fires that guided other bombers carrying high explosives as well as more incendiaries.

From late 1943 the RAF used two radar-beam systems called Gee and Oboe to guide its Lancaster and Halifax bombers to cities on the Continent. In addition, the bombers carried a radar mapping device, code-named H_2S, that displayed reasonably detailed pictures of coastal cities such as Hamburg, where a clear contrast between land and water allowed navigators to find the target areas. In order to "spoof" the Germans' radar warning system, RAF planes dispensed "window," which consisted of clouds of tinfoil strips that masked the bombers' movements.

THE BATTLE OF BRITAIN

From July through September 1940, during World War II, the Royal Air Force (RAF) fought a desperate battle against unremitting and destructive air raids conducted by the German air force (Luftwaffe). Victory for the Luftwaffe in the air battle would have exposed Great Britain to invasion by the German army, which was then in control of the ports of France only a few miles away across the English Channel. In the event, the battle was won by RAF Fighter Command, whose victory not only blocked the possibility of invasion but also created the conditions for Great Britain's survival, for the extension of the war, and for the eventual defeat of Nazi Germany.

Smoke rising from the London Docklands after the first mass air raid on the British capital, Sept. 7, 1940. New Times Paris Bureau Collection/USIA/NARA

Shortly after the withdrawal of British forces from the European continent in the Dunkirk evacuation (late May–early June 1940), Germany's armoured forces completed their blitzkrieg invasion of France. The French government collapsed on June 16 and was replaced by a regime that immediately sued for peace. This left the British suddenly alone in their "island home" as the last bastion against "the menace of tyranny," in the words of their prime minister, Winston Churchill. Speaking before Parliament on June 18, Churchill announced:

What General [Maxime] Weygand [commander of the Allied armies in France] called the Battle of France is over. I expect that the Battle of Britain is about to begin.... Let us therefore brace ourselves to our duties, and so bear ourselves that if the British Empire and its Commonwealth last for a thousand years, men will still say, "This was their finest hour."

On the German side, no plans had been made for an invasion of Britain before the Germans launched their offensive against France, nor were any made even when the collapse of France

was assured. German leader Adolf Hitler evidently counted on the British government's agreeing to a compromise peace on the favourable terms he was prepared to offer, and he still seemed to doubt the necessity of an invasion even when at last, on July 16, he ordered preparations to begin.

The German army was in no way prepared for such an undertaking. The German generals were very apprehensive of the risks that their forces would run in crossing the sea, and the German admirals were even more frightened about what would happen when the Royal Navy appeared on the scene.

An aircraft spotter scanning the skies above London, c. 1940. New Times Paris Bureau Collection/USIA/NARA

They had no confidence in their own power to stop the enemy, and they insisted that the responsibility for doing so be placed on the Luftwaffe. Air Marshal Hermann Göring expressed confidence that his planes could check British naval interference and also drive the RAF out of the sky. So it was agreed that Göring would try a preliminary air offensive, which did not commit the other services to anything definite, while the time for the invasion attempt would be postponed to mid-September.

Beginning with bomber attacks against shipping on July 10 and continuing into early August, a rising stream of air attacks was delivered against British convoys and ports. Then, on August 13, the main offensive—called Adlerangriff ("Eagle Attack") by Hitler—was unleashed, initially against air bases but also against aircraft factories and against radar stations in southeastern England. Although targets and tactics were changed in different phases, the underlying object was always to wear down Britain's air defense, and indeed the effort severely strained the limited resources of Fighter Command, under Air Chief Marshal Sir Hugh Dowding. The British disposed slightly more than 600 frontline fighters to defend the country. The Germans meanwhile made available about 1,300 bombers and dive-bombers and about 900 single-engine and 300 twin-engine fighters. These were based in an arc around England from Norway to the Cherbourg peninsula in northern coastal France. For the defense of Britain, Fighter Command was divided into four groups, and each group was divided into sectors. The sectors received

Members of the London Auxiliary Fire Fighting Services conducting a war exercise, 1939. New Times Paris Bureau Collection/USIA/NARA

reports from group headquarters about approaching Luftwaffe formations and mobilized squadrons of planes from numerous airfields to fight them off. The British radar early warning system, called Chain Home, was the most advanced and the most operationally adapted system in the world. Even while suffering from frequent attacks by the Luftwaffe, it largely prevented German bomber formations from exploiting the element of surprise. To fight off the bombers, Fighter Command employed squadrons of durable and heavily armed Hawker Hurricanes, preferring to save the faster and more agile Supermarine Spitfire—unsurpassed as an interceptor by any fighter in any other air force—for use against the bombers' fighter escorts.

German bombers (mostly lightly armed twin-engine planes such as the Heinkel He 111 and Junkers Ju 88) lacked the bomb load capacity to strike permanently devastating blows, and they also proved, in daylight, to be easily vulnerable to the British fighters. The Germans' once-feared Junkers Ju 87 Stuka dive-bomber was even more vulnerable to being shot down, and their premier fighter—the Messerschmitt Bf 109—could provide only brief long-range cover for the bombers, since it was operating at the limit of its flying range. By late August the Luftwaffe had lost more than 600 aircraft and the RAF only 260. Nevertheless, Fighter Command was losing badly needed fighters and experienced pilots at too great a rate to be sustained. The RAF was in a fight for its life—and, by extension, for Britain's life as well. Acknowledging that the country's fate hung on the sacrifice of its airmen, Churchill declared before Parliament on August 20, "Never in the field of human conflict was so much owed by so many to so few."

In addition to technology, Britain had the advantage of fighting against an enemy that had no systematic or consistent plan of action. At the beginning of September, the Germans dropped some bombs, apparently by accident, on civilian areas in London, and the British retaliated by unexpectedly launching a bombing raid on Berlin. This so infuriated Hitler that he ordered the Luftwaffe to shift its attacks from Fighter Command installations to

The dome of St. Paul's Cathedral in London, visible through smoke generated by German incendiary bombs, Dec. 29, 1940. New Times Paris Bureau Collection/USIA/NARA

London and other cities. Beginning on September 7, London was attacked on 57 consecutive nights. The bombing of London, Coventry, Liverpool, and other cities went on for several months, but it had the immediate benefit for the RAF of relieving pressure on its sectors in southeastern England and also bringing more German bomber formations into sectors farther north.

By mid-September, Fighter Command had demonstrated that the Luftwaffe could not gain air ascendancy over Britain. British fighters were shooting down German bombers faster than German industry could produce them. To avoid the deadly RAF fighters, the Luftwaffe shifted almost entirely to night raids on Britain's industrial centres. The "Blitz," as the night raids came to be called, was to cause many deaths and great hardship for the civilian population, but it contributed little to the main purpose of the air offensive—to dominate the skies in advance of an invasion of England. On September 3 the date of invasion had been deferred to September 21, and then on September 19 Hitler ordered the shipping gathered for Operation Sea Lion to be dispersed. On October 12 he announced that the operation was off for the winter, and long before the arrival of spring he decided to turn eastward against Russia. Plans for an invasion were definitively discarded; the campaign against Britain henceforth became purely a blockade of its sea approaches, conducted mainly by submarines and only supplemented by the Luftwaffe.

Children sitting outside the bomb-damaged remains of their home in the suburbs of London, 1940. New Times Paris Bureau Collection/USIA/NARA

Because Japan had only limited defense radar capability and few fighters that could operate effectively at the U.S. B-29 Superfortresses' bombing altitudes of 30,000 feet (9,144 m) and above, the Superfortresses faced only spotty opposition in their long-range assaults on the Japanese home islands beginning in November 1944. Nevertheless, unpredictable weather over the target areas, plus the action of the jet stream on bombs dropped from 30,000 feet (9,144 m), made high-altitude bombing imprecise. In response, LeMay ordered low-level bombing runs. Flying at night to avoid enemy defenses, B-29s dropping incendiary bombs from 5,000 to 9,000 feet (1,524 to 2,743 m) devastated more than 60 cities between March and July 1945.

THE JET AGE

Toward the end of World War II, the first operational jet fighter, the German Me-262, outflew the best Allied escorts while attacking bomber formations. This introduced the jet age, in which aircraft soon flew at more than twice the speed of sound (741 miles per hour [1,192.5 km per hour] at sea level and 659 miles per hour [1,060.5 km per hour] at 36,000 feet [10,972.8 m]) and easily climbed to altitudes of 50,000 feet (15,240 m). At the same time, advanced electronics removed the task of early warning from the pilot's eye, and guided missiles extended the range of aerial combat, at least in theory, to beyond visual range.

AIR SUPERIORITY

Flying at supersonic or near-supersonic speeds, often climbing into the thin air of the stratosphere, jet fighters were far less maneuverable than their propeller-driven predecessors. This made necessary a formation even more flexible than the finger-four. One solution was the fluid-four, in which two fighters flying 300 yards (274 m) apart would be trailed by another pair flying 2,000 to 3,000 yards (1,829 to 2,743 m) to the side, 600 yards (549 m) back, and 1,000 yards (914 m) above. Separation of a mile or more would allow the trailing pair to cover the lead pair from surprise attack. This tactic was favoured by the U.S. Air Force during the Vietnam War. By contrast, the U.S. Navy had developed the World War II Thach weave into the loose deuce, a more flexible formation—either pilot, depending upon the combat situation, could adopt the role of lead fighter while the other covered as wingman—and, as experience over Vietnam would show, one better suited for the jet age.

Because jet fighters had excellent climbing but poor turning ability, fighting in the vertical plane became more important than ever. The scissors maneuver acquired a vertical variation, in which two fighters would execute a series of climbing turns or barrel rolls, each with the aim of slipping behind the plane that climbed too fast. Speed—usually the greatest asset of the fighter—could easily become a liability, and many maneuvers were developed to preserve its advantage. One such maneuver was the "high-speed yo-yo," in which an attacking fighter, in pursuing a more maneuverable opponent in a tight circle, would pull up while turning; this would reduce his speed, allowing him to remain within the circle while placing him in a position to swoop down from above.

Supersonic speed actually accounted for a tiny fraction of flying time, since igniting the jet's afterburner could consume a fighter's fuel in minutes. Military cruising speed was almost always subsonic, with the afterburner being used only for pursuit or escape. In fact, fuel became such a pressing concern in jet warfare that fighters often could spend no more time flying combat air patrol than they spent flying to and from the patrol area.

Suppression of Air Defense

Beginning in the 1960s, radar-directed antiaircraft weapons proved so dangerous that they threatened to sweep aircraft from the sky. By flying low and fast, jinking (making quick, irregular changes in direction and speed), or diving in a steep spiral, aircraft often succeeded in evading these weapons, but only at the price of spoiling the mission. Air defenses had to be destroyed; in order to do this, aircraft had not only to outfly and outgun the weapons but also to foil their guidance mechanisms with electronic countermeasures (ECM).

In the Vietnam War the North Vietnamese deployed a formidable air-defense system based on Soviet-made antiaircraft guns and SA-2 surface-to-air missiles (SAMs). In response, the U.S. Navy and Air Force mounted complex air strikes employing aircraft of multiple types and capabilities. One such operation might begin with F-4 Phantom II fighter-bombers entering the target area first to drop clouds of radar-reflecting metallic fibres called chaff. These would be followed by F-105 Thunderchiefs modified into "Wild Weasels" by the addition of radar homing and warning devices designed to jam some enemy radars and locate others. The Wild Weasels would guide other F-105s armed with radar-homing missiles, which would destroy the radars and SAM sites and clear the target area for the main strike force.

That air warfare in the jet age had effectively become electronic warfare was confirmed by the Arab-Israeli War of October 1973. In the first two days of that conflict, Israel lost 40 aircraft to Egyptian and Syrian air defenses. In June 1982, however, the Israeli air force displayed a new mastery of tactics in the electronic age by destroying Syrian SAM sites in al-Biqāʿ Valley, Lebanon. The attack began with a wide array of ECM equipment—Boeing 707s modified into electronic warfare aircraft, E-2C Hawkeye early warning aircraft, and A-4 Skyhawks flying reconnaissance—to confuse and deceive Syrian communications and the radars of Syrian SA-2, SA-3, SA-6, and SA-8 SAM units. Small remotely piloted vehicles were sent over the valley; when the Syrians fired on these, Israeli F-4s spotted the SAM sites and destroyed them with radar-homing missiles and cluster bombs. Israeli F-15 Eagles and F-16 Fighting Falcons then destroyed the Syrian air force, downing more than 80 MiG-21s and MiG-23s.

The importance of destroying enemy air defenses and establishing supremacy in the air in order to assert mastery on the ground was reinforced during the Operation Desert Storm air offensive of the Persian Gulf War (1990–91). Allied air forces, led by the United States Air Force and Navy but including hundreds of French, British, Saudi, and Kuwaiti planes, had three objectives: to win air supremacy, to destroy strategic targets, and to degrade Iraqi ground forces in preparation for driving them out of occupied Kuwait. On Jan. 17, 1991, the allies launched the most intense bombing campaign in history, and by January 28 they had gained air supremacy. The Iraqi air defense system of aircraft, surface-to-air missiles, antiaircraft guns, and ground-controlled interception radars was rendered ineffective. Iraqi losses included some 35 aircraft downed in air-to-air combat, some 100 destroyed on the ground, and 115 flown to Iran to avoid destruction. Allied losses totaled only 39 aircraft, none in air combat. The allied air forces then destroyed targets vital to the Iraqi war effort. These included command, control, and communications facilities; ammunition; chemical and biological weapons facilities; petroleum, oil, and lubricant stockpiles; and manufacturing plants. Allied air forces also engaged in search-and-destroy missions against mobile launchers for Iraq's Scud missiles. Continuing the air war in order to maximize Iraqi, and minimize allied, casualties, the allied air forces disabled some 30 percent of Iraqi ground forces in the combat zone before the launching of the Operation Desert Sabre ground assault. Operation Desert Sabre lasted only 100 hours. Large numbers of Iraqi troops surrendered without fighting, collapsing under the cumulative effects of the allies' prolonged, massive air bombardment and the concentrated firepower and speed of the ground attack.

STRATEGIC BOMBING

The importance of ECM in long-range bombing became apparent in 1972, when U.S. B-52 Stratofortresses struck targets in North Vietnam. By flying under escort at night and at about 30,000 feet (9,144 m), the B-52s were reasonably safe from MiG fighters and antiaircraft guns, and Wild Weasel and chaff-dropping aircraft helped suppress the SA-2s. But the most important ECM was provided by jammers built into the bombers. These flew in cells of three in order to create "blankets" of radar suppression that largely foiled the SAMs.

The next generation of variable-wing bombers, such as the U.S. B-1 and the Soviet Tu-26 Backfire, were designed to avoid more sensitive electronic warning systems by penetrating enemy airspaces at extremely low altitude. Flying in groups was to be abandoned, since the large radar cross section and radio communication of several bombers would be easily detected. Instead, the new bombers were designed for solo missions and carried standoff weapons such as nuclear-armed cruise missiles, which could be launched against their Cold War enemies beyond the range of SAMs guarding the target areas.

In March 1999 the North Atlantic Treaty Organization (NATO), which had won the Cold War without firing a shot, launched a 78-day bombing campaign against Serbia to stop the mistreatment of ethnic Albanians in the province of Kosovo. By the time the Yugoslav government finally accepted a peace accord in June, aircraft from 13 NATO countries had flown more than 37,000 sorties, of which more than 14,000 were strike missions that dropped 23,614 bombs in an air campaign designed to destroy and disrupt the Yugoslav army and special police units in Kosovo. Strategic targets throughout Yugoslavia, such as the integrated air defense system, military command and control headquarters, petroleum storage facilities, and electrical power stations, were also attacked by aircraft and cruise missiles. Some of the alliance's most sophisticated weapons systems were used, such as the United States' B-2 and F-117 stealth bombers, which dropped bombs guided by inputs from the satellite-based global positioning system, or GPS. NATO had begun the campaign with great respect for Serb air defenses; in order to minimize risks from antiaircraft guns and missiles, combat aircraft flew no lower than 1,500 metres (5,000 feet). Only two NATO aircraft were lost in combat, but one was an F-117, supposedly invisible to radar. Air tactics in the jet age were indeed being shaped by electronics as much as they were by aerodynamics.

CONCLUSION

The American naval historian Alfred Thayer Mahan defined sea power as the ability to use the element to go where desired when convenient and to prevent the enemy from doing likewise. In a great naval war, when one side or the other has control over shipping in any portion of the seas, that side is said to be "in command of the sea." Attaining such command in areas of importance has usually been the first aim of the antagonists in a naval war, and to achieve this aim they strive to apply overwhelming force at the very beginning of combat. That force comes not only from surface warships but also from submarines, aircraft, guided missiles, and electronic countermeasures that interfere with the enemy's sensors and warning systems.

Submarines are famous for extending naval warfare into the third, or vertical, dimension. The air, far more so than the sea, is three-dimensional, as it has neither shallows nor bottlenecks such as narrow straits to use as natural control points. This has meant that in air warfare, too, complete command is almost impossible without the use of overwhelming force, usually applied first against the enemy's early-warning systems and ground-based antiaircraft weapons and frequently only afterward against the enemy's air forces. As the technology of both naval warfare and air warfare has grown more powerful and accurate, the reach of navies and air forces has tended to grow, so that war at sea and in the air now extends over the land as well, frequently far from the antagonist's home territory.

GLOSSARY

armament Weapons, arms.

ballast A heavy substance placed in such a way as to improve stability and control (as of the draft of a ship or the buoyancy of a balloon or submarine).

ballista An ancient military weapon, often consisting of a crossbow, that hurled projectiles.

bank A tier of oars, especially of an ancient galley, each representing a certain number of rowers on each oar or row of oars.

barbette An armoured structure protecting a gun turret on a warship.

biplane An aircraft with two main supporting surfaces usually placed one above the other.

bipod A two-legged support.

bireme A galley with two banks of oars used especially by the ancient Greeks and Phoenicians.

bonaventure A sail hoisted on the fourth mast of a medieval boat.

cantilever A projecting beam or member supported at only one end.

chaff Material (as strips of foil or clusters of fine wires) ejected into the air for reflecting radar waves.

coaxial Mounted on concentric shafts.

contrarotation Rotation contrary to another rotation.

corvette A highly maneuverable armed escort ship that is smaller than a destroyer.

cryptanalysis The art of deciphering or even forging communications that are secured by cryptography.

culverin A long cannon (as an 18-pounder) of the 16th and 17th centuries.

curtal A short-barreled cannon.

demicannon An obsolete cannon having a bore of about 6.5 inches (16.5 cm) and carrying a ball weighing from 30 to 36 pounds (13.6 to 16.3 kg).

destroyer A small, fast warship used especially to support larger vessels and usually armed with guns, depth charges, torpedoes, and guided missiles.

donnybrook A usually public quarrel or dispute.

dromon The Greek word for a liburnian.

floatplane A seaplane supported on the water by one or more floats.

frigate Originally a square-rigged warship intermediate between a corvette and a ship of the line; today an antisubmarine or fleet air-defense warship generally smaller than a destroyer.

fuselage The central body portion of an aircraft designed to accommodate the crew and the passengers or cargo.

gunwale The upper edge of a ship's or boat's side.

gyroscope A device containing a rapidly spinning wheel or circulating beam of light that is used to detect the deviation of an object from its desired orientation.

harquebus A matchlock gun invented in the 15th century that was portable but heavy and was usually fired from a support.

hull The frame or body of a ship or boat exclusive of masts, yards, sails, and rigging.

kamikaze A member of a Japanese air attack corps in World War II assigned to make a suicidal crash on a target (as a ship).

lateen Being or relating to a rig used especially on the north coast of Africa and characterized by a triangular sail extended by a long spar slung to a low mast.

liburnian A fast, light large-sailed sharp-prowed galley invented by the Liburnian pirates.

mizzenmast The mast aft or next aft of the mainmast in a ship.

ordnance Military supplies, including weapons, ammunition, combat vehicles, and maintenance tools and equipment.

penteconter An early Hellenic galley characterized by decks fore and aft and carrying fifty rowers.

photonic Of or relating to a photon (a minute packet of electromagnetic radiation).

pneumatic Moved or worked by air pressure.

polyreme A galley with more than two banks of oars.

pylon A rigid structure on the outside of an aircraft for supporting something (as an engine or missile).

quadrireme A galley with four banks of oars.

quinquereme An ancient galley propelled by five banks of oars.

ship of the line A square-rigged warship having at least two gun decks and designed to be positioned for battle in a line with other such ships.

subsonic Of, relating to, or being a speed less than that of sound in air.

tesseraconter A galley with 40 banks of oars.

transom Any of several transverse timbers or beams secured to the sternpost of a boat.

transonic Being or relating to speeds near that of sound in air.

trireme An ancient galley having three banks of oars.

trunnion Either of two opposite pivots on which a cannon is swivelled.

U-boat A German submarine.

unireme A galley having but one tier of oars.

zeppelin A rigid airship consisting of a cylindrical trussed and covered frame supported by internal gas cells.

WARSHIPS

Naval ships and craft are the subject of voluminous literature. For early history, William Ledyard Rodgers, *Naval Warfare Under Oars, 4th to 16th Centuries* (1939, reprinted 1967), and *Greek and Roman Naval Warfare* (1937, reprinted 1973), are older but still the most comprehensive sources on the classical era. J.S. Morrison and J.F. Coates, *The Athenian Trireme: The History and Reconstruction of an Ancient Greek Warship* (1986), treats in detail design evolution and technological developments. John H. Pryor, *Geography, Technology, and War: Studies in the Maritime History of the Mediterranean, 649–1571* (1988), explores both military and commercial navigation in the region. John Francis Guilmartin, Jr., *Gunpowder and Galleys: Changing Technology and Mediterranean Warfare at Sea in the Sixteenth Century* (1974), examines the way in which gunpowder changed the nature of warfare on land as well as at sea. Sam Willis, *Fighting at Sea in the Eighteenth Century: The Art of Sailing Warfare* (2008); and Jonathan R. Dull, *The Age of the Ship of the Line: The British & French Navies, 1650–1815* (2009), discuss and illustrate the general evolution of the sailing man of war and its role in the British and French empires.

The modern era is covered in Peter Hodges, *The Big Gun: Battleship Main Armament, 1860–1945* (1981); Norman Friedman, *Battleship Design and Development, 1905–1945* (1978), and *Modern Warship: Design and Development* (1979). On modern weapons systems, Norman Friedman, *The Naval Institute Guide to World Naval Weapon Systems*, 5th ed. (2006), is a comprehensive work; and Craig M. Payne, *Principles of Naval Weapons Systems* (2006), is an engineering text.

Historical characteristics of the major navies of the world are found in Roger Chesneau and Eugene M. Kolesnik (eds.), *Conway's All the World's Fighting Ships, 1860–1905* (1979); Robert Gardiner and Randal Gray (eds.), *Conway's All the World's Fighting Ships, 1906–1921* (1985); Roger Chesneau (ed.), *Conway's All the World's Fighting Ships, 1922–1946* (1980); and Robert Gardiner, Stephen Chumbley, and Przemyslaw Budzbon (eds.), *Conway's All the World's Fighting Ships, 1947–1995* (1995).

For characteristics by country, see: (*United States*): Norman Polmar, *The Naval Institute Guide to the Ships and Aircraft of the U.S. Fleet*, 18th ed. (2004); and Norman Friedman, *U.S. Battleships* (1985), and *U.S. Cruisers* (1984); (*Great Britain*): D.K. Brown, *A Century of Naval Construction: The*

History of the Royal Corps of Naval Constructors, 1883–1983 (1983); and Alan Raven and John Roberts, *British Cruisers of World War Two* (1980), and *British Battleships of World War Two* (1976); *(Japan)*: Hansgeorg Jentschura, Dieter Yung, and Peter Mickel, *Warships of the Imperial Japanese Navy, 1869–1945* (1977; originally published in German, 1970); and *(China)*: Bernard D. Cole, *The Great Wall at Sea: China's Navy in the Twenty-First Century* (2010); and Toshi Yoshihara and James R. Holmes, *Red Star Over the Pacific: China's Rise and the Challenge to U.S. Maritime Strategy* (2010).

On aircraft carriers, see Bernard Ireland, *Aircraft Carriers of the World* (2007); Norman Polmar, *Aircraft Carriers: A History of Carrier Aviation and Its Influence on World Events*, 2 vol. (2006–08), covering the periods from 1909 to 1945 and 1945 to the present; and Norman Friedman, *British Carrier Aviation: The Evolution of the Ships and Their Aircraft* (1988).

Information on landing ships employed in World War II may be found in Melvin D. Barger, *Large Slow Target: A History of the LST*, vol. 1 (1986); and Brian Macdermott, *Ships Without Names: The Story of the Royal Navy's Tank Landing Ships of World War Two* (1992).

Jerry E. Strahan, *Andrew Jackson Higgins and the Boats That Won World War II* (1994), is a biography of the man who designed the landing craft and covers the development and use of the boats.

The engineering characteristics of submarines are explored in Ulrich Gabler, *Submarine Design* (1986; originally published in German, 1964); and Roy Burcher and Louis Rydill, *Concepts in Submarine Design* (1994). Eberhard Rössler, *The U-Boat: The Evolution and Technical History of German Submarines* (1981; originally published in German, 1975); Erminio Bagnasco, *Submarines of World War Two* (1977; originally published in Italian, 1973); Dorr Carpenter and Norman Polmar, *Submarines of the Imperial Japanese Navy* (1986); and Richard Compton-Hall, *The Underwater War, 1939–1945* (1982), discuss underwater naval operations during this specific period. Antisubmarine warfare from World War I to the nuclear age is the subject of Robert C. Stern, *The Hunter Hunted: Submarine Versus Submarine* (2007).

NAVAL TACTICS

The most extensive work devoted exclusively to naval tactics is S.S. Robison and Mary L. Robison, *A History of Naval Tactics from 1530 to 1930: The Evolution of Tactical Maxims* (1942). Giuseppe Fioravanzo, *A History of Naval Tactical Thought* (1979; originally published in Italian, 1973), is an authoritative later analysis. Wayne P. Hughes, Jr., *Fleet Tactics and Coastal Combat* (2000;

originally released as *Fleet Tactics: Theory and Practice*, 1986), includes history but is more attentive to the art and science of tactics.

William Ledyard Rodgers, *Naval Warfare Under Oars, 4th to 16th Centuries* (1939, reprinted 1967), interprets galley warfare. The history of tactics in the age of fighting sail as presented by Julian S. Corbett in his numerous works, from *Drake and the Tudor Navy: With a History of the Rise of England as a Maritime Power*, 2 vol. (1898, reissued 1988), to *England in the Mediterranean: A Study of the Rise and Influence of British Power Within the Straits, 1603–1713* (1904, reprinted 1987), remains unsurpassed. A.T. Mahan, *The Influence of Sea Power upon History, 1660–1783* (1890), available in many later editions, is a classic naval history. Studies of tactics in the age of steam and steel include Bradley A. Fiske, *The Navy as a Fighting Machine*, 2nd ed. (1918, reprinted 1988); Romeo Bernotti, *The Fundamentals of Naval Tactics* (1912; originally published in Italian, 1910); and W. Bainbridge-Hoff, *Elementary Naval Tactics* (1894). Richard Hough, *The Great War at Sea, 1914–1918* (1983), explores the tactics of naval operations in World War I. The transition from battleship to aircraft carrier is discussed in Bernard Brodie, *A Layman's Guide to Naval Strategy* (1942). Studies of naval tactics in World War II are found in comprehensive histories,

such as Samuel E. Morison, *History of United States Naval Operations in World War II*, 15 vol. (1947–62); S.W. Roskill, *The War at Sea, 1939–1945*, 3 vol. in 4 (1954–61); and Friedrich Ruge, *Der Seekrieg: The German Navy's Story, 1939–1945* (1957; originally published in German, 1954; also published as *Sea Warfare, 1939–1945: A German Viewpoint*). Clark G. Reynolds, *The Fast Carriers: The Forging of an Air Navy* (1968, reprinted 1978), studies carrier operations.

WARPLANES

For military aircraft, historical overviews are offered by John W.R. Taylor (ed.), *The Lore of Flight* (1970, reissued 1986), a technically informed and well-illustrated work with separate sections on history, structures, engines, equipment, and flying, and containing an encyclopaedic index; and David Brown, Christopher Shores, and Kenneth Macksey, *The Guinness History of Air Warfare* (1976), a concise compilation of salient events and developments. Aircraft design is covered in John D. Anderson, Jr., *Introduction to Flight*, 3rd ed. (1989), an engineering overview of aircraft design and performance at a basic level, incorporating a technically accurate history of manned flight; and Edward H. Heinemann, Rosario Rausa, and K.E. Van Every, *Aircraft Design* (1985), a study of contemporary theory and practice. Aircraft propulsion is covered in Herschel Smith, *Aircraft Piston Engines* (1981), a technically informed history of power plants from the Wright era to the years immediately after World War II; and Edward W. Constant II, *The Origins of the Turbojet Revolution* (1980), a scholarly history of the development of turbojet engines. For early military aircraft, see Richard P. Hallion, *Rise of the Fighter Aircraft, 1914–18* (1984), a technologically and tactically informed account; and John H. Morrow, Jr., *German Air Power in World War I* (1982), an account stressing interactions between strategy and tactics on the one hand and social and economic factors on the other. Eric M. Brown, *Duels in the Sky: World War II Naval Aircraft in Combat* (1988), is an analysis of combat capabilities, based on personal experience, by a military test pilot. Robert L. Shaw, *Fighter Combat*, 2nd ed. (1988), focuses on modern jet aircraft but incorporates a solid historical base. R.A. Mason and John W.R. Taylor, *Aircraft, Strategy, and Operations of the Soviet Air Force* (1986), covers the development of military aeronautics in the former Soviet Union. Marshall L. Michel III, *Clashes: Air Combat over North Vietnam, 1965–1972* (1997), covers the technical and tactical aspects of the most hotly contested air war of the second half of the 20th century. For treatments of radar-evading aircraft, see Doug Richardson, *Stealth Warplanes* (1989; also published as *Stealth*), a review of the origins of stealth technology with informed speculation on contemporary and future developments. Two books that cover unmanned aerial vehicles are Bill Yenne, *Birds of Prey: Predators, Reapers, and America's Newest UAVs in Combat* (2010), a technical and historical overview; and P.W. Singer, *Wired For War: The Robotics Revolution and Conflict in the Twenty-First Century* (2009), a more critical look at the policy of remote-control warfare.

AIR TACTICS

Charles Harvard Gibbs-Smith, *Aviation: An Historical Survey from Its Origins to the End of World War II*, 2nd ed. (1985), and *Flight Through the Ages: A Complete, Illustrated Chronology from the Dreams of Early History to the Age of Space Exploration* (1974), provide basic introduction to the development of airplanes as a military force. John H. Morrow, Jr., *The Great War in the Air, Military Aviation from 1909 to 1921* (1993), is an authoritative overview of early air warfare. Morrow's *German Air Power in World War I* (1982); and S.F. Wise, *Canadian Airmen and the First World War* (1980), provide detailed coverage from the German and British perspectives. Raymond H. Fredette, *The Sky on Fire: The First Battle of Britain, 1917–1918, and the Birth of the Royal Air Force* (1966, reprinted 1991), shows the capabilities and limitations of strategic bombing. Robin Higham, *Air Power:*

A Concise History, 3rd rev. ed. (1988); and Bill Gunston (ed.), *Aviation: The Complete Story of Man's Conquest of the Air* (1978), are general surveys. Edward H. Sims, *Fighter Tactics and Strategy, 1914–1970*, 2nd ed. (1980); and Robert L. Shaw, *Fighter Combat: The Art and Science of Air-to-Air Warfare*, 2nd ed. (1988), focus on fighter planes. John B. Nichols and Barrett Tillman, *On Yankee Station: The Naval Air War over Vietnam* (1987, reissued 2001); and Marshall L. Michel III, *Clashes: Air Combat over North Vietnam, 1965–1972* (1997), address the air component of the Vietnam War; both focus on operations over the north, and *Clashes* is particularly useful in covering North Vietnamese tactics. R.A. Mason (ed.), *War in the Third Dimension: Essays in Contemporary Air Power* (1986), emphasizes continuity, innovation, and convergence in development of military aeronautics. Lon O. Nordeen, *Air Warfare in the Missile Age* (1985), provides an excellent overview of air tactics from 1964 to the 1980s. Matt J. Martin and Charles W. Sasser, *Predator: The Remote-Control Air War Over Iraq and Afghanistan* (2010), is a pilot's story of operating an MQ-1 Predator in combat.